THE HEAVY DANCERS

CONTENTS

FOREWORD

The heavy dancers are the image-conscious public persons who crowd the media of the world, 'summoning up the ancient spirits of the tribe as they prepare us for the ultimate war'. The more that they prepare for war, the more anxious they are to come before the public and assure it that they are devoted to the cause of peace. The peace movement has at least had this effect, it has made them more consummate in their hypocrisy. They command the present, and I send this book to press in a despondent mood.

This book is a sequel to the collection published in 1982, as *Zero Option* (in Britain) and as *Beyond the Cold War* (in the United States). In the past two years the issues have not changed but they have revealed their complexities. Several of the papers published here were written as contributions to peace campaigning, in Britain (with the Campaign for Nuclear Disarmament), in Britain and West Europe (with END, or European Nuclear Disarmament), or in the United States and Canada. The longest of them, 'The Defence of Britain', was written in a fit of fury through two nights and one day as a futile attempt to intervene in the media-conducted babble of the British general election.

Events in the past two years have forced onto the agenda of the peace movement issues which go beyond the plain demands for the renunciation (or freezing) of nuclear weapons systems. The Western peace movement has had its own problems of diplomacy with the East. Dialogue between citizens across the blocs has been made more difficult by security measures. And the underlying political question of the division of Europe can be evaded no longer. This question is raised in the first section and explored more fully in the third.

Everything previously published has been edited here with a respect both for the readers and the text. I have cut out repetitive or out-dated material, have restored some cuts, but have tampered no further. About one half of the pieces have not been published before. Many of these are in the last two sections.

Everything in the first three sections of this book should be self-explanatory, and can be understood in terms of the arguments presented. But I will admit that there is a hidden narrative—of debates within the peace movement, and between that movement and its opponents—which is not presented. When I first set aside my trade as historian five years ago, to take my part in the peace movement, we had to labour for a year or more to break through the 'consensual' silence. There followed a year or so in which the response (except from the direct apologists of nuclear weapons and strategies) was comparatively benign. Some of the Western media found us to be well-intentioned, if misguided, while the Soviet bloc media found us to be 'men and women of goodwill', even if our arguments were 'incorrect'.

That false Spring was blown away as abruptly as was an earlier Spring in Prague. Through 1983 and 1984 the peace movements were targeted by the Western media as witting or unwitting agencies of the Soviet Union; while those of us who expressed criticisms of Soviet militarism and support for independent peace groups in the East found our arguments suppressed or falsified in the mainline Western media at the same time as we were denounced in the Soviet Union and the Warsaw bloc.

I have had a sensationally bad press in the past two years on both sides: whether in *Encounter* or *Commentary* or in *Rude Pravo* or in various Soviet sheets. On one side it has been insinuated that I might be a Soviet agent, and on the

other I have been plainly accused by Soviet ideologists of
being an agent of the C.I.A. The attack from the other side
has been reaching a crescendo as this book has been in
preparation for the press. For some reason I have been
singled out, by the polemicists of the Soviet Peace Committee and the World Peace Council, as an operator working
for 'NATO's psychological warfare agencies'—maybe the
most hideous operator of all, although by no means alone,
since the list of my supposed fellow-agents now includes
END, the Bertrand Russell Peace Foundation, the Dutch
Interchurch Peace Council (IKV), my colleague in END,
Dr Mary Kaldor, and the network of Western non-aligned
peace movements (the IPCC) which includes most of the
major European movements and several major North
American affines.

It seems clear that influential Soviet operators, who were
willing to tolerate some 'incorrect' views (from Dutch
Christians and German Greens and Italian Eurocommunists
and British END) within Western peace movements so long
as these offered a prospect of halting cruise and Pershing II
deployments, have now reacted with extreme impatience
and would prefer to drive us out, even at the cost of splitting
these movements and detaching a pliant pro-Soviet portion
to their own side. This portion would then come within the
influence of the World Peace Council and would have some
nuisance-value as an auxiliary to Soviet diplomacies.

All this is going no now as this goes to press. The attempt
to split these movements will not succeed, and is based on a
misunderstanding of their character and objectives (a mis-·
understanding which is shared by President Reagan and by
Mrs Thatcher). But it is an ugly business which diverts
energies and leads to confusion and ill-will. And now I must
make an absurd confession. I had thought that it would help
readers if I wrote an introduction to this collection in which
I replied to my critics (and traducers) on both sides cf the
world, and in which I enlarged upon the 'hidden narrative'
which is only sketched here: for example, upon relations
between Western peace groups and independent groups or
voices in the East (with the Moscow Trust Group, Hungarian

Dialogue groups or with Czechoslovak Charter 77). I not only 'thought' about this, but I set down to write this brief introduction while this book was stalled in the press. And, alas! I emerged, after two months, clutching a brief introduction which had grown to the length of a short book. It had burst the bounds of this book, burst through the patience of my publishers, and, also burst the dimensions of the cover which was already printed.

We have therefore (the Merlin Press and I) hit upon a unique solution. This book will be published in one place and the introduction in another. The introduction will be available only in *samizdat*, to paid-up members of the peace movement, who must sign an undertaking that on no account will they pass copies to the editors of *Encounter* or to Mr Yuri Zhukov, the President of the Soviet Peace Committee. It is called *Double Exposure*, and is available, in plain paper wrappers, from the Merlin Press, 3 Manchester Road, London E.14 for £2.50 post-free.*

I could have closed the book at the end of the third section with 'The Liberation of Perugia'. But when I wrote that piece my mind kept moving in retrospect to that time when I was not an activist in the peace movement but was a soldier in what I supposed (and still suppose) to have been a necessary anti-Fascist war.

I searched around in boxes and files, some of which had scarcely been opened for thirty years. Are we now being persuaded that a remedy for the nuclear menace is to build up more and more 'conventional' arms? Then, as a member of the last generation of Europeans to experience an old-fashioned 'conventional' war, may I testify on that matter? (My 'Overture to Cassino', written in 1947 or 1948, was intended as the entry into a 'war novel' which mercifully the world was spared.) Are we today still locked into arguments as to which side must bear the blame for the first onset of the Cold War? Well, then, may I recall the experience

---

* By the way this is not just another of my bad jokes. The booklet really is published and it is available.—E.P.T.

when the soldiers of both sides met in mutual incompre-
hension in 1945 on the 'Drava Bridge'? I am not sure what
either of these stories 'mean'. They are offered to the reader
as raw evidence. 'The Place Called Choice' was written in
1950 and submitted to a poetry competition in the Festival
of Britain. It did not win a prize. In the past thirty years
I have taken it out of the drawer once or twice and fiddled
with it, until I now have no way of assessing whether it has
any merit. But it does have a certain interest as a document. I am sometimes asked by younger people what
I—or my generation—thought (felt?) when the first atomic
bomb was dropped on Hiroshima? The short answer,
I fear, is that few of us had any understanding of the
bomb or its effects, and we knew only that World War II was
at last at an end. It was only later, commencing with John
Hersey's *Hiroshima*, first published in the *New Yorker* in the
summer of 1946, that the bomb began to implode within
Western consciousness. And even then it is extraordinarily
difficult to recall our responses with honesty. But 'The Place
Called Choice', in its second and third sections, can at least
document that, by 1950, the meaning of nuclear weapons
was breaking through.

I don't know what the bits and pieces at the end of the
book add up to. This is a pig of a book, for the author as
well as the reader. Some of the bits, in any case, are poems
whose meaning can't be cashed in the same currency as
political analysis.

But I think that political readers (and also politicians)
ought to have to deal with such things. What may endanger
our species most of all may be the imaginative nullity of all
those heavy dancers, the hole left in our public life where
poetry ought to be. I don't of course mean my poems: I
wish that these were better. But what may be wrong with
politics now is that it is the exercise of power with poetry
left out. And what may be wrong with poetry is that it has
been pushed out of any central place and put into poetry
books.

In any case, let us try the experiment of putting the two
back together.

In the final section I could have dug up tracts of writing from the *New Reasoner* (1957-60) and the early *New Left Review* (1960-62) to illustrate for how long some of us have conducted a dialogue with 'dissent' in the Communist world and with liberation movements in the Third World—a dialogue which is now assuming significance in the perspectives of the peace movement. But my homages to Tibor Dery and to Salvador Allende are sufficient reminder. And my exchanges with Roy Medvedev in the Soviet Union and my essays on C. Wright Mills and Thomas McGrath in the United States are reminders that what has been creative in the intellectual life of the past forty years will not be found in the orthodoxies of either bloc but in the critical dissenting voices within each. I have said that the heavy dancers command the present. But these critical and sometimes lonely dancers are the ones who may command the future.

Worcester, November 1984.

THE WAR MOVEMENT

THE HEAVY DANCERS*

We all have opinions. We all agree that other people have a right to their own opinions. We even agree that they can try to change our opinions, and march around with banners in the streets.

But how do ideas and opinions change? How can opinions actually have *effect*—upon politics, upon power?

The innovative area of culture—the area in which opinions change, new ideas and values arise—this is the most sensitive, most delicate, the most significant area of all our public life. If we can't or won't change our ideas—if we blunder on with the habits of the past—then society gets snarled up.. Or it begins to die from the head downwards. As British society is doing now.

I'm going to argue that this delicate innovative area of our culture is in some ways more manipulated—more marginalised—and more threatened than for a long time. New ideas still do arise, but they are either coopted into a manipulated 'consensus' or they're pushed out into a margin of public life, where people can still march around with banners in their hands—but their hands will never be permitted to touch the levers of power.

There are many ways in which new opinions have arisen in the past. Let's look at only two. I'll call these, first, the

---

* Channel 4 'Opinion', 8 November 1982 and *New Society*, 11 November 1982.

activity of specialist intellectual craftsmen or women; second, the traditions of popular 'dissent'.

By the first I mean all those working in the laboratories of the spirit and the mind, with paint or sermon or pen or with thought and scholarship. I'm thinking of artists and philosophers—of Puritan lecturers and preachers—of satirists, polemicists, dramatists.

These people were never, until recently, out on the edge of the nation's discourse. They took a central part in it. It's true that this discourse was narrow and class-bound, and most of the nation were left to listen outside the windows.

But the means of communication which these intellectual craftsmen used didn't require vast capital to buy a newspaper or else access—by kind permission—to broadcasting media. The small printing-press, the pulpit, the stage—these weren't beyond their reach.

Since these voices were part of the nation's discourse, it follows that this discourse—and especially that part of it which we now define as 'politics'—was a different one from today's. These voices didn't only ask *how* questions: how do we fix the Corn Laws? How do we deal with the poor? They also asked *why* and *where* questions. Why—and how far— should we permit the state to have power over citizens? Where is industrialism leading us?

We're scarcely able to ask these questions, in the central arena of 'politics', today. They may be asked still—but they're kept outside there, on the margins. This is partly a result of our amazing advances in technology. A large part of the popular press is bought, and some part of the public mind is bought with it—by the way, the capitalist press *is* capitalist, as recent deals above the heads of editors, journalists and readers have reminded us. The broadcasting media have different problems.

I'm not here to knock broadcasting. The best British television is good. It's much better than most of what is chucked at the public in the United States. What's generally appalling, on British telly—and on all channels—is not only the prejudicial handling of particular political issues, but also the definition of what 'politics' is, and of who has the right to be in that set of frames.

They go on and on, in these frames, to the point of tedium, with the *how* questions only. How do we get inflation down? How should we cut up the defence budget between Trident and the fleet? A national 'consensus' is assumed—but in fact is manufactured daily within these frames—as to questions of *why* and *where*.

For example, all political discourse must assume that we're agreed on the need for economic growth, and the only problem is to find the party which can best fix it. But across the world people are asking questions of *why* and *where?* Do we have the right to pollute this spinning planet any more? To consume and lay waste resources needed by future generations? Might not nil growth be better, if we could divide up the product more wisely and fairly?

These questions can't be asked in that set of frames. They aren't proper 'political' questions. This is partly because of the insufferable arrogance of the major political parties. Long ago they had the audacity, through parliamentary control of broadcasting, to confiscate this part of the nation's intellectual life to themselves. Politics was defined as party politics, and then it was carved up, unequally, between them.

If John Milton or William Hazlitt were still around, and wanted to break in with a question of *why* or *where*, the managers of all the parties would gang up to keep them off. On every side a producer has to skirt around all these fenced-in estates with their party-political gamekeepers and notices saying 'PRIVATE—TRESPASSERS KEEP OUT'.

So we've got this extraordinary situation. The British people aren't totally stupid. Television acknowledges this with the high quality of certain programmes—in sciences, natural history, the arts. But the central national discourse, as to the ends and purposes of social life—this is sub-adult, managed and inane. *Gardeners' Question Time* is more adult and expert than Sir Robin Day's.

A body-politic without an inquiring spirit to ask *where* and *why* is like a car bumming down a motorway with an accelerator pedal but with no more steering than can just keep the car on the lane. We hurtle onward, faster or slower, but we can't take exits, go somewhere else, nor even stop and turn around.

I've mentioned poets. What a remarkable contribution to our nation's political discourse they've made—think of Langland, Chaucer, Marlowe, Milton, Marvell, Pope, Wordsworth, Blake, Shelley, Byron. . . Their voices weren't some extra condiment, like HP sauce, shaken on the British plate. They weren't interior decorators who made the place more pretty. They were part of what life was about, they asked where society was going.

Yeats's poem, *The Second Coming*, for example, is one of the most necessary, and full-throated, political statements of this century. Yet I couldn't begin to translate it into party-political terms—nor could Yeats himself. The poem measures itself prophetically against our tormented century, the bloodiest century in time. It's not about party-political questions, but it questions the values from which any adult politics should start. If you find any politician, whether of right or middle or left, who can't respond to that poem— then *watch him!* or *her!*

I don't suppose that this programme will be able to summon in poets with poems of that high order. This isn't my point. I'm saying that the broadcasting medium ought to be an open thoroughfare for the nation's opinions, just as the coffee-houses were in Dr Johnson's London or the hustings, pulpit and platform have been. And that the 'Trespassers Keep Out' signs ought to be torn down.

I spoke of another innovatory area from which Trespassers —or new ideas—arise. This is the tradition of popular 'dissent'. I'm thinking of the alternative nation, with its own vibrant but unofficial culture—the true Dissent of John Bunyan, but also the political dissent of Cobbett, the Chartists, women's suffrage pioneers.

There have been times when this tradition didn't lay claim to political influence at all. Bunyan and his fellows were proud of their spiritual apartheid in the 'Valley of Humiliation':

This is a Valley that nobody walks in, but those that love a pilgrim's life. . . Then said Mercy, I think I am as well in this Valley as I have been anywhere in my journey. . . I love to be in such places where there is no rattling with coaches, nor rumbling with wheels; me-thinks, here one may, without much molestation, be thinking what he is, whence he came, what he has done, and to what the King has called him. . .

Some of the most humane innovations in our country's life came in, eventually, from this alternative culture. Its influence was brought to bear on the segregated world of Britain's rulers—campaigns for the vote—for rights of press and opinion—the rights of labour and of women.

But whenever this alternative culture has come to the edge of touching power, it has suffered a crisis of identity. Its very reason for existence has been to *resist* power—to throw back its pretensions and intrusions. And power—or 'the establishment'—has endless resources to flatter, corrupt, or co-opt the occasional dissenter who's allowed a place in power's rituals.

This isn't imaginary. It's happened again and again and it's still happening. So political 'dissent' is caught in a double-bind. It exists to protest, and to campaign in alternative ways. If it accepts a place on the official media, then it falls within the official consensual frames. Worse, by permitting a brief image of 'angry' protest, it may seem to prove that opinion is free in this country—it can give legitimacy to the wholesale murder of free opinion which is going on all around.

You may throw up your hands at this point—*nothing* will satisfy these people! But our case is stronger than you may think. It's not only that the questions normally asked within the official frames prejudge the issues, by only asking *how* questions. It's also that the *how* questions themselves are carefully framed and adjusted: only the proper *how* questions can be asked, in the proper way.

For a century the powers of the British state have enlarged and enlarged. The alternative political culture has never touched these places of power. On the contrary the alter-native political culture is watched *from* these places, by covert agencies like MI5 and the Special Branch. By careful procedures of 'positive vetting', applicants for sensitive civil service posts are screened, and persons of independent views or unconventional lifestyles are kept out. In this way are pre-selected for the senior posts in the state only those persons who are subservient to the reasons of power, and resistant to innovation. It's a sieve designed to make sure that only the unoriginal and the mean-spirited get to the top. This is one reason why our country is dying from the head downwards.

These non-elected and self-vetted persons arrogate to themselves powers which would astonish our ancestors. It's supposed that they alone can determine what is the 'national interest' and invoke the awesome imperative of 'national security'. In this they protract into the present the traditions of an old anti-democratic imperial elite, whose last colony is this island.

So far from being free we are—in relation to these guardians of the 'national interest'—among the least free peoples of the advanced nations of the west. We have no Freedom of Information Act. No safeguards against mail interception and phonetapping. Our press is hedged around with Official Secrets Acts. In recent years our jury system has been fiddled with, our rights of public meeting and demonstration have been curtailed, and a heavy section of chief constables have pressed for heavier, undemocratic powers.

We've forgotten what any 'freeborn Englishman' knew 200 years ago—and what Americans still remember—that the state exists to serve us: we don't exist by permission of the state. Why have we forgotten? Why do we let these people get away with murder?

What they got away with, in 1982, was the Falklands war. It is as if, in normal times, they let the media play around with free opinions, since this flatters the British people's self-image. But in times of 'emergency'—and they alone define what an emergency is—they move in sharply and take over the controls.

In the case of the Falklands war, the lie beamed to us on all channels, from the *Jimmy Young Show* to the mainline news, was that our task-force was acting with the blessing of the UN Security Council, in defence of the rule of law, and in support of Resolution 502:

U.N. Security Council: 3 April: Resolution 502

1. Demands an immediate cessation of hostilities;
2. Demands an immediate withdrawal of all Argentine forces from the Falkland Islands (Islas Malvinas);
3. Calls on the Governments of Argentina and the United Kingdom to seek a diplomatic solution to their differences and to respect fully the purposes and principles of the Charter of the United Nations.

I happen to support this resolution, which was passed just after Galtieri's invasion and before our task-force had been sent on its way. Moreover, world opinion supported it also. This resolution carried with it a quite remarkable weight of international support:

U.N. Security Council: Voting, 3 April

In favour:	France, Guyana, Ireland, Japan, Jordan, Togo, Uganda, United Kingdom, United States, Zaire (10)
Against:	Panama (1)
Abstained:	China, Poland, Soviet Union, Spain (4).

You'll see that despite their hostility to anything smacking of 'colonialism' five Third World nations voted for it. Despite Hispanic kinship with Argentina, Spain abstained. Despite our supposed adversary postures, the Soviet Union and China refrained from using their vetoes. Only Panama sat in the dog-house.

Resolution 502 gave a real basis for an international exercise in enforcing the rule of law: for making the UN actually *work*, for once, through resolute diplomacy and sanctions. Instead, it was seized on by Mrs Thatcher to sanction. . . the rule of war. It was imprinted on British opinion, by every means, that Resolution 502 was a Security Council imperative, demanding instant Argentine withdrawal from the Falklands, and licensing every British military action to bring this about.

But it was nothing of the sort. The resolution had three parts, only one of which was brandished aloft by our government, while the other two were withheld from the British public's view. The relation of these three parts to each other was a question on which world opinion (and lawyers) did not agree, and which should have been referred back to the Security Council.

In the next weeks, while the task-force sailed to the Falklands, our government, with the aid of the United States, did everything in its power to prevent the Security Council from meeting on the issue again. When it finally did so—and called for an immediate ceasefire on the island and the implementation of Resolution 502 in its *'entirety'* and *'of all parts thereof'*, the terms of the voting had dramatically changed:

U.N. Security Council: Voting, 4 June

In favour:	China, Ireland, Japan, Panama, Poland, Soviet Union, Spain, Uganda, Zaire (9)
Against:	United Kingdom (1)
Abstained:	France, Guyana, Jordan, Togo (4)

You'll notice that I haven't put the vote of the United States there. General Haig and Mrs Jeanne Kirkpatrick were having a tiff, and the US vote was cast first with Britain, and then taken back and cast as an abstention. I've estimated its total value as nil.

You'll also notice that it is Britain this time, and not Panama, in the dog-house. That's quite remarkable. It was Mrs Thatcher's extraordinary achievement, in only two months, to run through all that credit of international goodwill and to have run up an equivalent debt of world censure. At the height of the Falklands 'victory' Britain stood alone in the Security Council, condemned or snubbed by every nation, just as Begin's Israel stands today.

But did you know that? Neither the media nor Mrs Thatcher went out of their way to tell you. That UN vote was passed over in silence. But to receive the world's censure is a serious thing. If the world is to survive, then every nation's citizens must develop an internationalist conscience, and attend to such censure as a matter of utmost gravity.

I'll be tougher. You perhaps suppose that during the Falklands war you weighed up the pros and cons for yourself and formed your own opinions. But many of you did *not*. You sucked in your opinions at the pap of an authoritarian state. The managers of our state moved in and did a job on the public mind. They issued us with public lies: refused us necessary information: and—do you remember?—when *Panorama* attempted a mild debate, there was a hullabaloo from the Tory benches.

If they could do this three months ago, then they can do it again tomorrow. Whenever they want they can manufacture 'public opinion' and then tell us it is our own. They are doing this still today.

I've gone into this, not to defend Galtieri's invasion (I don't). My own opinion is that if we'd honoured Resolution 502—in all its parts—world opinion might have enforced a negotiated solution less bloody to both parties, less painful to the islanders—but also less intoxicating and less politically advantageous to Mrs Thatcher. By resorting instead to the archaic and barbaric rule of war, we rocked an already-dangerous world, sank our country's reputation in the eyes of the world with the sinking of the *General Belgrano*, and gave a cue to Mr Begin for his own exercises in 'self-defence'.

Behind this lie more sensitive questions. What *is* the true security of our nation? Who decides? What claims can the nation-state rightly make on the loyalties of citizens? Might it be possible that the threat to our security today comes from outmoded notions of national interest? From the so-called security services? If the world is to go on—and it may well not—may it not be necessary for citizens in every country to develop international—or non-national—codes-of-honour, which may on occasion refuse the claims of their own nation-state? Should we always obey the Official Secrets Acts even when we stumble across evidence which threatens the liberties of the people or world peace? Just as Lollards or religious reformers in the old days put the Bible or their own con-

sciences above the dogmas of the church, should we stand
now on our consciences against the armed state?

We are living in abnormal times. Never has civilisation
been nearer to the end of the line, with so much banked-up
destructive power, such scattered and confused spiritual
defences. Remember how Yeats's poem begins, with an
image from falconry. The hawk of violence has been loosed
from the wrist—perhaps from our own wrists of bigotry and
apathy. . .

> Turning and turning in the widening gyre,
> The falcon cannot hear the falconer. . .

Next it will stoop—on us and our world.

It has been loosed from the wrists of normal people. The
most dangerous people of all are those who would have us
believe that everything is *normal*—that we need only to go
on as we are and trust them to manage things—the people
who would rock us to sleep in a cradle called 'deterrence'.

It's often true, in history, that the 'normality' of one time
turns out—a few decades later—to have been absurd. The
comfortable and powerful, who thought that they were
actors, were only puppets whose arms and heads were moved
by other strings.

If we could make a true national discourse again, an
opinion open to questions of *why* and *where*, we might be
astonished to find, behind the rituals of 'normality', the
absurdity of the rituals of our own time. I'm thinking of a
poem by one of my oldest friends, an American and a life-
long 'dissenter', Thomas McGrath. As you read it, put your
own features on the heavy dancers of our time. I can see
them now—the party-political pundits, the heavy chief
constables, the chat-show conductors, the paid defence
'experts', the Falklands liars—all of them now, going about
their normal business—with painted faces, feathers in their
hair, moving heavily in their primitive dance—summoning
up the ancient spirits of the tribe as they prepare us for the
ultimate war. The poem is called *Prophecy:*

Alas the long sad generations
Of machines!
Bit by bit that dark star
The Pentagon
Is crowded with devices
That speak in unknown tongues.
They take over the conference rooms,
The General's Washroom,
Finally: the Little Chapel
Of the B 52s. . .

And now no one knows what they are talking about.
The human concepts given them long ago
Change.
Something happened to the concept of honour
When the oil over-heated;
A bit of dust on a diamond connection
Has wiped out security;
At certain temperatures even the idea of Patriotism
Freezes.

And so it is that this morning the Generals and Bankers
Are discovered, carrying the water,
Carrying fetishes and the coloured earth up to the steps
Where now, painted, with feathers stuck in their hair,
They dance heavily: heavily,
Heavily calling out to the Unknown Ones inside.

THE SOVIET 'PEACE OFFENSIVE'*

Neither moralism nor fellow-travelling sentimentalism can be of service in guiding the peace movement in its difficult relations with Communist states. We are dealing, just as we are with the NATO states, with immensely powerful entrenched military interests and with leaders who seek to advance their own objectives.

The problem with the Communist rulers is that they are the ideological look-alikes of their opposite numbers in the West, thinking in the same terms of 'balance' and of security through 'strength'.

The Soviet rulers may have no aggressive plans, but 'the deterrent' remains immensely serviceable to them in freezing the *status quo* in Europe and in holding together their increasingly-restive client states. At any time from 1980 to 1982 they could have halted the build-up of the SS-20s, just as they could commence direct reductions now. It is as painful to them as it is to Mrs Thatcher to lose a single missile.

At a recent Prague summit meeting of the Warsaw Pact powers (January 5th, 1983) a package of proposals was issued which takes up several of the themes raised in the Western peace movements in the past three years: nuclear-free zones in Europe, the prohibition of nuclear tests, a zone of peace in the Mediterranean, a nuclear-free belt (taking up

---

* From the *Guardian*, 21 February 1983 and *The Nation*, 26 February 1983.

and extending the proposals of the Palme Commission)
running through Central Europe.

What could possibly be wrong with this plethora of Soviet
peace proposals? In many cases the proposals are good, they
offer advantage to both sides, and they deserve vigorous
support. What is wrong is what the proposals do *not* offer
(or what they close off from discussion) and their manipulation of European domestic politics to the advantage of the
Soviet Union.

What the Soviet proposals close off from discussion are
the most sensitive and troubling questions in the relations
between the two blocs. The aim of Soviet diplomacy is to
encourage Western European nations to edge from beneath
American hegemony at the same time as Soviet hegemony
is reinforced over Poland and the rest of the Eastern bloc.
At the same Prague summit a secret session was held on 'the
need to re-establish the leading role of the Party'. While a
peace offensive is being directed towards the West, the
East is being placed under quarantine lest the infection of
peace should spread.

If Soviet policy were to bring some measures of disarmament closer, then it might be possible to put up with it.
But it will not. It envisions that in 1983 Soviet diplomacy,
aided by the Western peace movement, will succeed in
dramatically reversing the post-war balance of political
relations. The Russians count on public opinion, direct
action and elections blocking or dislodging cruise and
Pershing missiles from one Western state after another, and
uncoupling Europe from US strategies. Thus NATO
modernization will be thwarted by the actions of West
European peoples, the seat will be knocked from under the
American negotiators at Geneva, and the Soviet Union will
regard with a benevolent eye the wreckage of NATO.

I am not filled with alarm at such an outcome, nor would
CND back away because it would give to our opponents, for
the ten millionth time, opportunity to accuse us of being
'one-sided disarmers' and Soviet dupes. Since this is a
potential Cuba crisis in reverse, there would be no harm if it
was, this time, the West that was outfaced and forced to back

down, even at the cost of leaving the Soviet Union with some notional 'superiority' in a category of weapons that is itself notional. This might, in a single episode redress the Russians' historical inferiority-complex (in nuclear matters) and NATO's assumption of the prerogative of superiority.

Yet this is not what is going to happen. In serious political terms it is unrealistic to expect that such a (welcome) loosening up of NATO could take place alongside a *hardening* of the Warsaw bloc. Established power, drawing upon immense reserves of ideology and of wealth, will rally to the defence of the old Cold War 'West', while at the same time repression in the East would sap the very springs of action of the Western peace movement.

The force generated by this movement in the past three years has always had a particular political accent: impatience at the domination of Europe by *both* superpowers; a desire to set nations free from their client status, to open frontiers and resume a flow of ideas and people between East and West. These desires are an integral part of peace conscious-ness, not an 'extra' which might be added to nuclear dis-armament. They go along with disarmament, both as pre-condition and as consequence. They were clearly stated in the original END Appeal of April 1980.

The Western peace movement derives its strength precisely from its political independence, its 'unacceptable' demands upon both blocs. If it should sleepwalk into dependency within a Soviet games-plan, its support could fall away as rapidly as it arose. The movement could be painted by its opponents into an unpopular pro-Soviet corner. We could come to the end of 1983 with Chancellor Kohl reinstalled in power and even (God forbid!) Mrs Thatcher.

The Soviet peace offensive is strictly for export. It goes along with a worsening climate of Cold War at home. Trials of Solidarity leaders continue in Poland. Arrests of independ-ent peace workers are reported in the GDR. On the same day as the Prague summit a leading spokesperson of Charter 77 in Czechoslovakia, Ladislav Lis, was arrested: among 'in-criminating' documents seized by the security police were drafts of his messages to the Western peace movement. In

Moscow the distinguished historian, Roy Medvedev—an early signatory (in 1980) of the Appeal for European Nuclear Disarmament—has been given, for the first time for some years, an official warning under the catch-all ('anti-Soviet activities') clause, Article 70.

For months hostility has been visited upon the small group of scientists, doctors and academics who formed last June in Moscow the Group to Establish Trust. Visitors from the Western peace movement have recently had long talks with the Group. They are convinced of their bona fides and are humbled by their dedication in the face of a record of persecution which far outdoes what happened to the Quakers in the 'Sufferings' in England in the late 17th century.

Sergei Batovrin, the young artist who founded the group, had eighty-eight of his antiwar paintings confiscated at an exhibit the group sponsored on Hiroshima Day, August 6. He was confined for some weeks in a psychiatric hospital and was placed under house arrest five times in November; his apartment has been repeatedly searched by the KGB.

Other members of the group have been temporarily detained on trumped-up charges, interrogated and sacked from their jobs; their telephones have been cut off and KGB cars have been stationed outside their apartments. Oleg Radzinsky, a young teacher, was arrested at the end of October; he was recently transferred from the Lefortovo Prison to the Serbsky psychiatric institute. Reports that he is in poor health are causing concern among his friends. Two supporters of the group in Siberia were arrested last July for collecting signatures on a peace petition from workers in a sawmill; they too are now in a psychiatric institute.

The group has sent urgent signals to sympathisers in the West that it expects the arrest of all of its members any day. A case is being prepared against them, and they have been accused in *Literaturnaya Gazeta* of being 'dying carrion-crows' and (absurdly) of supporting the massacre of Palestinian children. In a letter in the current *END Journal*, Prof. Yuri Medvedkov, a distinguished geographer, writes: 'We risk our liberty and even our lives every day but to be outside the peace movement is impossible to us. It's the

point of honour, the point of being humans.' And Batovrin
concludes a recent interview:

> We are not just talking of the persecution of a small group of peo-
> ple. . . The fate of the world depends upon whether each person
> understands that a peaceful future requires a peaceful defence of
> the right to struggle for peace.

It dismays and astounds me that there should be any
hesitation in the Western peace movement about coming to
the group's defence. Genuine peace movements have always
defended one another's rights: the right to communicate, the
right to opt for alternatives to military service, the right just
to exist. END is aiding, with a little success, members of the
Turkish Peace Association now on trial. Support for these
groups surely should not require discussion.

Yet a clatter has gone up, rather widely, that suggests that
'human rights' have 'nothing to do with' our only proper
concern: disarmament. The unavowed premise underlying
this clatter is the mirror image of standard Western apologetics,
now transferred to the East: the Soviet Union is only 'responding' to the Western weapons buildup; unlike Western
nukes, Soviet nukes are only for 'defence'.

But nuclear weapons are no nicer when they are wrapped
up, on that side as on this, with professions of peaceable
intent. It is helpful to be reminded (as we often are) of the
prodigious Soviet losses in World War II. Those losses fostered a historical consciousness that contrasts with that of the
United States, where there are still popular notions that war
is always for export; it never visits the American home. That
callow, boastful and menacing voice is not heard in the Soviet
Union; there is no appetite there for a war of conquest or
expansion.

History's legacy to Russia is paranoia, a tetchy sensitivity
to any 'instability' near its borders, a readiness to see in any
foreign ideas—even in a flight of doves—the conspiracies of
Western imperialist agents. Those weeping Soviet grand-
mothers who still deck with flowers the graves of the last war
have dry eyes for Afghanistan, as they had, in 1968, for

Czechoslovakia. The Soviet people will support their rulers
in preparations for any war that is 'in defence of peace'.

I am sorry to rehearse these plain truths, which I will be
told are 'anti-Soviet'. But it is time for the peace movement
to wash the sleep from its eyes. If we are entering into
political relations with the Communist states, then we must
do so as actors and not as the acted upon. If the Soviet
leaders are in earnest about some measures of disarmament,
and if they need the force of Western peace opinion to
achieve their objectives, then we must insert our own transcontinental demands into the negotiations.

The Western peace movement has never been just about
particular missiles. It has been about human neighbourhood,
communication, survival: the hope for what Ian McEwen
has called 'womanly times'. It has refused to adopt the
abstracted logic of the two great adversary blocs. The
Western peace movement is expressive of a political and
cultural sea-change which touches sensitive places in our
consciousness, subverts the pat certainties of thirty-five years
of Cold War, questions the game-plans of the old alliances.
It is in one sense an opening to the East: not to the East of
armed states but to the East of our fellow creatures.

The peace movement is a phenomenon analagous to the
'thaw' in the East after the death of Stalin. One reason the
thaw came to an abrupt end was that the clever statesmen of
NATO saw in it only Soviet 'weakness' to be exploited for
their own advantage; there was no corresponding thaw in the
West. If the Soviet leaders make the same error in 1983, and
seek to exploit what they perceive as 'weakness' and disarray
in the West to their own advantage, then not only NATO but
the human story itself may be finally screwed up.

This is the moment for the Western peace movement not
to fall in behind this or that makeshift of arms control but
to enlarge our demands upon both parties to the maximum
possible—and perhaps impossible. The opportunity that we
have now may never be repeated. We must strike directly at
the structures of the Cold War itself. A freeze on weapons
will not be enough. At the same time we must work for a
general and simultaneous thaw in both blocs.

The time to induce this mutual thaw is now, when Western peace consciousness (which *is* the thaw) is still growing, and when the Soviet leadership (which wants desperately to halt NATO modernisation) is bidding for the Western peace movement's favours. We must make it clear that we find it intolerable that independent voices in the East are harassed or silenced; that we will not scurry around to conferences in Moscow or assemblies in Prague so long as that repression continues; that we intend to act as free citizens of a healed world and that we do not require permits from Zhukov or one of his clerks to talk with citizens on the other side; and that, if it has to come to that, it is as easy to sit down in front of the Soviet Embassy as on Greenham Common.

I am not proposing some Cold War 'linkage' between disarmament and human rights. Our refusal of nuclear weapons has always been unconditional: this demand is dependent on no prior condition whatsoever. Rather we must press, in the same moment as we refuse weapons, for an opening of frontiers and prisons. Neither the cause of peace nor that of liberty can wait upon the other: it is natural that they go forward together. A genuine thaw in the East will make the cause of peace in the West unstoppable. Renewed repression in the East will feed the roots of a renewed Cold War.

There is a marvellous peroration in the declaration of the Prague summit about 'the broadest possible intercourse' between East and West. It calls for 'the extension of the mutual spiritual enrichment of the European peoples, propagation of truthful and honest information, and cultivation of sentiments of mutual friendliness and respect'.

Amen to all that. But what has this got to do with negotiations between statesmen? (Whoever heard a statesman propagate 'truthful and honest information'?) This is work for free citizens, not for arms controllers. We already have the work in hand. If the Warsaw Pact leaders really want a general and reciprocal thaw in the relations between peoples, then they need do very little. They can start now. They could open some frontiers; they could open the doors of some prisons and psychiatric institutes. They could call off the KGB surveillance of members of the Group to Establish

Trust, equip the security men with thermal underwear and send them off to watch an SS-20 site.

If we are to seize this last chance of putting Europe back together, the best thing we can ask of the current set of statesmen, East and West, is to get out of the way.

THE WISDOM OF SOLOMON*

If you board a flying machine at Kennedy or Logan Airport and turn right at Greenland, you will reach the European continent, an old place where in every state they speak a different language.

Across that continent, from the Baltic Sea to the Black Sea, there is an artificial line. One major city is even cut in two by a wall. On each side of this line are large and growing nuclear and conventional military establishments; there are also continuous ideological hostilities and skirmishes between rival security services. Two world wars have broken out in Europe, and, next to the Middle East, Europe is as likely a starting point for World War II as any.

Europe also is doing its best to screw up the Third World. The arms trade is one of the few vigorous parts of the slack Western European economy, and socialist France is especially mercenary and amoral in its salesmanship. The Soviet Union, whose most important production centres are in Europe, is the United States' leading competitor-colleague in this dirty trade.

When President Carter halted arms exports to certain Latin

---

* My article, 'The Soviet "Peace Offensive",' caused offence among some peace workers in both Britain and the United States. On April 16th, 1983, *The Nation* published a polemic against my views by Norman Solomon, in which I was accused of confusing the issues of disarmament and human rights. My reply was published in the same issue of *The Nation* and in part in *New Society*, 2 June 1983.

American tyrannies because of human rights violations, Britain, West Germany, France and Israel were only too eager to step into the market. To be sure, the implicit understanding was that these arms were to be used only by one Latin American country against another, or by their military dictators to slaughter their own poor. But the war in the Falklands, as a testing ground for advanced European military technologies, was a stupendous production from the studios of Nemesis Inc.

It may be overdue that we Europeans should become more Eurocentric in our political concerns: that is, should consult one another and try to resolve some of our own problems. If we could set matters right in our own backyards, we might be less of a danger to the world.

For the past three years the Western European peace movement has been signalling its unequivocal refusal of NATO's modernized weapons: cruise and Pershing 2 missiles. Unequivocal and unqualified: we are not interested in discussing any compromise. There has to come a point at which the nuclear arms race stops—whatever arguments of 'balance' are employed—and we in Western Europe are committed to stopping it here, at Greenham Common and at Comiso. We are even chided sometimes, by friends in the American freeze movement, for our 'unilateralism'.

I don't say that we will succeed. I say only that this is where we are and we can do no other.

Nor do we stand in particular need of lessons from Yuri Zhukov, the president of the Soviet Peace Committee. Yet we have been receiving from him, and from several official sources in the Soviet Union and Eastern Europe, rather a lot of instruction in the past few months. Zhukov, who is a *Pravda* editorialist and a very big Soviet noise, is displeased because we are not acting according to his script. We have not confined ourselves to refusing NATO weapons but have criticised Soviet nuclear weapons as well; and we have refused to align ourselves with Soviet policies in Poland and Afghanistan. We have also voiced our solidarity with independent peace groups in his country.

For these reasons we are now being unmasked by Soviet ideologists as 'anti-Soviet', Cold War and even 'pro-Reagan' elements—'infiltrated' into a movement which, in its recent incarnation, we happened to start ourselves! And Zhukov and his friends in the World Peace Council are trying, in an old-fashioned, 1950-ish way, to split our movement and bring it under Soviet hegemony. There are selective conferences in Moscow, pressing messages to us from several embassies, a great 'Peace Assembly' to be held in Prague in June 1983— and much more. We find this politically inept and morally offensive.

Our perception is this. For three years we have set every-ting else aside to campaign against NATO's new weapons. And in three years we have not extracted one real concession from the East. There are, it is true, some admirable proposals on paper from the Soviet Union and the Warsaw Pact powers, just as there are a few (rather less admirable) proposals on paper from NATO. But in terms of action, nothing. The two concessions we have explicitly pressed for have not been made.

First, we have asked—on two occasions, in April 1980 and in August 1981—for the Soviet Union to stop building up the number of its SS-20s. No answer; until a total was reached in 1982 clearly in excess of the corresponding Western weapon-ry. Second, we have asked them to stop harassing and im-prisoning independent peace workers on their side. The answer to this has been worse than no: repression is being tightened.

The SS-20s may not bother North Americans, since their range does not extend across the Atlantic. We argue that the cruises and Pershings would gravely disturb the strategic equilibrium, and that the terms 'intermediate' and 'theatre' weapons are misnomers. They are in fact forward-based US strategic systems, operated by US personnel, which can reach deep into Soviet territory. I think I was the first polemicist to say that they would set up 'a Cuba crisis in reverse'.

But the SS-20s are highly visible to Western Europeans, and a never-ending barrage of NATO propaganda ensures that this is so. They are targetted now on Bonn and London and Rome. If Europeans find that disquieting, it is, no doubt, a regrettable Eurocentric failing on their part. Norman Solomon reassures us that the presence of these weapons can be explained by the Russians' 'self-perceived defensive needs'. But I do not think that Soviet self-perceptions will limit the SS-20s' destructive power.

Solomon apologises further for these peacekeeping weapons by making several fallback references to an essay by Roy and Zhores Medvedev. The conclusion of the Medvedev's historical discussion of the leading role the United States has played in the nuclear arms race is that this has created 'a pervasive inferiority complex' in Soviet military circles. It ought not to be treasonable to suppose that there could be circumstances in which an inferiority complex (armed with nukes) could be as dangerous to life on this planet as the technological ego-tripping that characterises US weapons deployment.

I have not allocated 'greater blame' or even 'equal blame' to the Soviet Union for the nuclear arms race. Historical blame is beside the point: both sets of weapons are a present danger and both must be stopped.

The stopping of them is a political problem. In the West there must be a massive mobilisation of public opinion. There is a world of difference between the leaders of NATO (who are determined to deploy their infernal new weapons) demanding one-sided cuts from the Soviet Union and the Western peace movement (which is not only expressing but acting out its unqualified refusal of those weapons) calling on the Russians to make concessions in advance of the new weapons' arrival.

The object of the request is to prevent the weapons from ever coming. A direct Soviet concession of this order, in response to the peace movement, would so augment the force of Western peace opinion that we could sweep the weapons off the future's board.

Please remember that no European nation, East or West (the Soviet Union excepted) is represented at the Geneva negotiations. Yet the negotiators there are bargaining about intermediate-range weapons, the possible instruments of a 'limited' nuclear war in the 'theatre' of Europe. Western European nations can take part in the bargaining in only one way: by refusing to allow their national territories to be used as sites for the missiles. This refusal requires an act of political will, supported by powerful, aroused public opinion. The deployment of an unnecessarily large number of SS-20s is the best argument our domestic political opponents have, and it is one which is employed, day and night, in every newspaper and on every TV station. Some reciprocation by the Russians—not endless futuristic paper proposals to be fed into the labyrinth of superpower negotiations, but direct concessions to Western peace opinion—would begin to draw our opponents' poison.

I am not wedded to this course. I am ready to defer to the wisdom of Solomon—and, no doubt, to the wisdom of Yuri Andropov also. Soviet politicians and military leaders are 'realists'. What can our scruffy, undisciplined and argumentative millions—our idealistic and ill-marshalled demonstrators, our peace campers untutored in protocol, our pathetic declarations of nuclear-free zones in towns and counties, our movers of resolutions at party conferences and church synods—really promise to deliver?

To the Russians, we are background music only, and music not even loud enough to swing a German election. Andropov and his colleagues will take no more notice of us than an occasional glance at an opinion poll. They will attend to the *real* music—the rantings of Margaret Thatcher in Westminster, England, and of President Reagan in Orlando, Florida—to form their assessments of the true intentions of the ruling groups of the imperialist West. They do not have much reason to trust in Western democracy, nor any experience with its procedures. They have already ordered their own cruise missiles.

Our problems have been made worse in recent months by inept Soviet interventions in Western political life (including the peace movements), accompanied by continued repression in the East. Solomon is indignant that I even raise these matters, and I quote his comments since I have been looking at them for several days with growing despair:

> The Russians' essential perfidy is repeatedly alluded to by Thompson
> in references to repression in satellite countries like Hungary, Czecho-
> slovakia and Poland. We are encouraged to think that what happens
> in Eastern Europe is an index of the Kremlin's sincerity about
> wanting a halt to the nuclear arms race. But if we talk about Buda-
> pest, Prague and Warsaw, let us also talk about Santo Domingo,
> Santiago, and the countrysides of El Salvador and Guatemala [where
> the United States has been helping to finance an extermination drive
> against the Maya Indians].

This passage is so innocent of political analysis that I don't
know where to begin. I will start with an anecdote about a
recent conversation between a Norwegian peace activist and a
Soviet official. 'The European peace movement built up to a
"hot autumn" in 1981,' my Norwegian friend said. 'Why do
you suppose it was not followed, in 1982, by an even hotter
spring?' The Soviet official was puzzled and searched in vain
for a reply.

What my Norwegian friend was referring to were the unprecedented demonstrations—totalling more than 2 million
people—in Western European capitals in October and
November 1981. (We have been told that these rallies helped
breathe new morale into the American peace movement.)
And why were there not 3 million or 4 million demon-
strating in spring and summer of 1982? The answer is martial
law in Poland and the repression of Solidarity. A hope that
had been growing, a hope of healing our split continent by
the convergence of popular movements, was abruptly ended.

It is nonsense to try to extract something called 'the
nuclear arms race' from the ideological and political context
of which it is an integral part. In Europe we live in visible
contact with one another (whether antagonism or reciprocation); but, even if it is less visible, the United States and the
Soviet Union are tied into the same political context. Martial
law in Poland threw whole sections of the Western European
peace movement—notably the Eurocommunist masses in
Italy—onto a lame, defensive leg. In my view, the recent West
German elections were lost to the cause of peace in part

because of the clumsiness of Soviet interventions. And West German voters might have had reason to feel uncertain about the Kremlin's 'sincerity' at a time when peace activists were being harassed in East Germany and the 'Swords into Plough-shares' badges were forbidden on their arms.

It is of course true that US intervention in the West German elections was more foul and more flagrant than the Russians'. The point is that NATO's interventions and solici-tations were effective, and the Russians' were *counter-effective*. NATO's were effective because they exposed and exploited the nasty ideological sores on the other side. It helps neither anàlysis nor political action to apologise for those sores or to pretend they don't exist. .

Nor should we join in the old propaganda game in which human rights and human wrongs are turned up one by one like cards in the game of 'Snap'. This game is played by the ideologists of both superpowers for the delectation of the readers of *Commentary* and *Literaturnaya Gazeta*. It is a game of distraction, a grand confuse-a-citizen or confuse-a-comrade show. It is a game we should expose as one of the mental chains that hold humanity down. Let us never, for the shadow of one moment, engage in arguments that excuse offences against life or liberty on one side because similar or worse offences can be pointed to on the other. These remain two offences, there is no way in which one cancels out the other. The point is to end them both.

We are driven, of course, to take part in this game of swapping human wrongs by the barefaced hypocrisy of our own rulers. When President Reagan and Prime Minister Thatcher have the gall to claim their side is the protector of human rights, and to use the claim as Cold War propaganda and as legitimation for the preparations of the ultimate human wrong of nuclear war, how can we do other than throw that claim back in their guilty faces? Turkey has the worst human rights record of any European country; it is a partner in NATO, and a partner currently being nudged by certain US operators to flex its military muscle threateningly to destabilise Papandreou's Greece. And if we cast an eye across the globe, it is probable we would find that the most savage offences against human rights are now being committed in Latin America, often under US license and with US aid; the United States supports and condones these barbarities—some of which arise from indigenous contexts— by pleading the irrelevant categories of the Cold War.

But if we agree that the United States (or the West) is the greatest sinner against human rights, we solve no problems by simply crossing the floor of the Cold War and adopting the perceptions of the other side. We must situate ourselves in an alternative position and develop a 'third' perception, one which could bring into a single coalition the forces of peace and democracy in the First, Second and Third Worlds.

The political issue raised by my article was not the matter of human rights in general but the integral relationship between the ideological and security structures of the two opposing blocs and the nuclear arms race. In this context, certain human rights are highly sensitive and visible questions, which impinge emphatically upon the problem of disarmament.

My argument is that there is unlikely to be any permanent disarmament—or any disarmament at all—unless there is a reciprocal thaw in both blocs, an opening of direct communication and exchange between citizens, and that renewed repression in the East, in particular of independent peace voices, will weaken Western peace movements and could— if they do not take precautions—paint them into an ineffectual 'pro-Soviet' corner.

Solomon ignores this argument, and I am persuaded that he does not understand it. It may be less obvious to Americans than to Europeans. But I doubt whether he means to understand it, since he resorts to the strategy of leaving the argument unexamined and smearing it with the imputation of racism. 'It is worth pondering,' he writes, 'that Thompson devotes rigorous attention to Soviet-sponsored repression in client states primarily populated by white Europeans, but ignores brutal repression in US client states populated largely by nonwhites.' And he goes on:

For English-speaking whites in the West, it is all too easy to presume that the twinned international efforts for peace and freedom are more undermined by the jailing of a dissident in Prague or Moscow than by the execution of political prisoners in Guatemala or the Philippines, though a nuclear superpower is responsible in each instance.

And I and the European peace movement stand condemned for our 'Eurocentric fixation'.

This is a predictable form of argumentation by people who suppose themselves to be advanced radicals, and it consists of strewing the ground with tripwires of guilt ('English-speaking whites in the West', 'Eurocentric', etc.). In seeking to circumvent these tripwires we are forced to skirt the most relevant political problems also.

By all means let us talk about the situation in Guatemala and El Salvador when it is relevant, as it now very urgently is. Let us also ('Snap!') talk about Afghanistan. If Solomon comes to Europe he will find that much talking about them is going on, although it is not always easy to know what we can do. But what is happening in those countries has rather little to do with nuclear weapons, and it does not even need a superpower to do it, although that helps. It is as old as, and older than, the Maxim gun. Insofar as the violence of the superpower confrontation is being worked out in these peripheral client states, one way of aiding the victims is to challenge the Cold War itself—in its central military and ideological emplacements—and to strengthen the links between nonaligned movements and nations. This is what we are trying to do.

What Solomon fails to consider is any policy by which the peace movement might break down the confrontation of blocs; nor does he consider the mechanics of twinning the nonaligned peace work on both sides.

Just one example: we are being urged by the World Peace Council (a Soviet-oriented body) to send representatives to the Assembly of Peace to be held in June 1983 in Prague. We are not, as it happens, being simultaneously urged by the Atlantic Council (a private group which promotes co-operation between Europe and the United States) to send representatives to an officially sponsored peace assembly in, say, Guatemala City, to protest against Soviet SS-20s, so we cannot get out of both (or into both) by playing Snap.

Here are a few of the difficulties we have with the invitation to attend the peace assembly in Prague: (1) Czechoslovakia is a Soviet client state, although the Czechoslovak people supposed themselves to be sovereign until August 1968, when (2) the intervention of Warsaw Pact forces taught them better. This intervention was provoked by (3) a reform movement within the country's ruling Communist Party, not by any Western imperialist provocation. (4) The forces that entered Czechoslovakia in 1968 remain in occupation to this day, although it was claimed then that their stay would be temporary. (5) In 1977, after the signing of the Helsinki Accords, a Czechoslovak civil rights organisation, Charter 77, was set up, in which some former Communists of 1968 were prominent, to press for the observance of those accords. It has been consistently harassed, and members imprisoned. (6) Last year the spokespersons for Charter 77 addressed several messages to Western peace groups, suggesting that the movements in the East and West recognise and support one another and work for peace, for true detente and for the observance of civil rights. (7) This January one of the people who signed those letters, Ladislav Lis, was arrested, and he remains in prison. Parenthetically, in 1968 Czechoslovakia's government-sponsored Peace Committee had the temerity to protest at the Warsaw Pact invasion—perhaps the only recorded case of an official peace committee in the Soviet bloc protesting against an action of the Warsaw Pact. The committee was promptly disbanded and a new, compliant peace committee was appointed. And (8) this body will be the host organisation of the great Assembly for Peace. To raise money for the assembly, the government has 'invited' working people to pay a 'peace tax' from their wages—for example, to sign over their pay for one Saturday morning shift—which payments will be voluntary, of course, but the refusal of which may call down upon the recalcitrant ones unwelcome attention.

Many Europeans find this whole scene to be a can of

worms. But what can we do about it? To refuse to go to the
conference might be seen as a refusal to 'talk with the other
side', which everyone now wants to do. To go might be seen
as a condonation of the Soviet occupation of Czechoslovakia
(a legitimate demand on any European disarmament agenda
is the withdrawal of those forces) as well as an acceptance of
the repression of civil rights workers who have been trying to
open a dialogue with the Western peace movement. This
question has put us at sixes and sevens and divided us more
than any propaganda ploy by President Reagan could do. In
the end, some European peace workers will refuse to go, on
one principle or another; others will go with open eyes to see
if anything can be done, and others will sleepwalk through
the whole affair in an exalted peace-loving trance. The media
in the West will expose us all, without discrimination, as
Soviet stooges. The event will do only harm to the cause of
peace and will alienate democrats in the East from Western
peace forces. Many of those democrats are patriots claiming
to be exercising their constitutional rights, and they do not
thank us in the West for writing them off as 'dissidents'.*

It is only by attending to such details that we can see the
emptiness of the wisdom of Solomon. According to any
universal scale of human rights and wrongs, the execution of
Maya Indians in Guatemala, the raping of women and the
burning of villages is certainly more foul than the 'jailing of
a dissident in Prague or Moscow'. But in the complex politics
of peace, the major adversaries are NATO and the Warsaw
Pact, and the lines of antagonism and reconciliation run not
through the countrysides of Guatemala and El Salvador but
through Berlin, Warsaw and Prague. The future of the world
depends, in the end, on the peoples of the Soviet Union and
the United States finding some mode of mutual reconciliation (and disarmament); and the people of Europe could be
either a prize of war or a hyphen bringing them together.

I have to reply to Solomon that the twinned international

---

* CND's National Council, after a full and fair discussion, decided to
send two observers to Prague. While at the Assembly the observers
also had meetings with members of Charter 77.

efforts of peace and freedom *are* more undermined by the jailing of a dissident in Prague or Moscow than by the sack of a Guatemalan village. This is not because the first is worse than the second; it certainly is not. It is because the first may be more sensitively situated within the delicate and complicated politics of peace. If not just any 'dissident', but, say, Ladislav Lis of Charter 77 or Oleg Radzinsky of the Moscow Group to Establish Trust Between the USSR and USA is thrown into prison, it is a defeat for communication between citizens of East and West and a serious reversal for the cause of peace. It signals that the Communist authorities are not yet willing to reciprocate our efforts with the least thaw of their own.

The making of an honest political discourse between East and West is an extraordinarily complex business, with misrecognitions on all sides and with the security agencies of both blocs doing all they can to screw up the dialogue. It is not enough to rush across to the other side with an outstretched hand. The Kremlin may be sincere in wishing to see a halt in the nuclear arms race, but it is equally sincere in taking measures to insure that the infection of the peace movement is halted at its borders. Yet if we are steady and nonprovocative, I do not think these measures will be able to stop it. And, as I have said, if there is no mutual thaw, I doubt if we will succeed in stopping nuclear arms.

I am glad to learn that many US peace organisations have come to the defence of the Moscow Group to Establish Trust and its kindred groups in Leningrad, Novosibirsk and Odessa. It is not that these beleaguered handfuls of independent-minded citizens—who may be worn down into silence by incessant harrassment—are the only Soviet citizens concerned with peace. They symbolise the principle of trust and direct citizens' detente, and hence of internationalism against state power. If that principle is abandoned, the poison of compromise with power will enter all our work.

I had almost forgotten Norman Solomon. I find his tone offensive and unfraternal, and I object to his accusations of treason and racism, but I don't hold him an enemy to the cause of peace. If he wishes to be useful to that cause in his writing, however, there are certain habits he should kick.

One habit is that of using human rights as the coin of propaganda, as if a debit on one side can be scored as a credit to the other. This habit, which is widespread on both sides of the Atlantic, reveals how far we are from truly endorsing the consciousness of nonalignment. We remain in bondage to the schema of the Cold War, exchanging one ideology for its mirror image.

Another habit is that of setting up tripwires of guilt as an alternative to arguing. This strategy of discourse is very much of our time, among radicals and conservatives alike. It is sad to see it at work in the peace movement also: it is a kind of competitiveness, in which those who were once eager to prove themselves more revolutionary-than-thou (more anti-racist, more antisexist, etc.) must now prove themselves more antinuclear-than-thou.

The temptation to adopt that strategy grows as the confrontation becomes sharper. High moral commitment, the willingness to fast or to enter prison, is necessary and valuable in our movement, but I am bothered when guilt and a sense of emergency are allowed to displace political analysis, and even to license a flight from rationality.

Norman Solomon is too eager to take upon his white Western English-speaking nuclear terrorist back every one of the world's sins. I will allow him, and the United States, many of those sins; but it is indecently greedy to claim them all. There are plenty of European operators—and not all of them in the West—who have helped screw the world up, and keep the Cold War gelid. The present rulers of Britain are a reminder that Europeans have lost neither the inclination nor the power to multiply the world's human wrongs. And it is not even true that every person oppressed south of the Mexican border is oppressed at the sole behest of US imperialism. There are ruling families there, descendants of conquistadors, who would not thank us for implying that they are not 'white', and who are vigorous and self-motivated oppressors. And, although it is not quite decent to say so, if one scans the globe with care one may even detect a black rogue or two.

To take upon one's shoulders all the guilt of the world is itself a sort of patronage of lesser sinners and a default on internationalism. It is to say that only The Worstest, the US of A, can do evil in earnest; the rest of us are evildoers only as American clients and proxies. But if the United States were blown away tomorrow, I dare say the world could go on doing wrong.

It puzzles us Europeans, this new image of American radicals as a group of self-flagellants bent to the ground by the weight of their sins. For it does not correspond with our experience. We find that Americans are often struck from a very different mould, and draw upon different and honourable American traditions. If they were blown away tomorrow, we would gravely miss them.

What Solomon has obscured is that I was not calling for less but for *more*. I was summoning support for an assault, not only upon certain weapons-systems but upon the structures of the Cold War itself, from which those systems continually arise. And I was calling on the peace movement to exert whatever influence it has to impose a thaw upon both East and West.

To attempt this extraordinary (but essential) overthrow of ideologies and power, the European and American movements must act together. We are not different kinds of people but the same kind of people working in different places for the same ends. Even Normon Solomon and myself. Now that we have had our fun at the expense of each other, I dare say that we will both turn back to the same kind of work.

AMERICA AND THE WAR MOVEMENT†

There are two ways into the disarmament argument. One is from the globe itself: the threat to the species, the ecological imperative of survival. The other is from the injury done to people by the deformations, whether economic or cultural, of their own war-directed societies. And the problem is this: both arguments are being won, yet none of the structures of power have been shifted an inch by the argument, and not one missile has yet been stopped in its tracks.

The dangers to the biosphere posed by nuclear war are discussed in *The Aftermath*,* an expert collection of studies originally published as a special issue of *Ambio*, the journal of the Royal Swedish Academy of Sciences. The papers set forth the consequences of nuclear war in epidemiological terms, its effects on the ozone layer, on global food supplies and fresh water, on ocean ecosystems and on much else.

The message has been delivered before, though rarely with such authority. No serious attempt can be made to refute it. There can no longer be any doubt that the procurers of nuclear weapons threaten the human species and most mammalian species besides. Yet the procurers continue with their business, and simply enlarge their public relations staffs to handle meddlesome scientists, bishops, doctors and peace movements. Where we had only an arms race five years ago, we have an apologetics race today as well.

---

† From *The Nation*, 24 September 1983.
* *The Aftermath*, ed. J. Peterson (Pantheon Books, New York), 1983.

Beyond Survival** is towards the other end of the spectrum. It is a collection commissioned in the euphoric aftermath of the vast Manhattan demonstration of June 12th, 1982, and the editors and contributors suppose that they are addressing politics. And so, in some part, and helpfully, they often are. But the politics which they address are less those of power—its reasons and its irrationalisms—than those of building the alliances and coalitions which make up the disarmament movement.

Hence *Beyond Survival* appears at times to be introversial to an outsider like myself: the movement is placed upon a couch and undergoes analysis. Most of the analysts are competent, and all recommend new ways of bringing into a single coalition the constituencies of the poor (although they do not often use this term), the blacks, the feminists, the Hispanics, the labour unions, the gays, the environmental lobbies, and any other groups around which might have occasion to protest.

All this is offered cogently enough to help on the vigorous discussions already going on within the multiform American disarmament movement. And the emphasis upon the urgent need to enlarge the goal of the movement to take in opposition to US military interventions (whether nuclear or not)—that is, to transform the disarmament movement into a peace movement—is welcome, and is forcefully presented in an essay by Noam Chomsky.

My reservations concern the absence of a different kind of 'politics', by which I mean the objective analysis of power: its strategies, structures and controls: and the strategies (national or international) for contesting that power. The politics of most of these essays is deduced from subjective inferences. We explore the self-image and grievances of disadvantaged constituencies, and deduce that all of these would be less powerless if they could only meld their protests into a common movement—an ever bigger June 12th movement going in more revolutionary directions. 'Will we cling

---

** *Beyond Survival: New Directions for the Disarmament Movement*, edited by Michael Albert and David Dellinger (South End Press, Boston, USA, £8.00).

to divisive prejudices,' asks David Dellinger, 'and deny
connections between the approaching War to End War and
the abuse of millions because of their race, sex, sexual preference, or age in a society dominated by the blindnesses
of class arrogance?' And the movement itself then comes to
be its own self-sufficient goal. It appears as a kind of therapy:
'take up thy couch and walk!'

Race, gender, sexual preference, ageing and class are all
thrown together there as if they were all occasioned by the
same forces of oppression (by capitalism? patriarchy?
imperialism?) and all to be resolved by the same forms of
resistance. It would take me too long to sort that set out:
yet some of the grievances indicated (offence to the aged) are
beyond mortal repair but might be softened by reform of
manners and sensibility, others might be mended by reforms
of law and institutions, and yet others (class) may require
more revolutionary remedy.

Mass movements may be therapeutic (they often are) but
this cannot determine their strategies and goals. The peace
movement is engaged in a long rolling contest with the
strongest establishments of armed power in the history of
the world—and the strongest of all in the United States—and
it cannot afford to lose the contest. It might even be thought
to be patronising to tell blacks (or women or Hispanics or
gays) that they should support the disarmament movement
because they are oppressed or disadvantaged and therefore it
is in their self-interest to. . . etc. etc. These constituencies are
made up also of citizens, who are open to the same rational
arguments and appeals to solidarity as any other.

I am arguing the case for a more objective mode of political
analysis than is now current, and for a plainer vocabulary of
international bonding and solidarity. The politics of individual
ego-fulfilment have had a long run, and they have made some
real gains—and power has looked down upon it all with
benign self-assurance. Indeed, power has opened its portals a
crack and has allowed the winners to come in. Among the
small advance party of United States officers trained to
launch cruise missiles which arrived several weeks ago at
Greenham Common in my own country, it was announced

(with self-congratulation) that there was one woman. I
confess that I read of this example of affirmative action with
confusion and shock. What kind of 'individual rights' ideology is it which affirms the right of every person to exploit or
to exterminate their fellows?

It is a marginal point, and most of all in Mrs Thatcher's
England. The larger point is that, if the survival of human
civilisation is truly threatened (and I suppose that it is), then
the politics of self-expression and self-fulfilment of particular
interests must be placed under some political self-control:
they cannot be pressed always to the point of dissension and
inner division. And the political self-control must arise, not
from subjective inferences, but from a shared perception of
the objective crisis which threatens all interests alike, and
hence from shared strategies and shared goals.

Since the crisis is now global, then the shared perception
and the strategies of resistance must increasingly become
international. This is where the American peace movement
(whose work is crucial to civilisation's survival) faces quite
exceptional difficulties. *Inside* the United States many
persons feel themselves to be most bruised and restricted by
the structures of racism, sexism, etc.; and of course they
must and will contest these oppressions. But *outside* the
United States, in Central America and increasingly in West
Europe, it appears that it is arrogant American hegemonic
nationalism which is most threatening (and which may even
descend in the shape of a black F-111 pilot or a female cruise
missile launch-officer). American military personnel are now,
after all, *everywhere:* in El Salvador, in the Sudan, in the
Lebanon, in England and West Germany, in Turkey and in
Greece, in Diego Garcia and South Korea and Honduras and
around the Persian Gulf. What are they doing there? And by
what right? It is to ask us un-Americans to show superhuman
exercises of self-restraint if we are not to pray, at times, for
a reversion to good old-fashioned Middle American isolationism. There is nothing wrong with authentic American
nationalism, if it is concerned with America's own cultural
and historical traditions: but will it please go home and stay
indoors?

I have written 'hegemonic nationalism' and not 'imperialism'. Of course United States imperial interests and strategies
palpably exist (albeit with some inner contradictions). Yet
the naming of power in the United States simply as 'imperialism' may make the whole problem seem too tidy. For it
suggests that the problem may be easily isolated, as a powerful group of interests somewhere over there—the Pentagon,
the multinational corporations—whereas what must be confronted is a whole hegemonic 'official' national ideology,
which permeates not only the state and its organs but also
many 'liberal' critics of the state (in the Democratic Party),
which saturates the media, and which even confuses
opposition groups within the society.

People in vast regions of Middle America know almost
nothing of the world across the waters (where their fellow
countrymen are being rapidly deployed) except the fragment-
ary ideological fictions offered in their local media. Yet it
is this ideologically-confected national self-image—the herded
self-identification with the goals (any goals) of the nation-
state, the media-induced hysterias during the Iranian hostages
crisis and in the Falklands/Malvinas War, the manipulation of
the minds of vast publics as to the benign motives of their
rulers in invading Afghanistan or the Lebanon or in intruding
into Central America in support of 'national interests'—which
constitutes, quite as much as weaponry, the threat to survival.

The most dangerous and expansionist nationalist ideologies
are those which disguise themselves as missions on behalf of
human universals. Such ideologies build upon the generous,
as well as the self-interested, impulses of the evangelising
nation. (Middle America believes that US militarism is about
the export of 'freedom'). This was true of the French in
Napoleonic times and even of the British at the zenith of
empire (the 'civilising mission', the 'white man's burden').
These ideologies have now shrunk back (almost) within their
own historical and cultural frontiers, and are (almost) content
to be simple nationalisms once more, celebrating unique
historical experiences and cultural identities.

Today they are the Soviet and the American nationalist
ideologies which have become expansionist, and which walk

the world in the disguise of universals: the victory of World
Socialism or the Triumph of the Free World. And of the two
it is the American which is the most confusing. Because the
United States population is made up of so many hetero-
geneous in-migrations, it is possible to fall into the illusion
that America is a reservoir of every human universal, rather
than a peculiar, local, time-bound civilisation, marked by
unusual social mobility, competitiveness and individualism,
and with its own particular problems, needs and expectations.

Because of the youth and rapid growth of America,
nationalist ideology is more artificially-confected there than
in any other nation. It did not grow from experiential and
cultural roots, fertilised and watered by a watchful imperial
ruling-class, as in Britain. It was, like other artefacts of the
New World, a conscious ideological construction, in the work
of which ruling powers in the state, the media and the
educational system all combined. The ideology consists, not
in the assertion of the superior virtues of the (German/
British/Japanese) race, but in the pretence that America is
not a race or nation at all but is the universal Future. It lays
arrogant claim to a universalism of virtues—an incantation of
freedoms and rights—and asserts in this name a prerogative to
blast in at every door and base itself in any part of the globe
in the commission of these virtues. As it is doing in Central
America now.

Characteristically, in the going rhetoric which still engulfs
this nation, 'human rights' require no more definition than
that these are goods which Americans enjoy (to a superlative
degree) and which other guys don't have. This truth is held
to be self-evident. It is a cause of immense self-congratulation:
and a means of internal bonding, ideological and social
control, vote-soliciting, and even attributed identity. If an
Other is required, as foil to all this glittering virtue, then this
is provided by Communism. But anti-Communism is
necessary, less because Communism exists, than because
there is an internal need within the ideology to define the
approved national self-image against the boundary of an
antagonist.

I rehearse all this because I wish to define the size of the

problem facing the peace forces in the United States. I do so
with respect: our forces in Britain were in no way strong
enough to throw back a similar gust of ideology (more local
but also more intense) during the Falklands War. We know
the consequences. President Carter's helicopter operation to
rescue the hostages in Iran was a fiasco, and he was turned
out of power. Margaret Thatcher's helicopter (and task force)
operation to rescue her hostages in the Falklands was a
triumphant success: and she has now been returned to power
in triumph.

The American peace movement—if it is to have any hope
of success—must perforce challenge not only the military-
industrial complex (or imperialist interests) but the hegemonic
ruling ideology of the nation. It must strive to deconstruct
this ideologically-confected national self-image, which now
gives a very dangerous popular licence to expansion and
aggression, and to disclose in its place an authentic self-
identity. I will leave it to Americans—to poets and to
historians—to say what this self-respecting self-image should
be.

When I said that we un-Americans pray for a reversion to
isolationism I was of course in jest. What we pray for—and
what we can now recognize with delight—is the rebirth of
American internationalism: but an authentic internationalism,
which conducts its relations with equals, and which conducts
them with like-minded popular movements and not with
client states or with servile parasitic élites.

It is only the positive of internationalism which will be
strong enough to contest and drive out the reigning national
(or supra-national) ideology. There is a concern and
generosity in American radical, labour, religious and intellectual traditions within which this internationalism has long
been nourished, although sometimes as a threatened minority
tradition. The greatest achievement of the American disarmament movement of the past two years has not been in
winning this vote or that, but in raising peace consciousness
throughout the continent, in questioning the self-congratula-
tory official image of America, and in providing a nation-
wide network of groups within which the level of inter-

national discourse and information is continually rising.

Yet this still must rise a little further. The foundation-stone of internationalism cannot be guilt: it must be solidarity. We need, in some new form, a 'Wobbly' vocabulary of mutual aid and of plain duty to each other in the face of power. And we need to hammer out together our international strategies, in which the American movement clearly sees itself and *feels* itself to be part of a whole 'International' of self-liberating impulses from imperialisms and war.

Let us take the example of the *Iowa* task-force, which New York and New Jersey officials and representatives (many of them supporters of the Freeze when it seemed a vote-winner) have invited into New York harbour. Maybe the citizens are already stirring a little, and are realising the incredible folly of basing a fleet of eight warships armed with nuclear-tipped cruise missiles, nuclear depth charges, ASROC missles (some nuclear-tipped) in the densest population centre in the world, and making New York thereby a prime counterforce target (and candidate for nuclear accidents such as collision and fire).

What few have yet understood is the political strategy behind this operation. All the fuss about the 'Euromissile' crisis is about 572 cruise and Pershing II missiles—forward-based US strategic missiles to be sited on European territory. But quietly behind these are now coming the 4,000 plus sea- and air-launched cruise missiles. There are two clear political functions for the *Iowa* task-force. The first is as an 'insurance policy' in case the European peace movements should succeed in chasing cruise and Pershing off their territory. The fall-back will then be onto sea-launchers for cruise: if necessary over 300 missiles could be placed on World War II battleships (like *Iowa*), so that two ships could carry more missiles than the entire allocation to Europe.

This launcher (or launchers) could then lurk about off the coast of West Europe, in the North Atlantic, or could move into the Mediterranean. They would be more mobile than ground-launched missiles but also *less politically visible*. No-one could sit down in front of them; they would draw no demonstrations. They would get European NATO leaders off the political hook. If the missiles were thrown out of Comiso and Greenham Common, they would reappear, anchored off Staten Island.

The second function of the *Iowa* task-force (like similar task-forces, also armed with cruise missiles, based on California and Hawaii) will be as mobile intervention fleets: that is, as nuclear pirate fleets. The *Iowa* force could dodge from Iceland to the Indian Ocean: could appear menacingly off the coast of Lebanon or Libya, supporting the Rapid Deployment Force; or 'quarantine' some part of Africa.

Whichever way the 'Euromissile' crisis is resolved the shadows will advance across the Atlantic to your coasts. If cruise and Pershing go down in Europe, then the Soviet military may well 'reply' by increasing the number of their forward-based missile submarines, to bring American prime targets (of which New York must now be one) within comparable flight-time (some eight minutes) of the Pershing II to Soviet targets.

The European peace movements do not wish to export Europe's troubles to America. If things get worse for you, nothing will get better for us. We are living the same problem: we must live it together: and re-learn all that lost vocabulary of solidarity.

We shall also require solidarity in the face of power. It has been apparent that (at least since January) there has been an orchestrated NATO strategy of rolling back the peace movement, on both sides of the Atlantic, by the most careful employment of public relations, media management, the provocation of dissension, and, very probably, the infiltration of agents and provocateurs. The old NATO élites feel more threatened by their domestic peace movements than they do by their purported adversary (the Warsaw bloc); they fear that a whole way of managing the world, and of controlling publics and clients, may be slipping away into some dangerous and unstable unknown. (The Warsaw power leaders are suffering similar anxieties.) In that sense, the most important thing of all to them is not to be forced into defeat by their own domestic opposition. The MX is pointed, not at

Russia, but at the Freeze; the cruise missiles at Greenham will be pointed at CND.

This is to say that our peace movements are engaged in one of the sharpest confrontations of our national political lives. We must disabuse our supporters if they suppose that they are confronting certain weapons only—'the bomb'. The peace movements cannot opt whether to be more 'political' or not. They have challenged 'the bomb'—and behind it they have found the full power of the State. If they are to reach 'the bomb' they must now take on also a whole State-manipulated and media-endorsed ideology.

It is ideology, even more than military-industrial pressures, which is the driving-motor of Cold War II. What occasions alarm is the very irrationality—the rising hysteria—of the drive, when it is measured against the 'objective' economic or political interests of ruling groups or forces. It is as if—as in the last climax of European imperialisms which led on into World War One, or as in the moment when Nazism triumphed in Germany—ideology has broken free from the existential socio-economic matrix within which it was nurtured and is no longer subject to any controls of rational self-interest. Cold War II is a replay of Cold War I, but this time as a dead-ly farce: the content of real interest-conflict between the two superpowers is low, but the content of ideological rancour and 'face' is dangerously high.

If history eventuated according to the notional rational self-interest of states or of classes, then we could calm our fears of nuclear war. It is scarcely in the interest of any ruling-class or state to burn up its resources, its labour-force, its markets, and then itself. But ideology masks out such interferences from an outer rational world. Just at the moment when the adversary posture of the two blocs is becoming increasingly pointless—and when a cease-fire in the Cold War would be greatly to the advantage of both parties—ideology assumes command and drives towards its own obsessional goals.

We may call this ideology 'imperialist' if we wish (and on both sides). But in naming it as 'imperialism' we should avoid the reduction of the problem to simplistic preconceptions (for example, Leninist) of what imperialism is. No two imperialisms have ever been the same—each has been a unique formation. And none can be reduced to a mono-causal analysis: for example, the pursuit of markets and profits, guided by some all-knowing committee of a ruling-class. Even in Europe's imperialist zenith (which culminated in the direct occupation and exploitation of subjected territories) a wide configuration of motivations were always at play: markets, missions, military bases, naval and trade routes, competition between imperial powers, ideological zeal, the vacancy left by the dissolution of previous power-structures (the Moghul empire), populist electoral hysteria, the definition of frontiers, imperial interest-groups, the expectation of revenue or gold or oil (which sometimes was not fulfilled).

American and Soviet 'imperialism' are also unique formations, and of the two it is Soviet which is most threatened and insecure, and American which is most expansionist. The American formation is a whole configuration of interests: financial, commercial (or 'corporatist') and extractive (the search for reserves of fossil fuels, uranium and scarce minerals): military (the alarming thrust of the arms trade, with its crazily insecure financial underwriting, which, in its turn, must be underwritten by military guarantees); political (the establishment of hegemony not by direct occupation but through the proxies of parasitic ruling élites in the client nations): and ideological. This formation is plainly beyond the control of any all-wise committee of a ruling-class: the White House is simply rolled around every-which-way as the eddying interests break upon its doors. Now one interest, now another, penetrates into the Oval Office.

In this messy, indecisive formation it is clearly ideology which—in the person of the President and his closest advisors —binds the whole configuration together and gives to it whatever erratic direction it takes. The rhetoric of the Cold War legitimates the whole operation, and therefore the Cold War is necessary to power's own continuance: the Cold War's ideological premises must continually be recycled and its visible instruments of terror must be 'modernised'. But since this direction increasingly defies the self-interest of any of the participants, ideology itself becomes more hysteric: it combines into one mish-mash the voices of militant Zionism, born-again fundamentalists, traumatised emigrés from Communist repression, careerist academics and bureaucrats, Western 'intelligence officers' and the soothsayers of the *New York Times*.

There is now (in this sense) a 'war movement' in Washington and in London. It is made up of (a) particular military-industrial interest groups—searching for bases, fossil fuels, new weapons, markets for arms; (b) New Right ideologues and publicists, and (c) the confrontational rhetoric and policies of populist politicians of the right. The climate thus engendered is sheltering nakedly militarist adventures and interventions, legitimated within the cant of Cold War apologetics.

But the military confrontation between the blocs has less and less rational strategic function: nuclear missiles are now becoming symbolic counters of political 'posture' or 'blackmail', negotiations are about political 'face'. Both SS-20s and Euromissiles are superfluous to any sane armoury. And the cruise and Pershing missiles have got to come because they are symbols of US hegemony over its own clients, and their acceptance is demanded as proof of NATO's 'unity'. They must be put down in noxious nests in England, Germany and Sicily, in order to hold the old decaying structures of life-threatening power together. The rising military appropriations are all for glue to paste over the places where the post-war political settlement ('Yalta') is beginning to come apart.

Nuclear weapons are not designed for the continuation of politics by other means: they are already the *suppression* of politics, the *arrest* of all political process within the frigid stasis of 'deterrence', and the *substitution* of the threat of annihilation for the negotiated resolution of differences. And within this degenerative process, the simulated threat of the Other becomes functional to the tenure of power of the rulers of the rival blocs: it legitimates their appropriation of taxes and resources, it serves to discipline unruly client states, it affords an apologia for acts of intervention, and it is a convenient resource for internal social and intellectual control. Increasingly the symbolism of State terror is employed to menace domestic opposition within each bloc. Like a curving ram's horn, the Cold War is now growing inwards into the warriors' own brains.

The war movement in the West encourages—according to the Cold War's 'law of reciprocity' (whether missiles or ideology) —an answering ideological response in the East. In Moscow as in Washington and London the tattered scripts of the early 1950s are dug out of the drawers and the lines are rehearsed. (Some of the old actors are still around.) The *New York Times* and *Pravda* recite the old crap: 'KGB agents', 'agents of Western imperialism', 'un-American activities' and 'peace-loving forces'. . . indeed, some of the malodorous agents (of both sides) are actually sent in. But the true adversaries which power fears, and seeks to hem in within the old ideological controls, are now not without but *within* their own blocs and spheres of influence: the real enemies of United States and NATO politicians are Central American insurgency, European 'neutralism', and domestic peace and radical movements: the real enemies of the Soviet power-élite are Solidarnosc, Afghan insurgents, and the growing desire of East European peoples for greater autonomy.

There could be two ways back from the precipice to which a threatened and dying ideology is conducting us. One would simply be a reassertion within the power-élites of the United States and the Soviet Union of the claims of rational self-interest. What is the point of burning up the world when, with a little loss of rhetoric, it could be managed and exploited to their mutual advantage? If this way is taken, then the élites will back away from war: they will come to some agreement (above the peace movements' heads): go back into arms control and SALT: and draw up a new 'Yalta' for the entire globe, dividing it up between them according to agreed rules: Afghanistan and Poland for you, El Salvador and Nicaragua for me.

This way is so much preferable to nuclear war that it seems churlish to call it in question. Indeed, it has some support in

the United States, among élite groups which are now getting
into discourse with their Soviet analogues, and who give some
backing to the Freeze. Yet the trouble with this superpower
settlement, this Orwellian 'Yalta 1984', is that it could never
be more than a brief interim arrangement: it might last for
five or ten years. For the superpowers can no longer command
that the rest of the world—that Poland and Nicaragua,
Europe and Latin America—stand still. It is indeed a question
as to how much longer the élites can command their own
domestic publics.

So that, even if the élites of both superpowers snuggle up
together and attempt to take this first way back from nuclear
suicide, it can only afford a brief interval before the second
way to human survival is resumed. This is the way of the
'International' of peace movements, of non-aligned nations,
and movements for civil rights and for liberation, working
out—through many complexities—common strategies of
mutual support and solidarity. Their common aims will be
the enlargement of spaces for national autonomy, the peaceful break-up or melding of the blocs, and the refusal of every
syllable of the vocabulary of nuclear arms. No-one can draw
an accurate map of this way and show where it leads. We
must find out together as we go along.

QUESTIONS TO CASPAR WEINBERGER*

Mr. President. Ladies and Gentlemen. I also wish to express my pleasure that Mr Weinberger is here. I think that this is a recognition not only of the standing of this society but a recognition also of the depth of concern in Europe and in this country on the issues of peace. And I welcome it also as

---

* On February 27th, 1984, I debated at the Oxford Union with Caspar Weinberger, the United States Secretary for Defense, the motion 'That there is no moral difference between the foreign policies of the US and the USSR.' The debate had been originally scheduled for May 27th, 1983, but Mr Heseltine intervened to prevent the debate (long before the date of the general election had been announced to the British Parliament) on the grounds that 'such a debate in a year that might see a general election might not be advisable'. (*New York Times*, 20 April 1983.) Since Heseltine was then planning his electoral strategy—in which the peace movement, the Labour Party, and several other parties were to be lampooned with every resource of the Tory Party and most of the media as uncritically and one-sidedly pro-Soviet—it was clearly against the interests of his party that a public debate of this kind should take place just before the election. His intervention was a wholly improper and unconstitutional interference in public life and in the affairs of the Oxford Union Society.

Mr Weinberger and his side 'won' the debate by 271–232 votes. However, Mr Laurence Grafstein (a past-president of the Union who was one of the speakers on Mr Weinberger's side) has candidly noted (in the *New Republic*) that 'it was the presence of about a hundred Americans in the debating chamber which proved decisive'. Some of these voters had been specially flown across the Atlantic for the occasion!

I am grateful to BBC 2 (Special Projects) and to Mr Elwyn Parry Jones for sending me a transcript of my speech. I have corrected it for clarity and made a few cuts, but made no changes of substance.

one of those signs of the openness to debate of the American system: an openness which I have myself often benefited from. I have been able to say in the United States what I wanted to say on behalf of the British or the European peace movement. I have been welcomed at the National Press Club in Washington, at campuses and churches in the United States, and I know very well that I would not be able to speak openly in the same way in the Soviet Union.

Without this tradition and vitality of openness in American intellectual life, humanity would not now know the perils in which it is placed. If it had not been for the tradition of the United States scientists, of 'whistleblowers' like Daniel Ellsberg, or of arms controllers who have come out and made the most radical criticism of their own state policy—if it had not been for publications like the *Bulletin of the Atomic Scientists*, we would not even know about the nuclear winter that would follow even a medium exchange of weapons. We would not know this through Soviet sources, and we would not know it from British sources which are obsessed with 'official secrecy'.

This emphasises that we are tonight not discussing the relative merits of the two political systems. We are not discussing whether we would prefer to live in the Soviet Union or in the United States. There is scarcely any room for choice in this for any serious intellectual worker who needs the tools of his trade, who needs to be able to consult the libraries or to publish without censorship.

We are discussing tonight the foreign policies, not the internal social systems, the foreign policies of the United States and the USSR and the moral differences between them. And I can find none. Today the world is dominated by two towering superpowers, locked in each others' nuclear arms, aggravating each other, inciting each other in their ideological postures, rendering and reducing to client status their lesser allies.

Mr Weinberger will find some Europeans and many British in an ill-humour today. And he shouldn't be surprised. He is himself something of a philosopher, a rigorous thinker on questions of deterrence. In his *Defense Report* for the Fiscal

Year of 1984 he wrote out some of his reflections. Deterrence, he said is 'a dynamic effort', not a static one, and he set out a view of an entire 'continuum' over which deterrence had to be not only effective but constantly modernised and enhanced, linking the highest level of conventional arms to the lowest threshold of nuclear weapons: a continuum in regions, a continuum in ranges of missiles, a continuum in time itself, envisaging the possibility of an extended nuclear war. And this was a philosophy of 'enhanced deterrence'. Now enhanced deterrence is not a stable state, it is a radically unstable state. It has, in the worst-case analysis of the planners, an in-built accelerator, and these two systems are now acclerating towards each other at a growing pace towards a terminal collision.

We in Europe were found by some clever philosophers in NATO several years ago to be in a weak point in this 'continuum'. And for three years negotiations have been going on over our heads about a matter which could scarcely concern Europeans more: that is, the nuclear weapons sited on our own territory and which might be used in a European 'theatre of war'.

By no means all the blame for the enhancement of deterrence in Europe lies with the United States. Our own political leaders have been throughout consenting adults in the corruption and subordination of this nation to the hegemony of United States' military policy. Now the first flight of these missiles, owned and operated by the United States, are here on our territory and they are supposed to be for our greater security. Do we really feel more secure because cruise and Pershing have come? No-one feels more secure: neither Europeans nor the Soviet people nor the people of the United States.

We believe first of all that the military scenario has always been absurd. We have these serpents' eggs and more are coming. (By the way, perhaps we could ask Mr Weinberger when the next flight will come?) But I would like (since he is our guest) to warn Mr Weinberger before he replies that we have an engine in Britain known as the Official Secrets Act. And although he might be able to give this information to the

United States Congress—or even to the Soviet Ambassador—
if he gave it to the British people it might be an offence
against the Official Secrets Act since these are Acts to
prevent the British people from being informed about matters
deeply of their concern. We have the case now of a young
woman in the Foreign Office who is accused of a terrible
offence against 'official secrets'. And Miss Sarah Tisdall,
who is accused of this offence, is accused of having leaked to
an extreme revolutionary newspaper called the *Guardian* a
memorandum sent by our Defence Secretary Mr Heseltine to
Mrs Thatcher and others in which he explained how he
intended to con the British people and manage opinion at
the moment of the arrival of cruise. So that Mr Weinberger
must be cautious as to what he says about these matters in
this country.

All the serpents' eggs are now clutched on a site in Britain
whose location, thanks to the action of some of my fellow
countrywomen and their friends from North America and
Europe and elsewhere, has been rather well advertised. Even
the British people know where the cruise missiles are. I think
probably the Soviet Union knows where they are. And if the
'evil emperor' is anxious to make a pre-emptive strike (as we
are told by some people) than all the eggs could be smashed
in one basket in a perfect 'Pearl Harbour'. So no-one can
really be expecting this pre-emptive strike to come.

No, the missiles must move out first from the base. But
while these missiles are themselves so small that verification
is extremely difficult—and therefore arms control agreements
are being cast in jeopardy by cruise missiles coming—the
convoys which take them out to their firing-places in the
country are very well open to satellite observation. So it is
insane. The first sign of those convoys moving out would be
a signal to satellite observation that our govenment (or the
United States Government rather, because they are owned
and operated by the United States) was planning a strike; and
this would be an incitement to the Soviet military to make a
pre-emptive strike before their own missiles were struck. This
is insane. Although I would reassure Mr Weinberger that the
situation isn't quite as bad as that. We have got a fence

around these missiles, in fact we have got quite a tall fence. We have now got three fences and we have got them pretty well encircled by soldiers and by police and best of all by the Greenham Common women, and then outside by the peace movement of the nation. All we have to do now to make the missiles completely safe is to get the police to turn around and face the other way.

The second reason that we do not feel more secure lies in the predicted consequences of this action. The blocs have closed against each other. The counter-deployment is going on of SS21's, 22's or 23's, including deployment in Czechoslovakia and East Germany (which have hitherto been only very lightly, if at all, occupied by nuclear weapons). We have been saying up and down Europe for two years that the dragons' teeth sown in Comiso and Greenham Common would spring up as missiles on the other side. And so it has taken place. Any child could see that. Any child. Why can eminent statespersons not understand what Auden wrote in agony at the commencement of World War II?

> I and the public know
> What all schoolchildren learn:
> Those to whom evil is done
> Do evil in return.

The missiles are futile, of course. The Dutch women's peace movement have told me they have found out that the cruise missiles are actually cartons full of washing powder. It doesn't matter what they are: they are symbols and they are symbols of menace, of 'posture', of clientage and subordination in the recipient nations, of NATO or Warsaw Pact 'unity'.

But they are not only symbols. Nor are they all that there is. We know what is coming on behind them. Thanks to the openness of the American system we know much more about what is coming on on the United States' side. MX, BI, Trident (there and here), the Iowa task force with its load of sea-launched cruise missiles, the air-launched cruise missiles: 1,300 are in production now and in the fiscal year '85. And beyond that the vista of space weapons and space scenarios for war. And there are other little bits of things in Mr Weinberger's latest 1985 Fiscal Year *Report;* I think that there are five new short-range nuclear systems now being brought forward and two new chemical systems. There are (perhaps he will tell us?) plans for siting new ground-launched anti-ship missiles in the Western Isles and in Scotland?

I say that this is a condition of barbarism. And I put forward two documents, essential to my case. These are both part of the propaganda that led us to this disastrous situation. One is called *Soviet Military Power* and it has a foreword by Mr Weinberger. It is a 'Sears–Roebuck' catalogue of all the deadly military equipment, whether naval or air or on the ground, possessed by the Soviet Union. And the other, which was produced in answer to it by the Soviet propagandists, is called *Whence the Threat to Peace?* This also is a catalogue—rather better illustrated, because they could get the illustrations more easily from the United States' press—of all the marvellous military equipment being developed in the United States. They have even copied each other in maps. Here is a power projection in the United States catalogue, with a *huge* Soviet Union, with arrows going in every direction around the world. And in the Soviet catalogue, the Soviet Union is rather smaller and all the arrows are spreading out from the United States towards the five continents of the world.

The usual half-lies and propaganda statements are made in both these books. But the tragedy is that *both* these books are largely *true.* William Hazlitt said about a philosophical radical, the Rev Fawcett, in the 1790's that he had Thomas Paine's *Rights of Man* and Edmund Burke's *Reflections on the French Revolution* bound together in the same covers, and he said that, taken together, they made a very good book. But bind these two together and they make the most evil book known in the whole human record. They are a catalogue, an inventory of the matched evils of this accelerating system, a confession of absolute human failure. What moral difference is there between these two catalogues? What language of 'ought' can be found there? Is this the product of our most advanced civilisation? 'Was it for this the clay grew tall?'

The globe has shrunk now to a little gourd. It is controlled by two vast, mutually-exacerbating military structures at the summit of which there is extraordinary centralised power in the functions of the President of the Union States and the First Secretary of the Soviet Communist Party. We know now that throughout last autumn this power lay in the hands of two elderly men, one of whom was on a kidney-machine and half-dead from the neck down, and the other of whom (in the view of his critics) was on an autocue-machine and half-dead from the neck up.

The trouble with the statesmen and military leaders of both blocs is that they talk the same language. They both burn our taxes and our resources before the nostrils of the great Sacred Cow called the 'balance' or 'parity'. We haven't, on this side in this debate, played the game of 'snap'. We haven't tried to list the offences on one side and trade them against the offences on the other. Vietnam—Afghanistan; Central Europe—Central America, the joint competition in the foul trade in arms. If anything, I would say, looking over the last 30 years, that the Gulag has been shrinking over on that side, and is tending to enlarge in the area of dependency on this side, the client or proxy states of the Western powers. There is now a formidable United States presence everywhere: Oman, Turkey, Iceland, South Korea, Egypt, Diego Garcia—what are you doing in Diego Garcia?—Somalia—what are you doing there?

We have seen this process by which the Brezhnev doctrine was extended from Eastern and Central Europe to Afghanistan; while the Truman doctrine (taking over from Britain in 1947) proclaimed an area of special United States interest, first in Greece, Turkey, and the Near East, and was then extended by President Carter to the Persian Gulf. We see now before our eyes today an extraordinary notion of 'peace-keeping', in the Caribbean, around Nicaragua, or off the coast of Lebanon, where the *New Jersey* battleship is just steaming up and down lobbing half-ton shells into the villages in the hills above Beirut—lobbing half-ton shells—what is this? Congress doesn't understand, the American people cannot understand.

(By the way, it was reported in the *Washington Post* in July that there are eight Tomahawk cruise missiles in deployment on the *New Jersey*. It would reassure us very much to know that these missiles, with a range of 1,500 miles, do not have nuclear warheads? Because if they do have nuclear warheads they can reach deeply into Asia.)

What 'moral interest' is here? If anything I would say that, of the two, the United States administration under President Reagan has been more threatening in its military posture, while the Soviet Union has been more responsible for the ideological and security blockages which prevent any healing-process in the world to begin. But no micrometer can find a moral difference in the mutual postures of hostility. And I want to ask Mr Weinberger: what is this quarrel about? It is an irrational condition. It consists in itself. The superpowers feel threatened because they *are* threats to each other and have historically become so. It is an acquired inertia. It is a self-reproducing system.

When, at a certain historical moment at the end of World War Two, the armies met and caused a divide like a geological fault across the centre of our continent, we then had as a product of those particular historical circumstances and contingencies the origin of the Cold War. You can look back there for moral differences, but now, after 35 years, there is no more morality. This division has outlasted its historical tenure, the moment of its origin. Struck by the permafrost of deterrence occasioned by nuclear weapons arriving at that moment of division, there commenced a self-reproducing process in which the hawks feed the hawks of the other side.

Each side pretends to moral superiority. The Soviet Union pretends to be a socialist heartland but it fears most of all democratic socialist impulses; hence the crushing of the 'Prague Spring' in '68, hence the crushing of the self-activating working-class movement of Solidarnosc in Poland. And the threatening military posture of the West repeatedly gives to the old post-Stalinist rulers an extended historical tenure. It is the 'evil empire' claptrap, the 'sworn enemies' claptrap which Mrs Thatcher was using only last year, which causes prison doors to close on the other side, which leads to the tightening of security systems, which gives a justification and legitimacy to the post-Stalinist leadership which has out-lasted. . .

Lawrence Grafstein (interrupting): With the greatest respect, sir, do you really believe that Mrs Thatcher's voice or Mr Reagan's voice, shrill as we all agree they are, is respon-sible for the closing of prison doors in the Eastern bloc or in the Soviet Union?. . . I can't see how you could hold some-one's words responsible for someone else's deeds?

E.P. Thompson: I thank you for this correction. I said 'accomplices'. I hope that I said 'accomplices'.* This is a reciprocal process. Each time the West adopts a threatening and menacing posture there is an instant response from the other side which makes the position of the doves weaker and the position of the hawks stronger, which induces the enhancement of the security system and which makes more difficult the communication which our peace movement has been with great difficulty developing over the last three years.

We see this logic at work all the time. I want to give you one example of this. We now know that Mr Andropov was dying through the three months during which the NATO missile deployment was coming to fulfilment. There was then the makings of a succession-crisis, and the succession has now been decided. If we suppose that there are divisions (as many experts say) in the Soviet leadership, between the doves and the hawks, do you really think that the doves were being strengthened and encouraged as Pershing and cruise came into Europe? NATO acted precisely in such a way as to induce a response of fear and insecurity in the Soviet Union and to bring about the opposite result. And then the leaders of the Western world go to Moscow and proclaim that they want to have a 'dialogue'. . . with a coffin!

On this side we have the Western ideological use of 'human rights'. The cause is just but the employment of it is again and again the most odious hypocrisy. I need not remind you of the blind eye to offences in our own back-yard. I would

---

* I didn't!—E.P.T.

refer you to Amnesty International's report on *Political
Killings by Governments:* You won't find that it says that
political killings take place on that side of the world but not
in the 'free world's' area of influence. It's a very much more
jumbled picture than that and one which leads to a much
more complex reading. And secondly there is the double-talk
that goes on: the enthusiasm of President Reagan for workers'
control in Poland when the American air controllers were put
in irons; or of Mrs Thatcher for Solidarnosc, when by a
stroke of the pen seven or eight thousand British trade
unionists at GCHQ, Cheltenham, are suddenly told that they
have the same trade-union rights as Poles. I only want to say
this. The strategy of a Cold War ideological linkage between
human rights and Cold War is deeply counter-productive. No
one is ever going to get any human rights in Czechoslovakia
or Poland because a cruise missile or Pershing is pointed
at them.

Let me end by being constructive. Am I speaking for
'neutralism'? Am I saying 'a plague on both your houses!'?
Yes. But we—that is Europe—are also pretty plaguey. We are
a source of the plague, we were the source of World War One
and World War Two. And what we owe to ourselves, but also
to the American and the Soviet people, is a more active
strategy than mere neutrality. Neutrality isn't going to save
us from the nuclear winter if the superpowers engage. We
need to make a space between the two superpowers: a more
tranquil space, maybe by nuclear-free zones in the Baltic and
Balkans, a corridor in central Europe; by commencing a
healing-process of citizens, of scholars, of doctors, of
churches, a healing-process underneath the level of the states.

The European peace movement in the last three years has
not just been about certain categories of missile. Underneath
there has been a huge subterranean political-geological up-
heaval, the demand for greater autonomy both as individual
nations and of Europe as a whole. I think Americans will
understand when I say that we are on the edge of a moment
that they might remember from their own history. We are in
a place like 1771 or 1772. Europe is meditating now a
declaration of independence.

I want to ask Mr Weinberger what his solution is, beyond all the build-up of these missiles? What solution does he offer? I suggest that what we need is an 'Austrian solution' for Europe, and then for the world. Yes, the problem as Mr Shultz has said, is in effect 'Yalta'. But 'Yalta' has got two sides: one side is the Soviet presence in Eastern and Central Europe, and the other side is the heavy American military hegemony in western and southern Europe. And you will never reach a settlement on one side without a settlement on the other. That is the strategy we have to look for. I am making no moral apologies for the presence of Soviet troops in Czechoslovakia or in Hungary, but as realists we must know that they·will not withdraw unless there is some concession in the West and especially in West Germany. While West Germany is stashed with military forces will there be a withdrawal on the other side?

Americans should reflect how this situation came about. There has not been in this century any major war on American territory and forever may this continue. But if, some 40 years ago, invading armies had come by way of Canada into New England, had sacked Boston, Providence, New Haven, Albany, Rochester, Buffalo—had gone as far west as Detroit—had invested New York, so that New Yorkers died by one-third of the population—ate shoe-leather, burnt their books and their floor-boards, as the Leningrad people did—had got to the borders of Washington, as Hitler's armies got to Moscow—had then fought block by block right into the heart of Chicago, as happened in Stalingrad—had left 20 million dead—then the United States might have made, after that, a client buffer zone of Canada. That would not have been a 'moral' action. I'm making no apology for it. It would have been a consequence of history, a matter of state interest.

But those who served in World War Two would not have believed it, they would have been amazed if they had been told that 39 years after the end of World War Two there would still be Soviet forces in East Europe and United States forces in West Europe. At that time we had a vision, and that vision extended also to the United States and the Soviet Union, of a socialist and democratic world. We have

now to re-trace our steps back down to the point where
'Yalta' was fixed and try and unscramble it.

When friends come to help us its fine for them to stay in
the house for three or four days, but when they stay for
three weeks we get a little bit restive. After 39 years enough
is enough. So it's now our duty to start this healing-process
and its yours, Mr Weinberger, to assist us to this new objective whose end must be the withdrawal of these forces from
both sides. This is not anti-Americanism—it is not anti-
Sovietism. We'll send you home with flowers and we will
welcome you back to our universities or to our countries
as visitors with flowers once more. But it is in the interests
of the people of both sides to be rid of the burden, the
anguish, and the danger involved in this European connection.

The first moral difference that will appear will be when
either superpower makes an actual *act* of disarmament.
Then we can start to talk about morality. Until that happens
I rest my case on these two odious books and I ask Oxford
to support this motion in the name of a universalism at its
very foundation in the Middle Ages: a universalism of
scholarship which owed its duty to the skills of communication and learning and not to those of the armed state. As
William Blake wrote:

> The strongest poison ever known
> Came from Caesar's laurel crown.

I support this motion in the confidence that this house will
reject the poison of Caesar.

BRITAIN CRUISES ON

CARELESS TALK COSTS LIVES*

There is something quixotic in this—for a post-imperial island nation, with an ailing economy, to send out on three days' notice 26,000 men and a vast armada to the opposite end of the oceans in defence of a few hundreds of its own nationals threatened by an invading tyranny.

It is in defiance of all calculations of interest. There is no realism about it. And it is this which has caught, for a moment, the heart of half the nation. Those who suppose the British to be a nation of shop-keepers are riding for a fall. The British can also be a nation of romantics. They like to argue their politics, not in terms of interests, but in terms of oughts. This is true of the British Labour movement also. Inside every shop steward there is a Don Quixote struggling to get out.

The British are also a rather old seafaring nation, the island anchorage of the greatest naval imperialism ever known to the world. For 500 years the ships have set out, from the Thames and Medway, from Plymouth, Portsmouth, the Clyde, to quarter the globe and to accumulate that extraordinary empire by acts of aggression a great deal less decorous and less bloodless than the invasion with which the Falklands War commenced. It is odd that we should be so moralistic today about other nations' faults. We expect them to grow up instantly to our own senescent sanctity

---

* *Guardian*, 31 May 1982.

without passing through our own adolescent sins.

The whole British people had a part in this naval empire. It was not just a preserve of the ruling class. They were the common people who built and manned the ships and whose families awaited their return. Naval victories were a staple of popular ballad and broadsheet. Drake and Nelson were genuine national heroes, not invented from above.

There is a long resonance in this, and an old resource for Tory Populism. Naval officers have been the most competent cadre of the British ruling class—as seamen, navigators, administrators. Some even, through shared hardships and loyalties, became democrats or 'Friends of the People'.

And there is another ancient resonance, which one can sense to be vibrating now. The English nation came of age with the defeat of the Armada. The naval battles which first secured our empire were mainly with Hispanic peoples. Our privateers scoured the oceans, robbing the King of Spain of his treasure and singeing his beard.

The European maritime nations exported their rivalries and fought them out before astonished native audiences at the furthest ends of the earth. 'We did maik them such a breakfast as I do verielie think was neyther in the way of curttesy or unkindnesses well accepted.' So wrote Captain Thomas Best in a despatch of 1612 recounting the Battle of Swally Hole—one of those sharp engagements in which the English gained dominance over the Portuguese in the contest for ports in India.

'The Dragon, being ahead, steered from one to another, and gave them such banges as maid ther verie sides crack; for we neyther of us never shott butt were so neere we could nott misse.' The fight took place 'in the sight of all the army of the Muslim Governor who stood so thick upon the hills beholdinge of us that they covered the ground.'

Manners have changed today. We do not have to wait for Captain Best's despatch to come to us by sail around the Cape. We are told about it all—or we are told as much as some official thinks it proper that we should know—the next day by Mr Ian MacDonald. There has been some loss in the vigour of the language, as well as in veracity. But that is a

CARELESS TALK COSTS LIVES

small price to pay for progress.

And progress has made other gains. This is an electronic war, a war of top technicians. Our men-of-war no longer steer between the enemy and crack their sides. Torpedoes and missiles are launched at ranges of twenty or more miles. All that opponents may ever see of each other is a radar blip.

And there is no astonished army of the Muslim Governor now viewing the Battle of Falkland Sound. The audience, thick on the hills, are not only the sheep—or such of the sheep as have not already been changed, by the opposing forces, into mutton. It is also that of the arms traders and war gamesmen—the 'experts' of the whole world.

These are rapt in attention. Shares are rising and falling. Sea Harriers are up but aluminium frigates are down. Since the *Sheffield* was sunk the makers of the Exocet have already received new orders for sixteen hundred (or was it sixteen thousand?) missiles. Full order books for that. And 'lessons' are being learned. United States naval strategy is already undergoing a major review. Too late for us, of course. Progress is going on, and we are the price.

We can see, more clearly than we could two weeks ago, the features of World War III. It is not only that the Falklands War is being fought with nuclear-age technologies in which only the nuclear-tipped warheads are missing. It is also that the consequences of the militarisation of the entire globe have become transparent.

This is not just a matter of the export of sophisticated weaponry from the advanced to the Third World: sales to Argentina of the Exocet, of Skyhawks, of Sea Wolf and Sea Dart, Type 42 destroyers (sister ships to the *Sheffield*) and the rest. No doubt our forces in the Falklands are already reflecting upon that, and in due course the British public may give it a thought also.

It is also that, with the weapons, the advanced world is exporting—directly or indirectly—military juntas. Look where you will, the pressure is that way: Chile, Guatemala, El Salvador, Argentina, Poland, Afghanistan. If we want to crusade against fascist juntas, we need only scan the list of our own best customers for arms. Our loyal NATO ally,

Turkey, is a junta of that kind, with above 30,000 political prisoners in its jails and with the executive Committee of the Turkish Peace Association at this moment on trial. This year the United States has increased its hand-outs to Turkey of military aid.

The peace movement has been warning of this for years, but our government has noticed only when a junta blew up in its own face. It is not as if our governments (Labour or Conservative) were given no warning. In 1978, to his credit, President Carter cut off military sales to the Argentine on the issue of human rights. France, Britain, Israel and Germany eagerly stepped in to take up the slack. If (which God forbid!) one of our nuclear submarines should be sunk, causing a major reactor disaster in the South Atlantic, it would perhaps have been located by a Lynx helicopter (Westland Aircraft Ltd) equipped with Ferranti Seaspray radar and Decca electronic supports.

Helicopters in the Argentine have had other uses. It is said that some of the thousands of 'Disappeared Ones'—oppositionists seized by the junta's security arm—were simply dumped from the bellies of helicopters into the South Atlantic. An American business man recently overheard Argentine officers jesting about 'the flying nuns'—two French disappeared nuns who were dealt with in that way. It is a clean and convenient means of disposal.

That is an odious regime. Yet there is something a little odious also about the hypocrisy of our own politicians. We are now, very suddenly, in a war to the death with a fascist regime. Yet our government has no interest in liberating the Argentine people, or in strengthening the democratic opposition to General Galtieri. On the contrary, by taking recourse to military measures, instead of diplomatic and economic sanctions, it has strengthened the junta and given it a surge of populist nationalist support.

To be honest, I do not think that Mrs Thatcher—and still less President Reagan—want to see the fall of the Argentine junta. They would like to humiliate it, to be sure, and to see it reshuffled into more accommodating forms. But they will not wish to threaten *juntadom*, whether there or in Chile.

For if the junta fell under pressure from its own people, something far 'worse'—an Argentine Allende or Castro might come to power.

If the West had wished to destabilise the junta it had the means at hand. The Argentine is one of the most indebted nations in the world. And why? Because Western banks have loaned to Argentina the wherewithal to buy expensive Western weapons-systems. If Western banks had been willing to pull the plug and default the junta, in a few months unrest might have overwhelmed and overturned the military rulers.

But this would have been a desperate remedy with an uncertain outcome. It would have caused pain in the ledgers of the Western banking system. It was better to settle the matter in traditional ways, by the loss of blood rather than the risk of money. It was better to send out a task-force.

And do we realise—does *anyone* yet realise—what we—or our betters on the front benches of all the major parties—have done? In that quixotic moment of injured national pride and historical reminiscence, we have sent 26,000 men 8,000 miles away, without adequate air cover, to confront some of the most advanced weaponry yet devised.

The politicians squint at us complacently from the screens, one eye on the cameras, the other on the opinion polls. They are confident that they—or at least those poor bastards out there in the South Atlantic—will pull it off. Yet romanticism married to that kind of calculation of political advantage is a poor guide to reality.

Careless talk costs lives. It is costing lives now. Talk of paramountcy, sovereignty, flags, unconditional surrender; careless talk on the Jimmy Young Show and at the Scottish Tory Party conference; the careless roar of the House of Commons at feeding-time. Now they have got their meat.

It is impossible to write a line on the possible outcome of the Falklands War without hazard. To write is like rolling marbles on the deck of a ship in a storm. I write this now on Friday. What will we learn when it appears on Monday? Will Port Stanley have fallen to British marines? Will one of our capital ships have been sunk? Will a cease-fire have been enforced by world opinion?

I wish only to say this: we have done a dreadful and un-thinking thing. We have allowed a desperate gamble to take place with human life, in preference to a longer course of diplomatic and economic attrition. The gamble may pay off (and greatly to Mrs Thatcher's political advantage), owing to the immense resources, experience and skill of the British forces.

But it is not inevitable that it will, and it is necessary that someone should incur the odium of saying so. Our task-force is now at risk. Its air defences, always inadequate, depend upon two carriers. If the *Hermes*, instead of the *Atlantic Conveyor*, had been sunk, then the terms of battle would have tilted dangerously against us.

And what would happen then? Will 500 years of imperial naval history end in a tragic encounter in Falkland Sound? And how will the land forces be rescued and brought back? How, across those 8,000 miles, can we mount another Dunkirk?

Our politicians and much of our popular media have been guilty of appalling levity. The sinking of the *Belgrano* and the *Sheffield* ought to have enforced a change of tone, an interval of reflection. I would have been opposed to the sending of the task-force even if I had known that it would bring a quick, and almost bloodless, victory. Our proper course was always pursuance of the full terms of UN Resolution 502, in *all* its parts, and with the endorsement of world opinion. Our resort to force has already endangered the peace of the world by weakening the authority of the United Nations, which, ineffectual as it is—and as we have made it—is yet the only institution which points forward to an international rule of law.

But we are now, as I write, brought to a desperate situa-tion. A major British defeat could have appalling conse-quences within our culture: it could turn us into something much like a junta ourselves. Already the authoritarians of every hue are having their festival. After the careless talk has ended, the really ugly talk begins.

That is why the peace movement must now go out into those storms outside and rescue what is sane and pacific in our culture. If the first thoughts of all of us are with our brave lads in the South Atlantic—as it is obligatory for every politic speech to commence these days—then our second thoughts ought to be how to get them out of that cold and hostile place.

I can see no way in which CND's demonstration in Hyde Park on June 6th can not also be a demonstration to halt and to pass back into the hands of United Nations negotiations the outcome of the Falklands War. I know that there are some notable critics of our resort to force in the Falklands who are not nuclear disarmers; and I know that there are some nuclear disarmers who think that the Falklands War is not a proper issue to concern CND.

But I think that we must all, calmly and in good order and in the greatest possible numbers, go to the Park together. This is a crisis of historic dimensions, a crisis in our culture and our polity, and an ideological confrontation which we refuse at our peril. And, even more than this, it is our urgent duty both to our kin and also to their Argentinian fellow-sufferers in the South Atlantic.

We never know anything of the truth of wars until a few years have passed. It will all trickle out later—the crises of supplies, the official lies, the troops sickening in the ships, the equipment bogged down on the islands. We may also learn of episodes of skill and courage which we can celebrate with a whole heart—above all the extraordinary rescue operations (on both sides) of the hundreds who have already been tipped into those seas.

But now this is a war which must be stopped. Even if—as with the Peruvian or the Secretary-General's formulae—with a little loss of Mrs Thatcher's face. That is in the true interests of all parties, including the Falkland Islanders.

It is also in the interests of a threatened world. The peace movement did not deserve this tragic diversion. Militarisation is now global and the defences against militarist passions must be global also. There can be no gaps in that line.

I have heard it said that the British peace movement is finished, knocked sideways by the Falklands War. It was a fair-weather movement only—a peace movement which fainted at the sight of a real war. I ask you to walk out quietly and without provocation into that opposition, and to answer it with your numbers.

THE DEFENCE OF BRITAIN*

This is the most important general election to be fought in Britain in this century. Yet I am already weary of it, after only ten days, and I find that my neighbours and acquaintances are weary also.

The British people must take a decision on June 9th which will affect, in the most literal sense, their lives, and the lives of their children and of their children's children, if these are to have any lives at all. Yet we are not being serious about it.

The matter which we must decide concerns the defence of Britain and how this may be best conducted. When I consult the dictionary I find that 'defence' means 'protection' or 'means of resisting attack'. I take it that we all regard this as an important matter.

* A pamphlet written (and published by Merlin Press), in the middle of the 1983 General Election.

We would wish to protect this island against a foreign invasion or occupation. There may be a few things wrong with this country—in fact we are coming to realise that there are a great many things wrong in this country, with its economy and its social life—but we none of us suppose that they will be made any better by having Russians or Americans ruling over us.

'Defence' also makes us think of various good things, like our 'liberties' and our 'traditions' and our 'way of life', although I find that people are becoming more and more uncertain as to what their liberties and traditions are, and whose way of life (that of the security services or that of the unemployed?) is to be defended?

Yet whatever doubts we have, we all can think of things in the British way of life which we like, and we would want to protect these against attack. I would think, for example, of our jury system and of our free press.

But the strange thing here is that when we think of the things that are worth defending, it often turns out that the attack is coming, not from without our society, but from within. The Russians have not been tampering with our jury system—it is something which we might hope to export to them if times become happier—but this has been done by British police commissioners, judges, attorney-generals and the present Lord Chancellor. And a large part of our free press has been bought, over our heads, by money (some of it foreign money), making it more and more inaccessible to the common voice of our people.

So that the 'defence of our way of life' turns out to be something which cannot be done by paying over large taxes to a Ministry of Defence (which used to be called a Ministry of War) to buy more and more deadly nuclear missiles. A cruise missile cannot do anything at all to protect British liberties, any more than it can do anything to export liberties to people who live 'under the yoke of Communist totalitarianism'. No-one has even tried to explain how nuking other people will make them more free.

The 'protection' of our liberties against 'attack' has, for the greater part of our history, only rarely come to the issue of battles and weaponry. It has been done by means of law and pamphlet and sermon and the formation of democratic organisations—parties and chapels and trade unions—and by debates within the nation, and even (for this has not yet been bought over our heads by the property developers) by means of the vote.

This vote itself was a liberty which had to be fought for, won, and defended, by Radicals, Chartists and Suffragettes. It was never handed down on a plate from on high. But the 'fighting' was never a matter of buying bigger and more deadly weapons. It was done by acts of the mind and the spirit, by the persuasion of peaceful numbers, as at Peterloo, or the witness of supporters—in fact by such means as the peace movement still uses today.

The nuke and the vote belong to two distinct and opposed human technologies: mechanical brute force or the skills of civilised human life. They can buy the first (out of our own public revenue) but I hope that they cannot yet buy the second. The true defence of our liberties today requires defending these against the insatiable appetite of 'Defence'.

I must now explain to readers a certain difficulty about this pamphlet which they are reading. Over three years ago I wrote a small pamphlet called *Protest and Survive*. It made a little stir at the time, sold a good many copies, became adopted as a slogan, was republished in a Penguin book of the same title, and altogether it was the most ill-advised action of my life, for which I have been kicking myself ever since.

For I passed, with its publication, from being a private citizen and a free-lance writer and historian into being a famous (or infamous) Public Person, 'Professor' (which I am not) E.P. Thompson, on call at any hour of the day and sometimes night for the service of a huge, untidy, sometimes quarrelsome but always high-spirited and dedicated movement arising in every part of the globe which is called 'the peace movement'.

I did not call this movement into being. It happened of itself and I was happened by it. It was a necessary event. If, after 38 years of gathering nuclear threat, and the insatiable

and growing appetites of the nuclear armourers, some people
had not stood up and started waving banners to each other
across the globe, then one could properly have assumed that
the human spirit had rolled over on its back and given up
the ghost.

But I had myself become, with a few strokes of the pen, a
prisoner of this peace movement. After all, one cannot come
forward before the public and inform it that there is an
extreme and immediate danger that civilisation is moving
into a terminal stage—that everything we know of as civilisation may be at an end in some twenty or thirty years unless
this process is reversed—that whatever enfeebled populations
survive us amidst civilisation's radio-active ruins will carry all
the infirmities of genetic damage—one cannot utter a mouth-
ful like that and then say: 'Thank you, I am now going back
to look after my garden.'

No way. I had said that if we hoped, in this island, to
survive, then we must protest. And it follows that I must be
seen to be protesting with the protestors, or else I must eat
my words. If I could have seen a way to eat my words,
perhaps I would have done so, even though some of them
were large and unappetising. They were not nice orotund,
facile words, such as the 'True Peace-Keepers' use ('deterrence', 'security', 'negotiating from strength') which the
Great British Public is invited to swallow three times a day,
and which leave it burping contentedly before the telly.
Some of my words were too acid to swallow, and others
(like 'exterminism') would have taken an awful lot
of chewing.

I could not eat my words because I still consider them to
be true. I still consider civlisations's condition to be near-
terminal. I still think that we must protest if we are to
survive. Indeed, one or two of the more sombre predictions
which I made over three years ago have already come to
pass. The nuclear arms race has become very much worse.
The hawks of one side continue to feed and to fatten the
hawks of the other. The East and the West are hardening
the lines of ideological combat against each other. New areas
of the globe (Central America, the Middle East) are being

sucked up into the Cold War confrontation. Newcomers are
expected daily to enter the nuclear club: perhaps, very soon,
Argentina. As the Cold War confrontation hardens, so the
security state is visibly strengthened on that side and on this,
and a shadow is thrown upon civil liberties here in our 'free'
world as well as in the Communist world.

So I must, for a little longer—either until the forces of
peace win some little victory (and we have won no victories
yet) or until the sky becomes so dark that it is too late for
anything to matter—continue as a prisoner of the peace
movement.

There could be worse forms of captivity. For this work
has, in the past three years, brought me the friendship and
companionship of thousands of people—people whose
resourcefulness remind me of the best moments in our
nation's history, and even make me wonder, in incautious
moments, whether our people are really as dead and deluded
as our media and our rulers seem to intend them to be?

And there has been another compensation also. For I have
seen, in the past three years, a great many more places and
vastly more people in the world than I ever expected to see.
For the peace movement is a happening which is going on
now across all Europe and across the Atlantic and it has
somehow got down under into Australia and it has always
(since Hiroshima) been there in Japan.

Martin Eve, my friend and publisher, has just phoned up
to say that I can have 32 pages instead of 24. So in order to
fill up this page I will mention the foreign places where I
have been. These have been Holland, Czechoslovakia, West
Germany, Norway, Finland, Belgium, the United States,
Iceland, Ireland, Switzerland, Italy, France, Denmark,
Austria, Hungary, Sweden, and the Isle of Wight.

Everywhere I have met with the same rising peace consciousness, the same gestures and assurances of international
solidarity. I have met with extraordinary goodwill, extended
not so much to me as to fellow peace workers in Britain.
And this goodwill I now pass on to you.

I have peered through the fence at the cruise missile
installations at Comiso, the base in Sicily which is the twin

to Greenham Common. I have listened to leading musicians perform at a great peace rally in Iceland, whose ancient saga legends of the doom of the gods and the overthrow of civilisation chime in with the dark forebodings of our own days. I have spoken to a packed meeting in Derry (or Londonderry) where people from that deeply-divided community, Protestant and Catholic, came together to work for peace. And I have spoken at an 'unofficial' meeting in a private apartment in Budapest, where over 100 young people crowded the floor and the adjoining rooms to testify their desire for honest 'dialogue' between East and West.

All that is heartening, and it keeps one going. It is part of what the peace movement is about. The 'peace movement' is very much larger than those who join organisations or who wear its badges—it is also a mood, a happening, a raising of consciousness. It is not just—as some people suppose—a 'no' movement, no to nuclear weapons: it is also a 'yes' movement, yes to real exchanges and friendship between peoples.

But I was explaining about a certain difficulty with this pamphlet, and I also mentioned a visit to the Isle of Wight. There is a connection between these things. As I have said, three years ago I wrote *Protest and Survive* and it made a little stir. On May 1st of this year I was invited by the very vigorous branch of CND on the Isle of Wight to speak at a meeting, and, since I had never visited the island, my wife and I decided to take a day off walking on the downs.

It was a beautiful day, and the Island was spared some of the drenching weather the rest of us have been having. What came into my mind, as we walked the downs, was what an extraordinarily favoured part of this planet we have the good fortune to live upon, and also how favoured this planet itself is in a universe which is mostly made up of emptiness and fire and gas and dust.

It is a fit which is falling upon me more frequently, in the intervals of 'grass-roots activism', and I suppose it is a premonition of something: perhaps senility. It came upon me again, three days ago, when I drove across from Worcester to a rally of Christian CND in Carmarthen in South-West Wales. Mile upon mile a garden unfolded itself before me, with lush grass and with huge trees with late-opening leaves and lilacs in bloom; the wet spring had left these counties as the greenest place in the whole universe, the place with the strongest grass-roots of anywhere in the globe. It seemed to be a pity to leave this place in the knowledge that, in a few decades or so, it would be burned up.

I think that we are favoured, and that we owe a duty, not only to ourselves, but also to our ancestors who attended to the culture both of our fields and of our laws and institutions —who made them kempt and yet not too tidy nor too disciplined—and a duty also to hand on the place to the future. Despite the worst that agro-businesses and multi-nationals can do, despite the avarice of developers, despite the blasting of our inner cities, and despite the growing invasion of an arrogant state upon our rights, there is still enough here—not just to preserve but carry us forward—to bring us through to a humane commonwealth.

That sort of mood fell upon me also in the downs on the Isle of Wight. We are not well-fitted by our history to be the kind of people who just lie down and give up the ghost. There is something here that is still worth defending. Even if there is little opportunity for livelihood now in our shattered inner cities, there are people there who still inherit a culture which enables them to resist. And I thought of a pamphlet which I might write, as my contribution to the coming election next October. It would be a sequel to *Protest and Survive*, and it would be about the defence of all this—of our lives and of our liberties. It would be called *The Defence of Britain*.

In the next few days I mentioned the idea to a few friends, and also on my telephone. This was a great mistake. For someone who keeps my activities under surveillance must have carried the news post-haste to Mrs Thatcher, and she, hearing that I was about to write another pamphlet, with a great whirring of wings, like a pheasant trying to get lift-off into the air for fear of a fox, rushed across to the Palace and instructed the Queen to call an instant election.

She supposed that in this way she had put an end to my pamphlet, and, indeed, she and Mr Heseltine borrowed its title for their own election manifesto (a matter of plagiarism which I may not discuss here since it has still to be argued before the courts). And I supposed much the same. But the conduct of this election, in its first week, was so disgraceful and the treatment of the issues placed before the nation has been so trivial, and I have been made by this so generally angry, that the idea of a pamphlet came into my head once more.

I must explain my meaning more clearly. It is not that all the political parties have policies, on the questions which affect the nation in critical ways, which are equally meaningless and awful. That has been the usual situation in the past thirty years, but this time it is different. On the question upon which all other questions hang, that of nuclear weapons, several of the contending parties have very good policies: and the parties have been influenced in making these policies by the arguments of the peace movement over the past three years. In particular, the Labour Party, Plaid Cymru, and the Scottish National Party, as well as several lesser parties such as the Ecology Party, have admirable stated policies and I commend them warmly.

The members of the Liberal Party also have an admirable policy, and the Party itself *ought* to do so also, but in fact it does not. Instead it has a sort of shifty hole, called 'Don't Know', on the crucial question of cruise missiles. This is because of a successful exercise in a well-known British tactical ploy called moving the goal-posts.

What happened was this. The Liberal Party Conference met at Llandudno in the late summer of 1981 and debated the issue of cruise missiles very thoroughly. As it happens, both I and my friend Bruce Kent (whom the Papal Pro-Nuncio Monsignor Bruno Heims—a Swiss gentleman who usually occupies himself entertaining prominent Conservative Catholic laymen to dinner, and making the sauces with his own hand—has recently described as a 'useful idiot', but whom the British people, if they survive, will come to remember as the most useful Englishman of this decade)—

both I and Bruce were invited by the Liberal delegates to speak at the Conference at fringe meetings.

I will only say that this fringe meeting was one of the most searching and thoughtful discussions of the whole issue of nuclear weapons, and of the international questions attending upon this issue, that I have been privileged to take part in in the last three years.

Bruce Kent came back to spend the night with us in North Wales, and the next morning we walked down the mountain at mid-day to the pub. We had a radio with us and switched on the 1 o'clock news, when the first item was that the Liberal Party at Llandudno had, after full debate and by a firm majority, declared itself against cruise missiles. And I beheld the spectacle of Monsignor Kent, on a Welsh mountain-side, whooping and dancing a jig.

It seemed like a victory for democracy. The constituency workers had argued: they had done their research: they had selected their delegates: they had marshalled their forces: they had carried the ball down the field, and, POW! they had driven it directly into the goal. But what we had not allowed for was the cunning of Mr David Steel and the Parliamentary Liberal Party.

For these MPs (or the majority of them) simply strolled onto the field and carried the goal-posts away. I do not know where they put them, for they have not yet been found. (Last year's Liberal Party Conference was not even allowed to discuss 'Defence'). It turned out that the active Liberal Party workers, in their annual Conference, by no means had the right to determine such significant matters as party policy. This was, it transpired, a matter for their betters. Labour Party constituency workers will sympathise, since they have themselves often been through this goal-post-moving routine at the hands of the Parliamentary Labour Party in the past thirty years.

What was going on behind the scenes was this. The leaders of the Liberal Party, who have long been in the wilderness and who have long had a wholly unjust share of parliamentary representation in relation to their electoral support, were interested at that moment less in their own constituency activists than in a very large and somewhat tuneless cuckoo which had just fallen out of the Labour Party nest, and which called itself the Social-Democratic Party. In short, they had scented a chance to get back into serious political business again, and they were negotiating that odd two-headed political creature which is now beckoning us to the polls, under the name of the Dalliance.

Now the Liberal head of the Dalliance is against cruise missiles, or it ought to be if the decision of its own delegates is respected, but the other, SDP, head of the Dalliance is looking in the opposite direction. This makes it difficult to go anywhere in a straight line, rather like a three-legged race in which both parties are tied back-to-back. It therefore seemed advisable that, on the matter of cruise missiles, the Dalliance should have no policy at all and should just have a hole.

I do not explain all this out of disrespect for the Liberal Party, but simply out of disrespect for politics. I dare say that the Liberal Party's leaders have a good many second and third thoughts about cruise missiles, but they are obliged to keep these private to themselves for fear of being bitten by the other head of the Dalliance. It should be noted that our media, which have spent much of this election trying to get their fingers into a hairline crack between Mr Foot and Mr Healey, on the matter of Polaris, have left this huge fracture on defence policy within the Dalliance strictly alone.

A great many Liberal Party members have continued, with sadder hearts, to play a significant part in the work of the peace movement, including the work of CND. Many Liberal candidates remain true to the democratic decision of their own party conference and they deserve support accordingly. This is also true of some members and supporters of the SDP, who are more serious and well-informed upon international questions than one might suppose from the pronouncements of their leaders upon 'Defence'. It is probable that there are candidates of the SDP who are deserving of the peace movement's support—if they will answer its questions clearly and give the necessary assurances.

But I fear that I cannot offer the same references for Dr David Owen, whose statements on 'Defence' in the current election are intended to wean away the sucking Tory voter from the dugs of Mr Heseltine, and which fill me with dismay. One must add by the way—although the poor fellow cannot be held responsible for his image, since that is made up for him by his media advisors—that Dr Owen, when he pronounces frowningly on 'Defence' with all the pomp and pretentiousness of a self-assumed 'statesman', resembles nothing so much as that ferryman, Charon, whom the ancient Roman poets said would carry us across the river of Styx, a river which divides the world of the living from the underworld of the dead.

I have now conducted you on a brief tour of the British General Election of 1983, although I should add that there is another party offering itself at the polls. This is the Conservative Party. While some of its members, and more of its supporters, and perhaps even some of its MPs, are seriously concerned about matters of peace, the policy of its leaders on 'Defence' are ferocious and it has no policy at all on disarmament. It is not a party which can be returned to government without risk to our lives. I shall come back to this matter anon.

I must return now, however, to explaining a certain difficulty about this pamphlet. I left off at the point where I said that the conduct of this election, in its first week, was so disgraceful that the question of a pamphlet came back into my head once more.

The conduct of this election is disgraceful, not because the candidates or the party election workers are behaving disgracefully, but because the election has been confiscated by the media and is played according to its rules.

The first of these rules, with the television and radio, is that instantly an election is proclaimed the shutters are closed upon all opinions in the nation's head except those which are authorised by the Two Main Political Parties and the Dalliance. Nothing is allowed to be thought or said unless it is an authorised party-political thought, or unless it

is said by some media Presenter like Sir Robin Day or
Mr Brian Walden who have some special license to interfere
with the national mind. Anything else which might be in our
minds is extinguished until the polls are declared.

The second rule is that the media themselves decide what
are the 'election issues', and they do this by blowing up whatever is trivial, searching out 'colour' and 'Personalities', and
by trying to stir up little episodes of dissension within the
parties (but especially within the Labour Party) by picking at
old scabs and inspecting the sores underneath.

The third rule is to bludgeon us day after day with
meaningless opinion-polls, shoddily put together, and based
on illiterate or irrelevant 'yes/no' questions which refuse
electors the chance to express alternatives, complexities,
hesitations or doubts.

The result of all this is to side-track every serious issue
into by-ways, and to present the nation's political life as if
it was no more than a collection of comic actors slipping
about on banana skins and hitting each other over the head
with bags of flour. I do not know that any of the politicians
are particularly responsible for this treatment, although at
this moment the trivialisation is very much to the advantage
of Mrs Thatcher who is handled with a special awe.

Mr Michael Foot is managing to survive this exercise
remarkably well, and despite the worst efforts of the media
he is coming through as a fallible human being, with sincere
convictions, in the midst of a whole Tussaud's gallery of
infallible self-important image-conscious 'talking heads'.
Mr Foot does not come across as a 'strong' or cunning
candidate for Prime Minister, but simply as a man whose
appetite for power, for power's own sake, is now exhausted,
and who is ready to act according to principle and according
to his conscience—in short, in the view of the media, an
unfit politician.

Mr Foot apart—one watches this telly-carnival with
astonishment. Some of the 'debate' is about 'Defence', and it
was we, in the peace movement, who forced this upon the
political agenda. Yet, in the very moment that the agenda is
declared open, the arguments which we have rehearsed

throughout the country for three years have been hidden from sight or forgotten; secondary issues are blown up to immense proportions; false scent is laid across the track (how many jobs in 'defence' industries might be at risk?); and our case is presented to the people in a wholly distorted form like a grotesque cartoon.

Well, that is it. Three years of our labour is swilling away down the media drains. And there is no way, no way at all, in which the peace movement can get into this political 'debate'. For by these same media rules our voice is eliminated. Only 'party-political' spokespersons are allowed a place in the great revolving media wheel, and even then there may be only three spokes. Every other voice is excluded as marginal to the nation's political life.

What is strange about this is that (a few thousand devoted constituency workers of the various parties apart) the people who in the past three years have taken the most serious and committed part in the political life of the nation, and who have shown the deepest concern for the nation's destiny, are the members of the peace movement.

Week after week they have carried the argument to the people. They have held public meetings. They have discussed within chapels and churches and within political parties, trade unions and universities. They have gathered from every part of Britain to demonstrate in the streets. They have canvassed the housing-estates. They have raised money, in great part out of their own pockets, and they have conferred with fellow peace workers throughout Europe.

Some of them have done more than this. The women at the peace camp at Greenham Common, and the campers of both sexes at Molesworth, Upper Heyford, Faslane and other places, have testified to the seriousness of their political convictions in a way that makes the whole carnival of media politics look shoddy.

They endured, with caravans and makeshift shelters, one of the coldest winters of this century, in 1981-2, and although last winter was more kind, they have now been enduring the wettest spring in our records. And some of them have been willing to suffer for their convictions fines and imprisonments.

I know that some part of the public have been persuaded (by the media) that the 'Greenham Women' are an odd set of people and a general pain. Maybe one or two odd things have been done, and maybe some of them have endured so much that they have got a bit bossy and have come to think of themselves as *the* only true peace movement, with the rest of the nation, who have not been out there in the frost camping with them, left nowhere.

But since (if we except a few Queens and Duchesses) men have bossed this nation about for nearly all of its history, and have stirred up a good many wars in the process, it may not be a bad thing that some of the women are getting uppish just now. And if the media are really anxious to go after a bossy woman, they do not have to make the long trek from the pubs of Fleet Street down to Greenham Common. They need only go to their own front pages, where they will find our Governess seated like Britannia on the backside of the old pee, a Trident in her hand and the helmet of Deterrence squashed upon her head.

It is true that one or two things that the 'women for life on earth' have done, with a multitude of supporters, have been so odd that, although I am by profession a historian of the social movements of our people, I cannot think of any actions quite like them. And most of all I think of that astonishing day, December 12th, 1982, when, as if from nowhere, 30,000 women gathered quietly and without any sense that they were doing anything more dramatic than taking in the washing from the yard or popping up to the corner-shop, and formed that immense and life-affirming ring around the nine hostile miles of the fence of Greenham Common military base.

I was fortunate in being an observer on December 12th, not because the women had any need of me but because a car was in need of a driver. And I walked half way around the perimeter fence as the women quietly assembled, and as flowers and children's drawings and photos and poems and baby-clothes were pinned upon the wire. It was an extraordinary sight, and it was also strangely down-beat and self-conscious in a characteristic British way. To tell the truth, they did not do it with any great *éclat* or sense of theatre at all. No-one was quite sure exactly what was supposed to happen, nor even the exact moment when the miraculous linking was finally achieved. Some of the linked women were facing into the base, but at another part of the perimeter they had turned their backs upon the base and were looking outwards into the world. At one part there was a chant of 'Peace and Freedom!' and at another part some snatches of song.

It was a very untidy, low-key, British sort of do. Women had come from all parts of the country, and some had driven through the night. They came, they embraced the base and they greeted their sisters, they showed their presence, and then they drifted back home. (Some stayed, of course, to blockade the gates the next day.) But undoubtedly Other Nations would have done the whole thing better, and produced the whole drama with greater effect.

Yet the fact is that the women of Other Nations, who have done many ingenious and courageous things, have never mounted any action for peace with this particular quality of life-affirming symbolism nor on such a massive scale. It was an extraordinary event, which will very certainly be remembered in our history, and which carried a message outwards into the world which could not be misunderstood. It carried a quiet, unassertive, welcoming symbolism of a novel kind, unlike any other demonstration which I have ever witnessed. It did not only symbolise but it actually *was*, for a moment, an expression of international sisterhood, peace and love.

I have gone down a side-turning once again. I was explaining the ways in which the media's rules confiscate to 'party-political' routines the most serious political voices in this country. The peace movement has conducted the major political argument in this country over the past three years. Yet now that an election has come—and 'election' means a process of *choosing*—it finds that it must wait anxiously in the margin of events, while others who understand the arguments only imperfectly rehearse the debate, and adjust or devalue our priorities to meet the contingencies of a party-political yes-you-did-no-I-didn't sort of campaign.

And the rules of the electoral game are even odder than this. For it was decided some time ago, under the pressure of democratic opinion, that the amount of money permitted to be spent by any candidate in his or her constituency must be strictly limited and carefully accounted to the returning officer. And that any external intervention in election campaigning in a constituency which might be held to favour one particular candidate over another should be chargeable to the favoured candidate's expenses (which must come within the permitted limit); or, if such intervention can be shown to have been made without the candidate's authority, such actions may be found *illegal*, with dire and dreadful consequences to all concerned.

Those who know the American electoral system, where vast quantities of dollars are expended upon lobbying for votes, some of the money coming from hidden and disreputable sources (such as the arms industries) and most of it being spent on foul and libellous smear campaigns directed against progressive candidates, will appreciate the motives behind our own electoral rule.

Yet a gaping hole was left at the top of this law, by which the national expenditure of political parties is totally unlimited. Hence we have the position today, where the Conservative Party has raked in a huge quantity of money (most of it from businesses which will in due course pass the cost on to us by raising the price of their products), a sum which has been estimated in the press at various figures from four to twenty million pounds.

The Tories in fact have got so much money to spend upon buying the mind of the British people that they have not the least idea what to do with it, but are swilling it around all over the place, like one of those car-washes with huge rotating brushes. For example, they have been buying double pages of adverts in the daily papers, printed in outsize type so large that the reader crawls around inside it like an ant. Since I have not yet been able to get hold of a reducing-glass powerful enough to bring down this display to a readable type-face I don't yet know what these spendthrift advertisements say.

These are some of the reasons why I became angry and began to think once again of writing a pamphlet. It is too late, of course, to get it around the country. But at least the writing of it will relieve my spleen. The democracy of Britain finds itself once more, as it has done so often in the past, with a whole set of rules and laws like locked doors between it and full access to the democratic process, and with money like water-hoses playing with full force against its face. And CND finds itself, as George Cruikshank's 'Freeborn Englishman' found himself in 1820, with a padlock through its mouth.

I thought about this first on Sunday the 22nd of May. And I rang up Martin Eve to sound out his opinion. The project (he thought) was just feasible, although made more difficult by the fact that Monday May 30th has been styled as 'Whit-Monday' bank holiday, and is a day when not only bankers

but also printers close down their whole premises and have
a Revel.

If I was to write it (he said) then I must write it at once,
and complete it within three days. The whole thing would
put all my friends to great inconvenience and exertions, and
all for the purpose of easing a pain in my spleen. Yet as my
publisher and friend of many years, he was willing to
humour me in my dotage.

I have now almost completed my explanation of the
difficulties attending the production of this pamphlet. As
it happened I was unable to allocate the lavish space of
three whole days to the writing of it, since on Monday
May 23rd (as no doubt Mr Heseltine has been informed
already), my wife and I had to make a very quick and private
day-trip to Vienna to consult with Soviet friends. What with
this and that, the writing could not commence until 4 p.m.
on Tuesday, May 24th and the copy is to be delivered in
36 hours' time.

The difficulty, then, is that this thing is being written a
damned sight too fast, and through one day and two nights.
This has in no way eased my spleen, and that is no doubt
why the house has suddenly fallen empty of all inhabitants
save the dog which is cowering in the hall and my cat, who
normally sits on my shoulder to offer editorial advice, but
who on this occasion has fled to the kitchen. And that is
why this thing is coming out pell-mell and hugger-mugger
out of my unconscious, with Greenham here and the Liberal
Party at Llandudno there and the Isle of Wight somewhere
else. I have no time to ferret facts out of my files or to
deploy quotations or take breath for meditation, as I had
when writing, in thirty days rather than thirty hours, *Protest
and Survive.*

I have now completed the introduction to this pamphlet and
I believe that there are still a few pages left for the argument.
Fortunately we shall not need much space for this, since the
major part of this argument has, in the past three years,
already been conducted and won.

In *Protest and Survive,* three years ago, it was still necessary to explain with care what a nuclear war would entail, and to show why the proposed exercises in 'civil defence' were futile and could be interpreted only as efforts to tranquillise the public mind. That argument is settled now, and its settlement has been signalled by those numerous local authorities (as well as by the whole nation of Wales) which have declared themselves to be nuclear-free zones, and which have saved the ratepayers' money for more useful purposes.

So we have moved forward a little, and everyone in Britain who cares to know, now knows that a nuclear war would be an unthinkable disaster to this island, and scarcely a voice can be heard (as a few voices may still be heard in the USA) to suggest that such a war could be 'winnable'.

Indeed, most people are now persuaded by our arguments that cruise missiles on our territory, owned and operated by United States' personnel, so far from contributing to this nation's 'defence' or 'security' will actually increase its insecurity, by making these bases targets for attack and by placing the finger of a United States President firmly upon our own trigger. And even most of those who cannot yet see why these missiles must be refused, would accept them in this island with the greatest reluctance.

The evidence of this can be seen in the growing concern among Conservative voters, and some Tory back-benchers, over the question of a 'double key'. In fact cruise missiles are not operated by a key at all, but by a code; but no doubt some double-code could be devised.

We have been assured repeatedly that we ought not to concern ourselves about this matter, since the missiles can never be fired without a 'joint decision' of the President and the Prime Minister, and that an agreement to this effect was worked out many years ago which has had the assent of successive governments of both major political parties.

The peculiar thing is that this agreement, which concerns the sovereignty of the British people, has never been published nor set before parliament. And recent research in the archives has suggested that Winston Churchill (that is, the *real* Winston Churchill, who was once a person of some note, as older people may remember) was gravely dissatisfied with it, because it laid down conditions, not for 'joint decision' but for 'joint consultation'. And I have little doubt that if the real Winston Churchill had ever authorised the basing of a fearful new generation of foreign-owned and foreign-operated weaponry upon our territory—and I have some doubts whether he would, once he had taken a steady look at President Reagan and his advisers and formed an opinion as to their stability—then he would very certainly have ordered a double key, and he would have worn that key on his own watch-chain.

A few months ago Mrs Thatcher chose a new Defence Minister to succeed Sir John Nott; and she chose him with delay and care, not to defend Britain against the Russians but to defend her administration against CND. Mr Heseltine is a good sort of knockabout party-political busker, who cannot read deeply into things, who enjoys stamping about on the hustings, and who does not care very much what he says, nor whether it is true or not.

One of his first one-acters was to put on a contractor's helmet, invite the media into Greenham base, and show them around. It was clear that the bad press the government was getting about the 'double key' was bothering him, and, with the telly cameras whirring, he was asked a planted question by a deferential journalist. 'Aha!' came back Mr Heseltine's comforting response. The matter of the double key was no problem, no problem at all. In fact no key was needed. For we British had a recourse already. Every time a cruise launch-convoy sallies out of Greenham, it will be accompanied by a sturdy platoon of the RAF Regiment. And if our lads should notice that the Yanks were up to any unauthorised hanky-panky, then they would simply bonk them on their heads and place the whole convoy in jankers.

This tale was strictly for the British viewer and no efforts were made to convey it to America. In March I was invited to address the National Press Club in Washington on the question of Euromissiles, and the members received me with courtesy and straight faces. But when I told them this story about Heseltine I had them rolling in the aisles. And again and again, in the United States, it was made clear to me that many Americans cannot understand what has come over the British and why we put up with it. I am not referring to members of the huge and growing American peace movement, but to the professional reporters of the Fourth Estate. They do, after all, remember a time when it became necessary for their own people to make a Declaration of Independence.

I am now going to make a prediction, and by the time that this pamphlet is off the press you will know whether it is true. When Mrs Thatcher returns from the Williamsburg Summit she will bring back with her a 'key', a key specially presented to her by President Reagan himself, large enough to unlock the door to her second term in office.

It may not be a *real* key, of course. It may be a great big fulsome Presidential Promise, cut out in the shape of a key: that never, ever, will he blow this place up without telling her about it first. Mrs Thatcher will have this key placed in her hand, like one of those huge 21-year-old birthday cards, and she will be told that Britain has at last attained to its nuclear majority. And she will come tripping down out of the Concorde, waving the key in the air like Neville Chamberlain just back from Munich, and singing to the electorate in its last somnolent week—

> I've got the key of the door,
> Never been twenty-one before!*

---

* STOP PRESS. DOUBLE KEY. PREDICTION VINDICATED. 'Britain "will have Cruise firing veto",' according to the *Daily Telegraph*, 27 May. President Reagan said in an interview with television networks from nations attending the Williamsburg Summit that the issue of who would be in control of the firing of cruise missiles. 'I don't think either of us will do anything independent of the other. This constitutes a sort of veto power', he said. It is reported that this 'sort of veto power' was made up into an iced lolly shaped like a key and was pressed into the Prime Minister's hand on her arrival at Williamsburg. The ceremony was *private*, lest the German Chancellor might want an iced lolly also. In case Mrs Thatcher's lolly might *melt* before the election, the President's aides put another nougat key into her handbag, which will be produced if the opinion polls start to turn against her.

Enough of this show-biz. For if that is to happen, it will only be the beginning of it. The British public will then have to start puzzling out how to get a double-key to Mrs Thatcher, and to whoever might follow her (Good Gracious, perhaps Mr Heseltine!).

It would be better, of course, if cruise missiles were never to come at all. The majority of the British people have realised this. But some are still held back by real objections. And of these we will look at two. First, there are those who are distrustful of any act of 'one-sided disarmament', since they suppose that this would make it easier for the other side to go on arming without restraint. Second, there are those (often the same persons) who deeply fear and distrust 'the Russians'. We will discuss these two questions in order.

The first argument treats of missiles ('which of course *we* would never use') as if they were negotiating chips. They are—well, er, yes, they *are* missiles, but what they are *really* is a means of getting back at a new level into the balance game so as to get a position of purchase from which to negotiate downwards, multilaterally, with the Russians.

One trouble with this argument is that exactly the same argument is being used by the armourers on the other side. Their weapons, also, are only for 'defence', and *they* would never use them. They have to hang onto their SS-20s because they are negotiating chips. Another trouble—but I am bored out of my mind with this—is that all the counting of numbers and of balance, on both sides, is partisan and is skewed.

But Mrs Thatcher has some special troubles of her own. It is possible to argue, with honesty, that NATO should go on threatening to bring in cruise, as a bargaining-chip, provided that at the same time one is working earnestly and with good-will to find some urgent and fair settlement at Geneva. I think it is a bad argument, but it is not dishonest, and there are glimpses of honesty of this kind in the SDP's policies on the question.

This is sometimes called (with much self-congratulation) 'the multilateral approach'. It is a difficult approach to sustain, since its British advocates have got no-one to be multilateral with. The British have not been invited to the

Geneva negotiations, so that all that they can do is to wait anxiously outside the door. Since it is becoming abundantly clear that neither the Americans nor the Russians are going to give enough ground for an agreement, the waiting British multilateralists will at length have to lie down and die, with a good conscience, in a multilateral ditch.

But Mrs Thatcher just possibly could not only *sound* multilateral but *be* multilateral. For she has been offered a multilateral partner. Mr Andropov in some recent proposals suggested that he might bring down the number of SS-20s targetted upon Europe until they matched the sum of the British and French 'independent deterrents'. At that stage (he proposed) the Russian and Western missiles could be negotiated downwards and perhaps phased out together. He was offering Mrs Thatcher his arm, for a waltz on the multilateral ballroom floor.

One would have supposed that Mrs Thatcher would have accepted Mr Andropov's proposal with squeals of delight. For here she has been, throughout all her term in office, pining like a wallflower and dreaming of the day when she might find a partner to be multilateral with. And now that *handsome* Mr Andropov glides over the floor and selects her as his chosen partner!

But this was not her reaction. When it comes to questions of disarmament Mrs Thatcher is *very* hard to suit. She is most particular. Mr Andropov had suggested that he might introduce his SS-20s to her Polarises. This did not accord at all with Mrs Thatcher's strict sense of Victorian propriety. The Polaris, she said, was only a weapon 'of last resort', whereas the SS-20 (one supposes) is an ill-bred sort of weapon which might resort at any time and place.

For crying out loud, *what* does the woman mean? What *is* a 'last resort'? God preserve us, in that event, from the first and second resorts! Are we to shell out cruise missiles, and are the Russians to shell out SS-20s, as the small coinage of a nuclear war? And is Polaris to be preserved, deep on the sea-bed, only for the ultimate dark deed, the final passage of this island across the River Styx, where those scowling ferrymen (all of Mr Brian Walden's 'experts') are patiently

waiting? Or has she worked out some secret suicide pact
with Ronald Reagan, so that when, in 'the last resort', it is
time to go she may go with him?

I cannot stand the multilateral homilies which come out of
that woman's lips. When she croons in her husky way: '*We*
are the *trooo* disarmers*' I cannot even admire her gall. Prime
Minister, when have you ever made *any* proposal, in good
faith, to disarm *anything* (except, of course, the Russians)?
You have ordered every weapon that has come your way.
You have without hesitation welcomed into our island the
cruise missiles. You have been willing to beggar the country
to buy Trident. You have ordered the Tornado fighter-
bomber. You have turned down each and every proposal
from the other side, sometimes before it was even received
and read. Your administration has, in the United Nations,
voted against a resolution for a bi-lateral nuclear weapons
freeze. You have opposed 'no first use'. You have fought,
with unseemly gusto and with an eye for political self-
advertisement, the unhappy Falklands War.

I said, many pages back, that the Conservative Party has
no policy for disarmament. Mrs Thatcher certainly has
none. She is, quite simply, a one-sided armer. It has never
been clear to me why it is supposed that it is always right
for every nation to *add* to its armaments by unilateral
measures. Yet if any unilateral measure of *dis*armament—
any initiative to get the log-jam on the move—is brought
into public discussion there are at once cries of 'foul!' and
even of 'treason!'

It is the use of the word 'multilateralism' by such persons
as our Prime Minister which has brought it into disrepute.
For it has become, with her sort of person, nothing but a
hypocritical cover underneath which one-sided arming can
go on. As for effective measures of multilateral and
reciprocal disarmament, this has always been the objective
of the peace movement. Unilateral measures by this country
are, exactly, what may at last get this whole multilateral
process going. We have said this again and again and I will
not waste any more time on the point.

But how do we know (for this is the second question of

our honest objector) that if we do anything the Russians are going to respond? The plain fact is that we do *not* know that the Russians will do so, and we do not know that the Americans or the French or the Israelis or (perhaps next year) the Argentinians will respond either. How on earth can we be expected to make such a promise?

If one looks at that list, it seems just a little more likely that the Russians might respond than anyone else. For our weapons are pointed at them, and Mr Andropov is already there, on the ballroom floor, inviting our multilateral partnership. The Soviet Union, in the past year or two, has made quite a number of multilateral proposals—they have said they are in favour of a nuclear weapons 'freeze' and of 'no first use'—and while no doubt their statesmen will (just like the statesmen of the West) try to twist any agreement to their own advantage, at the moment they look a good deal more likely to be willing to come to some sort of agreement than does President Reagan, who has a quite insatiable appetite for new armaments and whose eyes are fixed now upon the star wars of the twenty-first century. In any case, looked at in terms of mere political calculation, Soviet statesmen would be incredibly foolish—and would lose the propaganda battle of the century—if Britain were to commence to disarm and if they were to find no way to respond.

I am not, now, in this pamphlet going to take in the whole 'Russian Question', since the pages are running out and since I must take this copy to be set into print in some three hours time. I have already written a good deal about this matter, as have other people in the peace movement who are more expert than myself. And there would be no harm if some of our opponents actually *read* some of the things which we have written before they started libelling us as being 'soft on Russia' and the rest.

For example, they might read my book, *Zero Option*, in which, among many choice articles, they will find a lecture, 'Beyond the Cold War'. They will find there that I am not a misty-eyed optimist but a pessimist about the Soviet Union: that is, I am deeply pessimistic about it so long as the Cold War and the armaments race continues. I sketch out there a process, which has now been going on for more than thirty years, by which the hawks of the West and the East keep on strengthening and feeding each other.

Every upward movement in arms on one side meets with an upward movement on the other, and this is true not only of arms but also of ideological hostilities. When President Reagan, speaking at Orlando, Florida, rants on about the Soviet Union being 'an evil empire' he is actually helping it on in that direction, since the Soviet rulers respond by tightening up their security system and by putting their military preparations into repair.

It is true that I do not regard the Soviet Union as an aggressive, expansionist empire but as a vast sprawling empire, perhaps already in decline, facing all kinds of internal stress and economic difficulty, unable to feed its own people with grain, and over-ripe for modernisation and (if things should go well) democratic changes.

If it is an expansionist power, then it is not doing well. Since the end of World War II it has lost its hegemony over Yugoslavia; suffered a disastrous breach with China; and its hegemony today over several East European states (Czechoslovakia and Poland) is maintained in some part by military threat. Its adventure in support of a failing client regime in Afghanistan is going on as badly as did several British adventures in that country in the last century.

In short, I see no evidence that the Soviet Union (which has an acute headache over Poland) has an appetite to gobble up more unruly nations in the West. Nor does it have, at this time, the economic or political influence to turn Western Europe into some kind of 'Finland'. On the contrary, the Soviet rulers are more anxious about the penetration of 'Western' influence into the East, and, if the Cold War were to come to an end, we might expect to see some 'Finlandisation' in reverse in Eastern Europe.

The panic scenarios which we are always being given, of hordes of Soviet tanks rolling towards the Channel ports, do not come out of reality but out of the Cold War textbooks of the past. What is needed now is the commencement

of some healing-process between the two blocs—a diminution
of the mutual sense of threat—which will, in due course,
enable the Soviet and East European peoples to make whatever changes they wish in their own societies and in their
own way. As for 'human rights', every time Mrs Thatcher
or President Reagan rant about these (while at the same
time hurrying forward new generations of threatening
missiles) they are making the situation over on the other
side *worse*. The cold warriors of the West are actually feeding
and strengthening those very forces in the East which are
holding back democratic change.

I have been watching this process very closely for a year,
since we Western peace workers are in touch with independent-minded persons in the East, who are working in
their own way and in the face of great difficulties for peace
and for change. I have observed with sorrow the way, every
time our Western cold warriors open their loud mouths,
it makes the position of our friends on the other side worse.
When Mr Heseltine does his show-biz at the Berlin Wall one
can actually hear the prison-doors closing on the other side.

I said, some pages back, that I was unable to commence
writing this pamphlet on Monday, May 23rd, because I had
to make a quick day-trip for a private consultation with
some Soviet friends in Vienna. These friends (whom I had
never before met) were a young Soviet artist, called Sergei
Batovrin, and his wife, Natasha. They are members of a
small independent Soviet peace group which was set up,
some eleven months ago, with the aim of promoting direct
communication and exchanges between the citizens of the
East and West, and, in particular, of Establishing Trust
between the USA and the USSR.

This initiative was not liked by the Soviet authorities at
all, partly because they dislike *any* private intiatives by their
own citizens (unlicensed by State or Party) and particularly
dislike direct communications between their citizens and the
West (which they suspect as being channels for 'Western
intelligence'), and especially, on this occasion, because working for peace in the Soviet Union is preserved as a State
monopoly and is directed at opposing the aggressive and

expansionist plans of the capitalist West.

In short, the Soviet authorities view the whole Cold War scene *exactly* as does Mr Heseltine, only upside-down; but since the Soviet Union is a tightly-controlled authoritarian state, the Soviet authorities are in the happy position of being able to hold down and control independent peace initiatives more effectively than Mr Heseltine can do. And instead of sending around libels on peace workers to Tory parties and to the popular press (as Mr Heseltine was reduced to doing), the Soviet authorities were able to send around to Sergei and Natasha's apartment—again and again and again— the officers of the KGB.

It has been an appalling scene, and if you get hold of END's publications you can read about it there. The Moscow Group, which has not given up and which does not intend to give up, and whose support, not only in Moscow but in other cities is actually growing, has been given a very rough passage. All of Sergei's paintings have been confiscated, Natasha has had to put up with KGB men pushing around her apartment and upsetting the baby, Sergei was put for a month into confinement in a psychiatric hospital, and, finally, he was given, for the third time, the choice between imprisonment and exile. After consultation with his friends he decided that he must go. And he and Natasha, their baby and Sergei's mother arrived, quite suddenly, in Vienna on May 19th.

There has not been a great hullabaloo about this in our media, although one might have thought that the story was good Cold War 'copy' and could have been used to beat up the Western peace movement. This is perhaps because when Sergei arrived at Vienna airport, and the microphones and cameras were thrust before him, he simply said that he and his friends were working for peace, and for 'trust' between East and West, and he meant to continue with the work.

He did not call upon the West to build even bigger wea- pons, nor did he ask for boycotts, nor did he accuse Western peace workers of being useful dupes of the Kremlin, and he did not even ask us to help his people by ordering cruise missiles. In short, the Western media found him to be a flop.

When Dorothy and I heard of the Batovrins' arrival we got

ourselves tickets to Vienna. It was a daft thing to do, and the most expensive day-trip of our lives, but it was a matter of impulse and not of thought at all. Our purpose was simply to take Natasha a bunch of English flowers. When your brothers and your sisters have been suffering in that way, and for the same cause, it seemed right that someone from our own peace movement should go and say thankyou and hello.

Sergei will be writing himself about his experiences and his Group's ideas. I will leave this to him. What he said to us, again and again, was that the work of peace was not only about halting missiles but also about dialogue between peoples, communication, and establishing 'trust'. Somehow or other, we must establish a new kind of relationship between the peoples of East and West. As for the Soviet people, they very certainly feared and hated any thought of war. If they supported their own rulers, it was because they supposed that they offered them 'Defence'. Just like us.

I put to Sergei the question raised by our objector. If Britain were to initiate disarmament, would there be a Soviet response? He did not know. He could give no certain assurance. But if Britain were to halt cruise missile deployment, the Soviet people would see that as 'an act of peace'. It might make more possible the real work, the work of establishing trust.

I regard this election, or *choice*, now before the British people as the most important in our time, not because I am an optimist but because I grow, with each month, more pessimistic as to civilisation's future.

The Soviet state is certainly a threat to liberty. But it is a threat, not to our liberties, but to the liberties of the Soviet and East European peoples—to people like Sergei and Natasha. We have, very urgently, to reverse this process and to create the conditions in which the cause of trust can grow.

The whole matter of cruise missiles seems to me now to be very simple. After all the numbers have been counted, and the balances have been struck, it is simply a case of leapfrog. If the arms race is to be frozen, or halted, it is inevitable that at the point of freeze either one side or the other will be ahead in this or that category of missiles.

It may be true that at the present moment the Soviet
Union is ahead in certain categories of Euromissiles (if they
are counted in certain ways), just as it is probably true that
the United States is ahead, in the number of warheads and in
refined technology, over the global scene. In any case, there
is so much surplus of killing power around on both sides
that all the arguments of balance have lost any sense at all.

The second simple point is that if NATO puts down cruise
missiles then the Soviet Union will put down its own
missiles in reply. Marshal Ogarkov has already promised as
much. So that everything will have got a great deal worse,
and we may even be into launch-on-warning systems, and on
our way, on both sides of the world, to becoming permanent
cave-dwellers or troglodytes.

But there is a third simple point, which even those candidates in this election who have admirable policies for peace
are not yet succeeding in getting across. And this is that we
may, truly, be coming to a point of final choice. If we miss
the bus this time around, there may not be another. And
that what we are making a choice between is also between
two kinds of Britain: a Britain which is independent and
which still has some influence and respect in the world, and
a Britain which is becoming little more than a servile NATO
security state.

When I was in the United States recently I noticed a
curious assumption which was coming, increasingly, from
the White House and its captive media. It was that the
question of cruise missiles was a matter which, in the last
analysis, would be decided by President Reagan. Either the
President would come to some bargain with Mr Andropov
or he will 'decide' to deploy cruise missiles to Europe.

But there is something a little strange in that assumption.
The cruise missiles may belong to the President, but we had
always supposed that the territory of Europe still belongs to
us. There may of course be some other secret agreement,
worked out many years ago and assented to by successive
administrations—but never published nor brought before our
parliament—under which we ceded our sovereignty to the

United States. If so, then well and good, and we can dispense with the comedy of elections.

But until some Ministry of Defence spokesman can show us this agreement, we must assume that we still own our own country. And since the matter of cruise missiles is being negotiated behind closed doors at Geneva, where no European nations are present, we have ourselves only one point at which we are able to enter the negotiations. And this is to refuse our territory for their use. That is the only way in which we can get into the negotiations at all.

The matter in Europe now stands like this. Holland will almost certainly refuse cruise missiles, because the Dutch people won't have them. That being so, the Belgians will probably refuse also. That is two down, with three still to go: Italy, West Germany and Britain. Meanwhile it is pretty clear that there will be no agreement at Geneva, and that, if we lose this election, the cruise missiles will start to come.

But if the British were to refuse cruise, then the entire situation in Europe would change. It would then become impossible to put the things down in Italy or Germany. There would *have* to be a whole new negotiation, and the European nations themselves would have to be parties to it. The Americans would have to be less pushy, and to regard the Europeans with a new respect. The Soviet Union would have, out of plain self-interest, to make some kind of response.

For the first time, in clear daylight, the whole logic which is carrying us to nuclear war would be checked and reversed by the conscious choice of a free people. No-one can say what this might lead on to. But if the peace movement of the world, which is now a powerful force, responded to the British choice and worked with effect, we might even move forward to Sergei's agenda: the making of a new relationship between East and West, the establishment of trust.

The British people have therefore had thrust into their hands a most awesome choice, which could, in a visible way, affect the future of the whole world: which might decide, indeed, whether that world, as a civilised place, goes on at all.

Behind this choice (it is becoming daily more clear) there is also another choice: a choice between two Britains. We have long been a declining power, and some good may come of that. In those old Victorian days, which Mrs Thatcher so loves, when we splashed red paint across the five continents, we were feared but we were not greatly loved. We still owe human debts to the peoples of Asia and Africa whom we pushed about and exploited which it will take a century or two to repay.

This is a time, however (when all our old imperial self-images have been shattered) to reconsider what kind of a nation we are. If we accept that we are now a second-class power, it does not have to follow that we have to be a client state of the USA (nor of a fiction called 'NATO'). Nor do we have to be second-rate. Nor do we have to maintain the inclination and the airs of a bully when we have long lost the power.

It is this which bothers me most about Mrs Thatcher and her chosen circle: Mr Heseltine, Mr Cecil Parkinson, Mr Norman Tebbitt and the rest. They have an appetite for our liberties. Since they have lost the power to rule over half the world, they would like to recapture the buzz by ruling over us.

The media these days has a great line in hunting 'extremists'. When they dislike anyone's ideas, then they set them up as extremists and pelt them day after day. They did this with Mr Benn, and with Mr Livingstone, and now they are doing it with Bruce Kent and the peace campers at Greenham Common.

Yet if I look around this country the most extreme people in our public life are Mrs Thatcher and her circle. I do not refer only to their policies on 'Defence', although there could not be any policy more extreme than perfecting and modern-ising the means to exterminate our human neighbours a few thousand miles away. They are extremists in their social and economic policies as well.

They are bent (under cover of the cry of 'freedom') to strengthen all the powers of the overmighty central State: to increase the powers of the police and the surveillance of citizens: to enlarge the Official Secrets Acts (which already make our press a laughing-stock on the other side of the Atlantic): to sell off the nation's assets: to interfere with our university autonomy: to interfere with our trade unions: to weaken the powers of our local authorities: to employ the resources of the civil service and of the public revenue in order to libel private citizens and to engage in party-political exercises (as Mr Heseltine has recently been doing).

In short, if the Soviet rulers are a threat to liberty—but to the liberty of the Soviet people—then we must also say that our rulers in Britain are a threat to liberty, but to our liberties at home.

There has taken place, quietly and little observed, a take-over of the old Conservative Party (I am thinking of the party of Harold Macmillan, of Butler, Heath and Lord Carrington) by a Tory Militant Faction. These rulers are now becoming deeply impatient with our democratic forms. They regard the rest of us, not as their fellow-citizens, but as their subjects.

The crisis of this came when the British people's attention was diverted to the South Atlantic last year. Differing views can be held about that whole sad episode, which is very far from finished and which Mrs Thatcher means to keep going as long as she can. But there can be little dispute that this was the time at which, from the courage and the bloodshed of other people at the other end of the earth, Mrs Thatcher took on a new 'resolute' image. And there was then annointed by the media, and appointed to service as her Lieutenant upon all public occasions, a new officer in our life, 'The Falklands Factor'.

This 'Falklands Factor' has nothing to do with the Falkland Islanders, who seem to be a taciturn and slow set of people, and many of whom now want to leave their islands. It has everything to do with Mrs Thatcher's 'image' and the Central Office of the Conservative Party's projection of it. In this image, every act of heroism and endurance, by 2 Para or by helicopter pilots, are to be ascribed to Mrs Thatcher and to Mrs Thatcher alone.

In short, the Falklands War, coming at a time when our

The Archmedia of Mass Annointing the Falklands Factor

economy and our social life were visibly falling apart, was the
greatest and most undeserved bonus which the Militant
Faction of the Tory Party could get. And it made them more
Militant, more factional, and more extreme.

The question is: is this really the kind of nation which we
wish to be, and is this how we wish to be seen in the world?
For I have travelled a bit since then, and have found that the
Falklands War was regarded by most other nations in a very

different light. It was seen as a bizarre episode, a sudden flush of imperial nostalgia, as if Britain had suddenly fallen through a time-warp into the 18th or 19th century. It made other peoples recall that Britain was still a nation to be *feared*. But fear is not the same thing as respect.

The Falklands War was the last episode of our old imperial past. It summoned up the nostalgias and the resentments of a nation in decline. It was played through by Mrs Thatcher with calculated gestures of Churchillian reminiscence. And there were times when this reminiscence caught the whole nation's breath—centuries of sea-born empire and piracy, and now once again the fleet putting out from Portsmouth, with the waving of flags and the watching crowds, on a mission to rescue our kith and kin from oppression at the uttermost ends of the earth. . .

Yet there is no way forward for any nation down the paths of nostalgia and reminiscence. That will become the rhetoric of rogues, and we will be screwed as their subjects. To become lost in the rehearsal of past grandeur (as Spain once did) is the path towards true decline.

That then is one kind of Britain we can choose: a security state, with a subjected people—a client state which still struts and postures in the world as a bully, which lets its staple industries decline while it exhausts its revenue upon an absurd and obscene great-power-symbol (the 'independent deterrent'), and whose written culture oscillates between cynicism and self-deluding nostalgia.

There has, however, always been an alternative Britain in these islands, and I suppose that my pamphlet may get through to some of them. I know all the dangers of national feeling, and I know more than most (since I am an historian) about Britain's imperial sins. Yet I cannot agree that the history of this island has been, in every way, a disgraceful one; nor that there is nothing in it that it is worth defending.

This has not only been a nation of bullies. It has also been a nation of poets and of inventers, of thinkers and of scientists, held in some regard in the world. It has been, for a time, no less than ancient Greece before us, a place of innovation in human culture. Here were worked out certain laws and democratic forms which have influenced the forms of States in every continent; here there were conducted, over centuries, great arguments of religious faith which were then carried across the Atlantic; here some of the first trade unions and co-operatives were formed, without whose example multitudes over the whole earth might still suffer extremities of exploitation; here, and in our neighbour, France, were worked out some of the clearest claims to human rights.

Therefore I say that the alternative Britain must stand to those rights now, and exercise them with the very greatest vigour. And in doing this we may be fortified by the knowledge that in defending ourselves, we may also be defending the future of the world.

Which Britain do we wish to be seen as in the eyes of international opinion? The Britain of the 'Falklands Factor', the strutting bully which made the world aghast by sinking the *General Belgrano*, an old battleship with a complement of more than one thousand souls, without warning and outside the exclusion zone which we ourselves had imposed and while it was steaming *away* from our fleet? Or the alternative Britain of citizens and not subjects which, summoned up all the strengths of its long democratic past and cut through the world's nuclear knot.

If we could only do that, then we could happily resign ourselves to leaving behind for ever the pretentions of a great power, leaving the world to say of our imperial past, as Malcolm said of the old Thane of Cawdor, 'nothing in his life became him like the leaving of it'.

You will recall that I have a padlock through my lips in the matter of the general election. I am not allowed to advise you as to how you should actually *vote*. I would advise you, of course, to vote for those candidates, of whatever party, which have the best policies for defending the lives and liberties of the British people.

These will best be defended by refusing cruise missiles and also by refusing a second term to Mrs Thatcher. Indeed, I would advise you to make your own judgments in every constituency, guided by two considerations only: the best way to refuse nuclear weapons, and the best way to ensure that Mrs Thatcher's administration is not returned.

I have a little difficulty with this last matter. It appears that if Mrs Thatcher is defeated, as a result of this pamphlet, which is not an authorised party-political production, then a breach of electoral law may be caused thereby. In which case it will be necessary to cancel the results of the entire general election and to play it through once again. But we have taken the advice of an eminent barrister, and, while it is a nice point and has not yet been argued in the higher courts, he thinks that the election might stand provided that I became a fugitive from the kingdom. He was very attentive to us, and gave us a full seven minutes of his advice, and he charged for his counsel only £800.

I have advised you what to vote *against*. As to what to vote for (apart from our defence) I can claim no clarity at all. I do not expect any alternative administration to work great wonders. I do not expect Mr Foot to be a 'strong' Prime Minister, but I expect him to be an honest and humane one which is something we presently stand greatly in need of. He is also a reading man, who knows something of our history and our democratic traditions; and to have such qualities in a Prime Minister would be a great novelty.

As for the other issues, and the issue of our employment most of all, it is not that I regard any one of them as unimportant. But all of them become trivial when set beside the defence of our liberties and our lives. And if these are not defended, then nothing can be solved. For we will move, with all our human neighbours, towards civilisation's 'final solution'.

This pamphlet was commenced in its writing at Worcester at 4 p.m. on Tuesday, May 24th and concluded on Thursday the 26th of May whence it was transported by messenger post-haste to Chilmark in the County of Wilts, three horses dying under the messenger on the way, and there set into type by Mistress Hems, whence it was taken by stage-coach to the City of London at the Merlin Press in the Isle of Dogges to be done by Master Eve into a little book.

CRIMINAL PROCEEDINGS, OLD BELIAL SESSIONS*
by Our Crime Reporter

At the Old Belial last week Miss Jane Candide, a junior employee in government service, was convicted of offences under all seventy-seven sections of the Official Mendacity Acts.

When charged the defendant did not enter any plea. After some moments of silence Mr Justice Canting informed her that if she continued to stand mute then, according to the ancient practice of the land she would be subjected to the *peine forte et dure:* that is, she would be taken to a dark place and laid naked on her back while weights of iron and stone were placed upon her chest until she was pressed unto death. (Anticipation in court.)

As Mr Justice Canting was about to pronounce sentence, a court usher remarked that the prisoner might be better able to plead if the gag were removed from her mouth. When this was done she said something in a low voice which the Court took to be 'guilty', whereupon the gag was instantly replaced for the remainder of the proceedings.

Opening the prosecution for the Crown, Mr Percy Cute, QC, said that there was no dispute between himself and his learned friend, the counsel for the defence, as to the facts of this case. For some time Her Majesty's Government, in consultation with its closest allies, had been planning to import a consignment of American Cabbage-Patch Scarecrows.

---

* *New Society,* 5 April 1984.

These Scarecrows, of a new and advanced design, were necessary for the defence of the kingdom. By their fearsome aspect they would keep in awe the scarecrows of the Enemy. And, even more they would cow and render subordinate the Enemy within—that is, the disaffected natives of this country.

There was no secret whatsoever about the matter of these Scarecrows. Her Majesty's ministers had proclaimed their imminent arrival in the loudest possible terms. Since their entire purpose was to terrify both the Enemy and the natives, publicity was of the essence of the matter.

However the Secretary of State for Offence, who was particularly responsible for this operation, was placed in difficulties last autumn by the growth of disaffection among the general populace.

'The whole operation was placed in jeopardy,' said Mr Cute. 'What was to be done? In these perilous circumstances Mr Hushpuppy, the Minister for Offence, took the bold decision (under instruction from our Great Ally) to "put the boot in". He agreed to sneak in the first consignment of Cabbage-Patch Scarecrows six weeks in advance of the publicly-announced date.'

Mr Hushpuppy had dictated a memorandum to his closest colleagues in the Cabinet, announcing this decision and describing the measures which he would take to mislead Parliament, con the British people, and manipulate the media. In short, this was a perfectly normal ministerial memorandum, of the most mendacious intent, and as such every comma lay under the protection of the Official Mendacity Acts.

It was this document which Miss Candide had leaked to an unauthorised newsheet. Mr Cute acknowledged that the leaking of secret information was a regular practice, in which senior officials of the security services and indeed ministers themselves frequently engaged. But this was proper. It conduced to the management of the natives. The material so leaked was nearly always false or defamatory of defenceless individuals. It was leaked only to authorised persons and to authorised media.

Indeed, when this was taken into account, it only threw

into a darker light the heinous nature of Miss Candide's crimes. For she had leaked information to the public which could give the game away by revealing to them the means by which their minds were controlled. Mr Cute feared that even now Miss Candide did not understand the depravity of her conduct. For, when interviewed by Det. Chief Supt. Gotcher of Scotland Yard, she had replied that 'she did not believe in telling people lies'. (Sensation in court.)

By this confession Miss Candide stood condemned out of her own mouth as a person disqualified in the most essential point for any form of government service. He would rest the case for the prosecution upon her own confession.

Mr Pleamarket-Creep, QC, defending, said that there was no dispute between himself and his learned friend, the counsel for the Crown, as to the facts of the case nor as to the depravity of the offence. He supposed that there was no disagreement as to anything anywhere in the Court.

His defence was that his client was a moron. She was an animal and she was not a political one. She had no ideas of her own. She had never joined anything. That is why she had done so well when she was positively vetted. Indeed, if it had not been for this momentary and inexplicable lapse into honesty, she was exactly the kind of moron qualified to rise to the highest ranks of government service.

At this point Mr Pleamarket-Creep concluded his defence, wrapped his silk around him, and lay down on the floor, where he was observed to screw up his face and wink at Mr Cute and then at Mr Justice Canting.

Mr Justice Canting began his judgment. He addressed himself first to counsel for the defence and assured him that grovelling would be of no avail in this case, the most flagrant of any that had ever come before him.

It was true, that plea-bargaining was an established practice of the courts, and one which was often of great service to the Crown. Why was this? Because it brought matters to a term and excluded from the process that archaic relict of past times, the jury. Trial by jury occasioned time, expense, and (far worse) uncertainty of conviction. The useful invention of plea-bargaining enabled the Court to move directly from the charge to the sentence. This was a great convenience. Indeed, he was happy to say that by such means the Old Belial itself might now be regarded as a Public Convenience.

He did not know whether there had been any bargain in this case. Very probably not. However, it was clearly in the interests of the Crown that there should be no jury in this case. How could a jury be selected with absolute certainty of conviction? His learned friend, the Attorney-General, had assured him that every possible precaution was being taken in the vetting of potential jurors. Even so, no certain way could be found to exclude subversive persons, such as readers of the unauthorised newsheet which had published Mr Hush-puppy's memorandum—every one of whom was an accomplice after the fact.

In these circumstances it was politic and proper for the Crown to take exceptional measures to ensure that Miss Candide entered a plea of guilty. It was possible that they had gone further than they had a warrant to do, in conveying the suggestion that in return she would receive a non-custodial sentence. But what of that? The object had been achieved, and he now had the prisoner defenceless before him.

Mr Justice Canting then addressed Miss Candide: 'Your offence is the most monstrous in living memory. I will deal with it under three heads.'

'First, by revealing the plan to sneak in Cabbage-Patch Scarecrows into this country you set in motion a train of consequences among the disaffected populace which could have led on to riot, rapine, arson, violent confrontation and blood flowing through the country lanes. It is true—and I will frankly acknowledge this—that when in fact the Scarecrows did arrive there was no riot, rapine, blood nor arson.'

'But it is an ancient practice of our courts that any old buffer who occupies this bench may introduce the most lurid and improbable worst-case hypotheses into his judgment and then give these fantasies full weight in his sentencing.'

'Prisoner at the bar, we must judge you not on the basis of what *did* happen, which was rather little. We must speculate upon what *could* have happened, when viewed by a fevered imagination, and then sentence you accordingly. So that I must, in respect of my own ghastly fantasies, regard you as standing before me convicted of arson, rapine, riot, burglary, barratry, bigamy, buggery, bastardy, battery, bankruptcy, and whatever else I can imagine.

'Second, by your action you have weakened the confidence of this country's allies in the trustworthiness of the Government. I use the plural only out of form. You well know which Great Ally I refer to. It is a matter of high import that this Ally should know everything about the most secret affairs of this country but that the British people should not.

'Until lately only inferior degrees of treason have been known to our laws, such as high treason, petty treason and the like. But the courts now recognise an infinitely graver degree of treason. This is Super Treason, or lack of deference to our Great Ally. You stand now before me convicted of super-treachery. Indeed, I am aghast. . .' (At this point Mr Justice Canting was overcome by emotion and raised his eyes to the United States flag which now hangs in the courtroom of the Old Belial.)

Concluding his judgment Mr Justice Canting said that Miss Candide's offence, under the third head, was even more grave (if that was possible) than the first two. She had flouted the Official Mendacity Acts, without whose salutary operation no government could continue.

These Acts had a venerable history of precedents reaching back to the thirteenth century. They were a staple of English Common Law. It had long been a principle of government to regard literacy or the provision of public education as a threat to public order. His learned predecessors had done everything in their power to prevent the people from reading the Bible in English. For several centuries they had succeeded in conducting proceedings in the courts in archaic Latin forms so that the condemned did not even know for what they were being hanged. The government had conducted a stubborn resistance to the publication of the proceedings of Parliament. Had it not been for the interference of a certain Alderman Wilkes and of other ruffians in the City of London (in the case of *Rex versus Hansard*), the public would remain in blissful ignorance of debates in the House of

Commons to this present day.

'But, alas! The floodgates of democracy have now been thrown open! On every side authority is menaced by public education and public prints! How, in the face of these hazards, is order to be maintained unless by the skilful exercise of mendacity, and the constant provision to the public of pre-masticated public information?'

In an impassioned conclusion Mr Justice Canting described the Official Mendacity Acts as a last dyke thrown up against the inrush of anarchy. The grand purpose of these Acts was well-known. It was not to deny information to the Enemy, who had his own means of finding out. It was not even to deny information to the natives of this country, although the Acts took care of this matter. It was to enable the Government to feed the public with a wholesome and regular diet of *dis*information.

'Great God!', Mr Justice Canting continued: 'The crimes of the prisoner endanger the very fabric of civilised life. If the operations of government are to be thrown open to every Tom, Dick and Harry—nay, as the fashion now is, to every Jill and Jane' (consternation in court) 'and if the criminal infection of truth-telling were to become common, how could any rule continue? How could we ensure the security of any Scarecrows? How could we prevent the displeasure of our Great Ally? Nay, how could we ensure the secure tenure of our own salaries and fees. . .?' (At this point Mr Justice Canting broke off and wept copiously into his wig.)

When he had composed himself, Mr Justice Canting delivered sentence. 'Jane Candide, you have been found guilty of riot, arson, rapine, super treason, and of truth-telling in contempt of all seventy-seven sections of the Official Mendacity Acts. These are all capital offences, but by some oversight the legislature has not provided for the capital penalty. The sentence is seventy-seven years of imprisonment.'

LAW REPORT: COURT OF APPEAL

Regina versus Herself, Ex parte the British People

Before Lord Cain (Lord Chief Justice), Lord Justice Shuffel and Lord Justice Flay.

Actions taken by Government effectually withdrawing all human rights from the British people were clearly actions taken on the grounds of national security. Therefore the court was not entitled to inquire into the actions which were taken in the exercise of the Royal Prerogative.

The Court of Appeal so held when allowing an appeal by Herself against the decision of Mr Justice Playfair, who had granted in the High Court a declaration of invalidity of an instruction issued by Herself that the constitutional rights of British citizens should be suspended during Her Good Pleasure.

The Lord Chief Justice, giving judgment, said that it was intolerable that the time of their Lordships should be taken with such trivial and factitious matters. An action might well lie against the British people and their counsel for barratry. An action might lie against Mr Justice Playfair for insubordination—he would refer that matter to the Lord Chancellor.

What were the facts in this case? For many years a vast, complex and exceedingly expensive organisation known as HAPPYFARM had been employed by the Government to poke and pry into the communications of our neighbours, our allies, and whomsoever the Government nominate as our enemies (which of necessity included a great part of the British people). For reasons of national security successive Ministers had lied through their back teeth about this operation, and had repeatedly assured both parliament and the public that HAPPYFARM was a low-cost operation exclusively concerned with sending food parcels to the Third World.

The importance of HAPPYFARM's functions and its delicate and confidential nature was obvious and needed no emphasis. There could be no dispute but that the activities were of paramount importance and must be protected from any public inquiry.

Unfortunately the cover of HAPPYFARM had been blown when a postal worker blurted out to the press that no food parcels were ever sent from there through the post-office. This had been a most serious breach of the Official Secrets Acts.

In these circumstances it became inevitable that the true functions of HAPPYFARM (i.e. general piracy of the air, telephone and post) should be officially acknowledged. And ministers took the view that thenceforth security would be best obtained by chaining all civilian operatives to their desks and by forbidding any conversation between them except in the presence of an accredited security officer.

These condign regulations were issued by Herself upon the authority of the Royal Prerogative. Counsel for the respondents (the British people) had argued in the High Court that these regulations were contrary to the letter and spirit of a great number of statutes enacted by parliament in the past two hundred years, and by some accident they had lighted on a judge (Mr Justice Playfair) who had upheld their plea.

His Lordship said that although his patience was already exhausted he would, nevertheless, for form's sake, attend to certain submissions of counsel for the respondents.

Respondents had argued that this nation was governed through a 'parliamentary democracy', and that parliament alone was empowered to abridge the liberties of the British people.

His Lordship agreed that parliament was indeed one among a number of authorities so empowered. Parliament had in recent years been mindful of its duties in this respect, and had brought forward several admirable statutes which had enlarged police powers, curbed the trade unions, taken away rights from metropolitan authorities and juries, etc.

But parliament was a strictly subordinate organ of the State, and it shared the power to abridge liberties with many other subordinate organs such as the National Coal Board and the Metropolitan Police Commissioner. The notion that parliament was anything more than an historic ornament was an outmoded and archaic doctrine.

The function of government was to govern according to law and law must be certain. But parliament was constituted through an electoral process which, despite every precaution, remained arbitrary and uncertain. Parliament must therefore itself be governed and be subjected to law: that is, to their Lordships themselves.

Counsel had also argued that over several centuries the Royal Prerogative had been abridged, citing among other precedents the case of *English Commonwealth versus Charles I*. It was true that there was some abridgement to be found here; indeed, he might say that in that case the Royal Prerogative had been cut short. (Sniggering in court.) But it was well known that this breach in the body politic had been repaired by 13 Ch. II St. 1, c. 1.

It had further been argued that the Royal Prerogative had been subjected to the authority of parliament in 1 Will. & Mary, Sess. 2, Cap. 2, vulgarly known as 'The Bill of Rights'. His Lordship had little time for such musty precedents. That document had not been drawn by judges or by lawyers. It included many loose phrases as to 'Vindicating and Asserting the Auntient Rights and Liberties of our Auncestors', which purported liberties could not be found in any book of law.

In particular respondents had cited the first proposition of the Bill of Rights: 'That the pretended Power of Suspending of Laws or the Execution of Laws by Regall Authority without consent of Parlyament is illegal.' And they had supported this by citing 'The Case of the Seven Bishops' (1688) in which the jury had found against the exercise of the Royal Prerogative to suspend and dispense with existing laws.

But all these statutes and cases were no more than regrettable necessities. They were sops thrown to a turbulent and disaffected populace as a means of quietening their minds.

They did not represent the true intentions of the governors. Indeed, in 'The Case of the Seven Bishops' the jury had found against the clear direction of the court. These precedents had long been set aside.

Finally, counsel had submitted that the Royal Prerogative had been invoked as a fiction by Herself in the pursuit of Her own ambitions, and that Her Majesty the Queen had neither been informed nor consulted and might indeed have disapproved of this exercise of the Prerogative in her name.

It was true, Lord Cain said, that this matter was not wholly satisfactory. In recent years the Royal Prerogative had passed over from Her Majesty to Herself, along with much of the deference and allegiance previously owing to the monarch. He was aware that it had been proposed that the forms and the reality should be brought into a match, and that Herself should be duly crowned and enthroned.

However, it would be foolhardy to meddle with the ornamental forms of the monarchy so long as the arbitrary and uncertain process of parliamentary election (to which he had just referred) had not been curbed and brought under a rule. What if some shocking accident were to occur and Herself be unseated? What if some popular fellow should attain not only to the post of Prime Minister but also, thereby, to the Prerogative? It might then be a time when the Royal Prerogative should revert once again to the person of the monarch, as a hedge against anarchy.

Indeed, when Lord Cain considered the hazards of a merely-biological succession (the Royal Family), he wondered whether some more certain safeguard of law and property might be devised? Even in the best of families there could be disputes, or persons who did not come up to the mark, as he had once had to make clear with some force to his learned brother, Mr Justice Abel. Might it not be wiser if the Royal Prerogative were to be vested in the office and the person of the Lord Chief Justice?

In conclusion the Lord Chief Justice said that the matter before them was clear and allowed for no argument. The object of government was to govern the British people. No power could reside in the governed. The Government of this nation consisted of a separation of powers in three parts, *viz.:* (1) The Director of the Security Services, (2) Herself, and (3) Himself (in the Office of Lord Chief Justice).

The name of the Director was always withheld from public knowledge as an Awful Secret. He was generally—although this was not essential to his functions—the agent of a foreign power, such as the USSR or the USA. He might not be questioned by parliament and he was responsible only to Herself. The function of Himself was to confirm, in arcane and pompous language, whatever the Director or Herself decided upon, and to act as a screen between them and the public.

Since the interests of national security were paramount (and were the true seat of power in this nation), it was the duty of the courts to endorse any action taken under the Royal Prerogative 'which could truly be said to have been taken in the interests of national security to protect this country from its enemies or potential enemies' (*Times* Law Report, 7 August 1984). Such enemies might be without this country or (more probably) within. And how was the truth of what was said to be determined? His Lordship found no difficulty here. Whatever Herself chose to say might, by definition, 'truly be said', since Herself had truly said it. Any further inquiry into this by the courts would be dangerous.

It was true that he could find no certain definition of 'national security' in his books. But what matter? He would enter certain *dicta* for the guidance of the courts. National security was whatever the Government pretended it to be. This matter had already been made clear by his learned predecessor in this office, Lord Chief Justice Lane, who had found (*Times* Law Report, 7 August 1984) that 'the ministers were the sole judges of what the national security required'. All that was necessary, in any exercise of the Prerogative, was that Government should indicate that it 'thought' that national security required these measures, and that this 'thought' arose from 'a *bona fide* belief'. Since Herself was distinguished by the strength of her *bona fide* beliefs we could be assured of firm government during her lifetime.

As for the Royal Prerogative, Lord Cain noted that it was a convenient fiction to enlarge the powers of Herself. The Prerogative covered not only national security but also the conduct of foreign affairs, the armed forces and the police, the regulation of the civil service, the inland revenue, the interception of citizens on Herself's highways, and by extension whatever else She wished.

Counsel's submissions as to infractions of 'human' and 'constitutional' rights were an intolerable abuse of the courts. Their Lordships could not find any 'rights' in their books. The law was concerned with persons in their view as obedient subjects and not in any supposed view as 'humans'. Their Lordships could not find any 'humans' in their books.

Nor could they find any British 'Constitution' in their books. While certain suppositious 'rights' had from time to time been granted as a means of managing disaffected opinion, these could at any time be suspended, and usually they were. Indeed, their Lordships recollected that until recent times Governments had very often suspended not only the purported 'rights' but also the bodies of their subjects, and for all their Lordships cared they might soon start doing this again.

The appeal by Herself was allowed. The respondents were ordered to pay all costs as well as the costs of HAPPYFARM and of the Trident programme. Lord Justice Shuffel and Lord Justice Flay remained mute throughout the proceedings.

Law Reporter: E.P. Thompson

THE DIVISION OF EUROPE

A BASIC QUESTION

Fifty-six years come tomorrow
Was Workers' October—kingdom of necessity
Turned arse-over-tit, kingdom of freedom come.

Let me look at my watch.
It seems a long time for the kingdom of freedom
To have shown the world nothing but its backside.

Comrade Central Committee, comrade high official
Of the Writers' Union, letter-signers, informers,
Stuck in half-a-century of backwards postures:
You bore us to distraction.

You're right: this *is* a bitter old capitalist world.
It needs changing. Some of us are trying.
But not in your way, arse-forwards,
Offering it to the world as a fully-human bottom.

Perhaps fully-human bases have superstructures?

May we talk to your other end?

September, 1973.

119

THE SOVIET UNION: DÉTENTE AND DISSENT (1974)*

Roy Medvedev's measured appraisals provoke in my mind reflections upon two moments in my own political experience.

The first moment is that of the crisis of the Second World War: the years 1942-45. Soviet intellectuals are now examining the evidence of these years, and are uncovering a record of diplomatic miscalculation, destructive terror, and military and administrative mismanagement whose consequences were appalling. Medvedev himself, in his discussion of *Gulag Archipelago*, focuses attention on Stalin's personal responsibilities: his 'criminal miscalculations, his inability to prepare either the army or the country for war, his ludicrously foolish orders at the outbreak of hostilities, his desertion of his post in the first week of war, and his prior destruction of experienced commanders and commissars. . .' all of which resulted in the loss or capture of some 4,000,000 troops.

Some Western socialist intellectuals have tended to focus attention less on the military conduct of the war than upon the diplomatic bargaining in Yalta and at Potsdam which determined the balance of power at its conclusion: the trading of spheres of influence, which resulted in the division of Europe which endures to this day, and which entailed, on

---

* From *Détente and Socialist Democracy: a Discussion with Roy Medvedev,* edited by Ken Coates (Spokesman, 1975).

the one hand, the imposition by Soviet arms of a military
and bureaucratic 'socialism' upon the peoples of Eastern
European countries, and, on the other, the consignment
of certain Western European countries to a United States
sphere of influence (whose consequences, in Greece and in
Spain, can be seen to this day).

Both these lines of enquiry seem to me to be important.
But there is a sense in which, for a man of my generation,
neither of them falls at the exact centre of the experience of
those years. For the experience was—as one lived it—that 'the
war' was 'won', and that it might very well have been lost. It
is true that as Solzhenitsyn, Medvedev and others show, it
was 'won' at a cost immensely and tragically higher than
might have been necessary. And it is true also, as many
younger Western socialists and Trotskyists insist, that in the
moment of 'winning' the war many of the democratic and
socialist objectives of the popular victors were betrayed by
their own leaders.

But neither of these reservations cancel out the historical
event: that the Allied armies and not the armed power of
Fascism emerged in control of Europe. The generations who
did not live through those years perhaps assume this outcome
too easily. If the outcome had been the opposite, they would
now be making very different kinds of assumption. For if
Franco, in the more exposed and precarious circumstances of
Spain, has been able to survive the war for thirty years, I can
see no overwhelming reason why Nazism and Fascism should
not have endured over the whole of Europe into the 1970s:
at the best one might have hoped for inner nationalist
fractures resulting in terrible internecine conflicts between
rival élites; at the worst a Euro-Nazism, armed with nuclear
weapons, might have submerged the entire world in imperialist wars. In any case, those of us who survived in the 1970s
would not be discussing these matters, since we would have
access neither to any printing-press nor to sources of
objective scholarship.

So that a 'victory', even if at tragic cost and partially-
betrayed, remains different from that kind of defeat. And
since no Western writer with the genius of Solzhenitsyn has

ever composed a *Gulag Archipelago* which takes into a single
view the repression in this century of intellectuals, Jews,
trade unionists, socialists, liberals, communists, and ordinary
people of all persuasions in Western and Southern Europe, it
follows that the matter is not as vividly present in the
imagination of those under 40 years of age as it remains to
those of us who are over 40.

It may follow also that there is a certain difference at a
deep, almost sub-conscious level—a level of experiential
assumption—in attitudes towards the Soviet Union. Put in
the simplest way: I cannot in the end rid myself of some kind
of very deep affirmative feeling towards 'the Soviet Union',
as the country whose valour saved all of us from a future of
Euro-Nazism. If the Western Allied forces and the resistance
movements contributed something to this outcome—and
perhaps contributed rather more than Russian school-
children are now told in their lessons on 'The Great Patriotic
War'—none of us can doubt that the Soviet people bore the
greatest part. So that all of us now living, including those
who were not yet born at the time of the battle of Stalingrad,
live by virtue of a transfusion from that Soviet blood.

At any rate, between 1942 and 1944 it appeared very
simple when one looked at a map. Nazism possessed absolute
control over an area and resources larger than the present
European Common Market: every unrestrained political and
administrative means was employed to fashion a military
machine of formidable efficiency and power. While the Allied
forces engaged in peripheral campaigns or in lengthy preparations for the opening of a 'Second Front' in Europe (content,
in fact, to see 'Germany' and 'Russia' bleed each other white)
the markers on the map moved to the edge of Leningrad and
of Moscow and deeply towards the Urals. Then they began to
move back, in a way in which, from the time of the
assumption of power by Mussolini, Hitler and Franco, they
had never moved back in Europe before. They moved back
with astonishing rapidity, as this hitherto invincible political
and military machine met, for the first time, its match; and
whole armies were encircled and engulfed. Even the simplest
Allied soldier, listening to the news in South Italy or on the

South Coast of England, knew the meaning of these gigantic German reverses. They offered expectation of ultimate victory: an enhanced chance of survival for himself or his family: a war which might not (as one had come to suppose) endure for decades but which might reach a more proximate termination.

For the Soviet people this achievement may have taken place *despite* Stalin and Stalinism, although this was not so easy to see from the West at that time. And the resilience of the people may have stemmed from patriotic rather than communist resources. But however this is seen, some residue of affirmative feeling towards something called loosely 'the Soviet Union' must always remain in my experience. Even when confronted by *Gulag Archipelago*—perhaps at such times most of all—one thinks of the Soviet people as a people with extraordinary, inexhaustible reserves; with an irrational resilience; a people who, when by every logic they are defeated, are capable of moving the markers back across the map once again.

For some of us, in those years, admiration was indiscriminate and self-betraying; and we can now see clearly Stalinism as the enemy of Soviet and Western revolutionaries alike. We can also see Soviet 'dissidents' in all their variety— Solzhenitsyn, Sakharov or Medvedev—as emblems of this astonishing resilience; driven back into the Urals of Soviet culture, they have decided, when defeat had seemed inevitable, to give not an inch more of ground. They are hemmed in in their own Stalingrad. Will we see, once again, those liberating markers moving back across the map? This is what Medvedev asks. I have tried to explain why this question calls up in some of us an ancient sense of solidarity.

The other moment in my own political experience which Medvedev provokes me to reflect upon lies in the years 1956-61. In the aftermath of the 20th Congress Western Communist Parties were thrown into turbulence, with major secessions of 'revisionists' and 'dissidents'. In Britain some of the seceders (the *New Reasoner* group) formed an alliance with younger socialist elements which gave rise to the 'New Left'. These events coincided with the influential presence of the Campaign for Nuclear Disarmament: in itself an induction of a new political generation into affirmative action.

The Campaign advocated the immediate, unilateral renunciation by Britain of the manufacture or possession of nuclear weapons. By some—indeed by all—this was seen, in part, as 'a moral gesture'; an initiative towards general disarmament and détente. But opinions were divided as to the political and diplomatic context of this policy. Some supporters of CND advocated the open or tacit continuation of Britain within the strategies of NATO. This would have entailed a continuing dependence, in the last resort, upon a United States 'nuclear shield' which, in the view of some of us, deprived unilateral nuclear disarmament of either moral or political credibility. We in the New Left advocated the policies of CND *plus* 'positive neutralism': that is, a policy which entailed also British renunciation of NATO and the adoption of mediating, neutralist policies aligned to those of Yugoslavia, India and the emergent Third World.

It was a critical part of our advocacy that we argued that with each effective movement of détente there would follow a relaxation in military and bureaucratic pressures within both the United States and the Soviet Union. Thus the relaxation of Cold War tensions was a precondition for further de-Stalinisation, and a precondition for resuming socialist and democratic advances, East or West. I was myself especially associated with this advocacy; and since recent events have thrown this whole perspective into doubt, I should perhaps convict myself out of my own mouth.

Thus I wrote in *Universities and Left Review* (No. 4, Summer 1958):

. . . with each month that the Cold War continues, a terrible distorting force is exercised upon every field of life. As it drags on the half-frozen antagonists become more sluggish in their reactions. Political and economic life is constricted, militarism and reaction are infused with new blood, reaction and the subordination of the individual to the state are intensified, and the crooked ceremonies of destructive power permeate our cultural and intellectual life.

The relaxation of the Cold War would create conditions 'in which healthy popular initiatives will multiply' and (in the words of the Programme of the Yugoslav Communists in the same year) 'shatter the basis upon which bureaucracy thrives and assist the more rapid and less painful development of the socialist countries'. If the British Labour Movement were to adopt the policies of unilateral disarmament plus active neutrality (outside of NATO) this would contribute simultaneously to the acceleration of processes of democratisation in the East and to the resumption of socialist progress in the West. The same perspective was still presented in the British *May Day Manifesto* (1968).

As Medvedev shows, we have been witnessing in 1973-4 an altogether different process. Summit agreements between United States and Soviet leaders, accompanied by some regularisation of relations and limitation of Cold War tensions, have intensified pressures upon Soviet 'dissent' and have been accompanied by the increasing discipline of intellectual and cultural life throughout the Communist world. Does this mean that our original argument was wrong, and was based upon a merely sentimental and wishful appraisal of realities?

Such a conclusion would be premature. It is mistaken to be too impatient in our expectations. There are inner contradictions to be expected within any wider political process. The logic which we proposed—that relaxation of Cold War tensions provides a precondition for socialist democratisation—has, although in a very general and uneven way, been seen at work between 1954 and 1974: and notably in the evolution of Eastern Europe. But insofar as democratisation threatens ruling bureaucracies and also the military-diplomatic controls of the Soviet Union, we have seen a zig-zag movement with very severe setbacks—notably in Czechoslovakia, 1968.

In the Soviet Union the contradictions are especially acute. On the one hand, the repressive institutions and the repressive ideology of pseudo-Marxism have found, for decades, their major source of justification in the function of the ruling bureaucracy (and of its organs of police and of intellectual control) in defending the Soviet people from the threat of attack, from without or from within. It therefore follows that if Nixon and Kissinger can be seen driving through the streets of Moscow—and if the threat from Western imperialism can no longer be seen as immediate—then the function of the bureaucracy is itself called in question, and its repressive ideology loses further credibility. Hence 'détente' is simultaneously a moment of enhanced danger to all those whose privileged and unrepresentative positions rests upon the invocation of this function. Hence the post-Stalinist bureaucracy finds that its legitimacy is called in question, not because our earlier argument was wrong, but because it was right. If the threat from the West appears to diminish, then the old functions can only be sustained by emphasising the threat from China. (But this also involves tormented readjustments of ideological orthodoxy, and of expectations as to from which quarter to expect 'the main enemy' within.)

Thus what we are now witnessing is a limited and calculated agreement, a détente based upon the regulation of great power interests from above. Both parties to the agreement wish to keep this détente firmly within control and to prevent the unleashing of popular initiatives. But insofar as *any* détente strips the reigning Soviet bureaucracy of its prime function and legitimation, this is sensed as a moment of acute danger. Controls over the life of the Soviet people are tightened at exactly this moment, to prevent that uncontrolled and self-generating liberation of (in the first place) intellectual and cultural forces which would, in the end, call in question this bureaucracy itself.

If this analysis is correct, then it also suggests to us certain lines of action which European socialists should take. What we are observing in the Soviet Union at the moment need not indicate a genuine and profound reversal of the tendencies towards democratisation but a temporary arrest to a process which, at any time, may be resumed. Since so much depends upon contingencies—as well as upon the jockeying for power of different interest-groups within the Soviet leadership itself—it would be foolish to attempt any prediction as to whether this arrest will prove to be long or short. What has to be challenged is the complacency of those Western socialists and liberals who assume that they are only spectators in this auditorium, and that the outcome will be determined solely by events in the Soviet Union or in Eastern Europe. So long as Western social-democracy remains confined (whether by active ideological complicity or by effective impotence) within the strategies of NATO and of a 'Europe' which excludes not only Moscow but also Prague, Belgrade and Warsaw, it is itself contributing to the outcome which it deplores. It is very easy for the Western intellectual to applaud those Soviet intellectuals who have the courage to challenge their own statist orthodoxy. But since Western intellectuals, for all their vaunted (and valued) freedoms, have been unable to detach decisively one single Western society from the military and diplomatic definitions of the Cold War era, the applause has an empty sound to it.

There have of course been gestures towards such a detachment: in French truculence towards NATO, in Brandt's *ostpolitik*, and (at the level of annual conference decisions) in the professed policies of the British Labour Party. Gestures and professions are better than nothing; and they indicate that, with greater resolution, actions may ensue. If only one Western nation were to effect a democratic transition to a socialist society, were to detach itself decisively from NATO and from dependence on the United States, and were to initiate an active, probing, self-confident diplomacy, offering manifold exchanges in trade and in ideas with 'the East', this might serve as a significant catalyst. An initiative of this kind—supported by popular initiatives, exchanges by trade unionists and intellectuals, exchanges in education and in tourism—could not be presented by orthodox Soviet ideologists as the old kind of threat to 'subvert' the Soviet system. It might give great encouragement to the most affirmative elements in Soviet and Eastern European 'dissent'; and, by breaking down the old ideological deadlock, by which we are offered the alternatives of a statist and repressive 'communism' or of substantial democratic rights and defensive liberties within a capitalist society, it would point towards further perspectives of socialist internationalism.

It is of course true that such an initiative—if taken by France, Britain, West Germany or Italy—would entail an element of risk. Militarist elements in the Soviet leadership might take it as evidence of 'weakness' in 'the West' and seek to exploit it accordingly. Thus we are supposing that, if such an initiative were to succeed, it would meet with corresponding initiatives from progressive forces in 'the East', at least strong enough to hold their more regressive and militaristic leaders in restraint. And the risks would be greatly enhanced by the diplomatic and economic sanctions brought to bear by the United States and NATO powers upon any defaulting member; by the consequent exposure of this defaulter to immediate economic and social crisis, accompanied by intensified internal class struggle. But the continued division of Europe and of the world entails much greater and continuing risks, which may be regulated temporarily but which can never be permanently ended by great power agreements. We can never move out of this international polarisation except through a process which, at the moment of depolarisation, entails great risk: and it is important that these risks be taken, not as a result of unforeseen accidents; but in a context of mounting popular internationalist initiatives.

This is to restate, in the context of the mid-1970s, perspectives which were argued in the late 1950s by Claude Bourdet and the French *Nouvelle Gauche;* by 'positive neutralists' within the Campaign for Nuclear Disarmament in Britain; by C. Wright Mills in the United States; and by Imre Nagy and the Yugoslav League of Communists. It is sobering to realise that, after fifteen years, the perspectives appear to many to be more, rather than less, utopian. Not many Western socialists today appear to have any confidence in the possibility of a peaceful and democratic transition to socialism; indeed, few appear to be examining what such a transition would entail and many would appear (from their actions) to consider that such a transition would be undesirable, preferring to develop the defensive institutions and the redistributive policies of the labour movement, so that they can get some milk from the capitalist cow for as long as she has milk to give. At the same time the younger Marxist Left, in all its varieties, falls back upon a rhetoric of 'revolution' which supposes a dramatic and violent transition to a socialism whose democratic features are problematic—a rhetoric which, whether one finds it distasteful or not, offers a perspective a good deal more utopian than the one I have sketched above. Finally, many dissidents in 'the East'—or many of those whose voices have been heard most clearly in recent years in the West—no longer hold to the perspectives of a regenerated socialist democracy which, to one degree or another, informed the Polish revisionists in 1956, Imre Nagy, the Yugoslav Communists of 1958, or Dubcek. One or two of them (if we are to judge by recent statements of Solzhenitsyn) might actually oppose any Western advance towards socialism, and would (like the Pentagon) see the detachment of any Western power from NATO strategies as a symptom of weakness.

Utopian or not, I think it is worth re-stating this old perspective for two reasons. First, it may serve to correct the rather self-satisfied stance of some Western liberals and socialists. For if one proposes this perspective, it can at once be seen that it might prove to be as difficult for a Western nation to resume initiatives independent of great-power polarities as it proved to be for Czechoslovakia in 1968. A comparable effort of self-emancipation by any Western nation has scarcely been attempted. While this does not in any way call in question the value of Western freedoms, it does suggest that Western intellectuals have efficiently preserved these freedoms for their own consumption by virtue of the fact that they have been ineffectual in using them to challenge the overall boundaries within which such self-expression remains 'safe'.

The limits of Western tolerance have not yet been exposed to a Dubcek-type test; or, if they have, that test was made in unusual circumstances in the southern hemisphere. And when Allende pressed against those limits, neither he nor any Western freedoms survived the test.

Second, the perspective only appears utopian because it is

presented in a way which proposes that an action be taken in advance of the necessary preconditions for that action. These preconditions are, exactly, an initial rebirth of socialist internationalism; a growing discourse between 'dissident' voices in both the East and the West; a discourse which, by proposing alternatives to the present polarisation of power, itself begins to create such an alternative, in a reawakened internationalist conscience, and in feasible national strategies. This is why one must attach the greatest significance to Roy Medvedev's initiatives. Honest political exchanges between Soviet or East European dissidents and Western socialists, unmediated by party officials and uninhibited by ideological imperatives, are a precondition for Eastern democratisation and for Western socialist advance alike.

This leads me to my final points as to how such exchanges might be conducted. If exchanges enlarge they will turn out to be deeply confusing, to overthrow many cherished expectations; to break down many ideological pre-suppositions. There is a sense in which the Soviet Union, after fifty years of severe intellectual repression and discipline, is a de-structured political community. Or it is, in one sense, altogether de-structured; and in another sense, it has only one, obligatory political structure, through the Soviet Communist Party. We are fortunate, in conversing with Roy Medvedev, to be conversing with a man who relates at many points to our own Western socialist traditions, and specifically to a Marxist tradition: we recognise common terms and signposts. But it cannot be expected that all conversation will be like this. On the one hand, from the de-structured political community we must expect that a people who have suffered from innumerable crimes which have been justified by a mandatory statist Marxist orthodoxy will show a profound distaste, not only for Stalinism, but also for all Marxist forms and terms. The Christian tradition will seem to some—as it seems to Solzhenitsyn—to have offered greater resources in defending the individual and the human conscience than any resources within Marxism. The children whose teeth have been set on edge by the sour grapes of paternal statist ortho-

doxy may suffer very large illusions as to the liberalism of the
West, and they may be (as Solzhenitsyn seems to have been)
seriously misinformed as to certain Western realities. In
contrast to statist ideology the Voice of America may be
mistaken for the voice of truth.

On the other hand, insofar as the only legitimate
structuring of political life is through the Soviet Communist
Party, we may expect to see unexpected and unpredictable
things here also. Any historian knows that social contradictions and tensions have a way of working themselves out,
not in neat predictable ways, but through whatever forms are
available. People make use of whatever forms history has
given to them to use. In a Durham pit-village in the 19th
century the very conservative Methodist chapel may turn
out to be the training school for a militant miners' leader; in
Catholic Fascist Spain we may find important radical and
liberation elements within the Catholic Church; and so on.
Since the inheritance of the Soviet Communist Party is in
fact enormously richer than its official ideological forms
would suggest, we can expect repeated evidence of social
tensions working their way through within—or despite—
these forms. The rhetoric of statist Marxism may be authoritarian and empty; but it remains, in form, a Marxist rhetoric,
and there are strong libertarian elements within the Marxist
tradition. To suppress those elements would involve (among
other things) suppressing the collected work of Marx.

This is why it is foolish to criticise Medvedev because he
has some expectations of renewed democratic changes initiated by elements within the Soviet Communist Party. But in
fact I find it foolish and beside the point for any Western
socialist or Marxist to spend time, at this particular stage, in
criticising Medvedev or any other dissident in any way at all.
What we ought to be doing is *listening*. In the first place,
and in the second place, we have to express solidarity, assist
our Soviet comrades in their efforts to consolidate a position
from which any dialogue becomes possible, listen carefully,
learn, attempt to understand the new ideas and the new
sensibility which has been growing up like tundra beneath
the orthodox snows.

The particular privilege enjoyed by the Western Marxist or Leftist intelligentsia is the privilege of irresponsibility. Since our actions are largely verbal and command few real social consequences, we can say what we like in the way that we like. An error of political judgment, an ill-advised telephone call, lack of security with an address-list, will not bring down the arrest of colleagues or their dismissal from employment. Still less will it plunge a whole movement into disarray. Some of us have got so used to this displaced, intellectualised context of Leftist discourse that we indulge in the luxuries of mutual denunciation at the drop of a hat. In the pursuit of a 'correct line' which might be followed, at the very most, by a few thousand people—and more often by a few score intellectuals—we denounce A. because he has a wrong formulation on Soviet State Capitalism and B. because he shows a tendency to humanism and moralising. Well, if we want to be like that, and if the discourse between East and West opens up further, we shall find a great deal to denounce. It will keep us happy for some years. There will be, for example, quite a lot of Soviet humanism and moralising, since a nation which has had a great many millions of people wrongfully and arbitrarily killed or imprisoned has got something to moralise about, and some knotty problems about morality, politics, the State and the individual conscience, to clear up. It will seem to some that the matter is not wholly closed by coming to the fine point of a correct formulation.

It seems to me that any helpful discourse between Soviet dissidents and Western socialists must be conducted in a receptive and provisional way. For the time being we should not be impatient for it to have an outcome in any agreed opinions or agreed internationalist strategy; the open and rational discourse—and the information and mutual understanding which this will bring—will remain as a sufficient objective. And if some of those from the East who join the discourse turn out to be deeply hostile to all Marxism, and in search of non-Marxist spiritual values, I hope the discourse will continue all the same. Indeed, when I read some self-styled Western Marxists—for example, the school of

M. Althusser, which appears to continue on its way oblivious
of the fact that the history of the Soviet Union raises certain
'moral' questions—I think that it would not matter all that
much if Marxism was Christianised a little. Or, again, perhaps
the problem is that as a State or doctrinal orthodoxy it has
already been Churchified too much.

As regards the supposed failure of dissident Soviet intellectuals to agitate among the masses. . . Perhaps I may end with
an historical analogy which might afford a little encouragement. When in 1792 Tom Paine published in England *Rights
of Man* every official and quasi-official means was taken to
suppress the man and his ideas. Paine was indicted and driven
into exile. The book was burned by the public hangman.
House-to-house enquiries were made as to his readers or
supporters. Resolutions were passed at county meetings. In
nearly every town and most villages in Britain there were
public bonfires, when Paine was burned in effigy, and the
populace were given drink to toast the 'Church and King'.
And all this worked very well. The chauvinist and regressive
impulses of the crowd (who had never had an opportunity to
read Paine) were flattered. Those intellectuals and artisans
who supported him were isolated in a sea of public hostility.
But a year or two later? What the authorities had overlooked
was that they had engaged in a superb advertising campaign.
Every old woman (as one reformer noted, in an isolated
country town) had heard about Tom Paine and wondered
what he had really written. The ideas and the pamphlets
began to circulate in the wake of an aroused national
curiosity. Soon a book had become a popular movement.
I could not say whether this is a relevant analogy or not.
I know little about the complexities of life in the Soviet
Union. But I do know that in history exiles have a way of
returning as heroes; and that at night bonfires light up the
surrounding countryside.

EXTERMINISM REVIEWED*

My 'Notes on Exterminism'[1] were written in May 1980, in the aftermath of the NATO 'modernisation' decision and of the Soviet invasion of Afghanistan (both in December 1979), and against the background of the US failure to ratify SALT II and of a bellicose and seemingly 'consensual' all-party militarist hullabaloo in Britain (*Protect and Survive* and so on). There was then no effective peace movement in Europe—something in Holland and in Norway, a first stirring of the new movement in Britain, but as yet very little in West Germany or Italy. The peace movement in the Far East was also quiescent. And Solidarity did not yet know its name.

The times favoured intellectual pessimism. I can accept the reproof of Raymond Williams and of those other contributors who detect some sentences in my 'Notes' that could support a determinism according to which the rival weapons systems, by themselves, and by their reciprocal logic, must bring us to extermination. I ought to have known better than to have gestured at Marx's suggestive image of the hand-mill and the steam-mill. Yet the 'Notes' did not only suggest that: there was also, already, in the European Nuclear Disarmament Appeal, the outlines of a strategy of resistance, and my essay concluded with a conspectus of this alternative—a conspectus which has taken on flesh in the past two years, in the realities

---

* Abridged from my concluding essay responding to the discussions of the notion of 'exterminism' in the volume *Exterminism and Cold War* (Verso Editions/NLB, 1982).

of the peace movements.

If the times are not quite as dark today, they are still dark enough. And I am unwilling to abandon the category of 'exterminism' without at least a tentative defence. The term itself does not matter: it is ugly and over-rhetorical. What matters is the problem that it points towards. There remains something, in the inertial thrust and the reciprocal logic of the opposed weapons systems—and the configuration of material, political, ideological and security interests attendant upon them—which cannot be explained within the categories of 'imperialism' or 'international class struggle'. And there are some plain misunderstandings of my argument.

Thus Roy and Zhores Medvedev[2] challenge my view that 'a situation could ever reach the point in the Soviet Union when "hair-trigger military technology annihilated the very moment of 'politics' "'. And they argue, in response, that 'the Soviet system is too conservative and densely bureaucratised for this to happen'. If the Party exercises comprehensive control of most sensitive aspects of intellectual and social life, 'how can one imagine that those military experts who manage the Soviet Union's ICBMs could possibly launch them in an emergency without collective decisions at the highest levels of the Party and state?' And the Medvedevs conclude that 'strict and comprehensive safeguards exist against any possibility of either a mistaken or deliberate initiative by any level of the military hierarchy alone'.

That may be so, if we stress *initiative*, although even here there is room for little accidents which perhaps do not receive Politbureau sanction, such as the episode of the Soviet submarine in sensitive Swedish waters. But if we accept the Medvedev's arguments in a literal sense, then we can only conclude that the Soviet Union is doomed by its bureaucratic and conservative procedures to be the loser in any nuclear exchange. For military-technological considerations have already shrunk the time in which any collective decisions of Party or state can be made. Nuclear weapons are so devastating that response to an attack—or pre-emption of an anticipated attack—must be almost instantaneous. And the whole absurd theory of 'deterrence' demands that such near-instantaneous capabilities can be displayed. In one example, the Pershing II is advertised as a highly accurate and swift weapon: if sited, as planned, in West Germany it will be seen as a potential weapon for first strike, capable of taking out Soviet ICBMs and command and communication centres in the western Soviet Union in a few minutes of flight. In the view of one well-informed American authority, Arthur Macy Cox, such a threat could be met by the Soviet military only by the introduction of LOW (Launch-On-Warning) automated systems, which would despatch a nuclear counter-strike on the trigger of an electronic alert signal. The collective decisions of Party and state would then be pre-empted within the circuits of a computer. And an influential lobby for LOW systems exists in the USA as well. Where would be the moment of 'politics' then?

This question ought to remain open for analysis a little longer. New contributions on this question, some of them coming from positions rather far from those of the traditional 'left'—notably Jonathan Schell's *The Fate of the Earth*—will ensure that it will not be tidied away. Schell is asking whether advanced civilisation may not be falling subject to a tendency towards its own self-extinction—a tendency which, if not reversed within a decade or so, might become irreversible? That is much the same question as is proposed in my 'Notes'. What name, then, are we to give to such a tendency? And what *is* a 'tendency'? Is this moment simply the product of an accidental coincidence—the coincidental invention of an appalling new military technology superimposed upon a particular episode of world-wide political confrontation? Or can we speak of entering—at some point after 1945—into a distinct historical epoch (perhaps a terminal one), with distinct characteristics governed by the reciprocal non-dialectical contradiction between two military blocs whose competition, at every stage, reinforces their mutual hostility and their exterminist resources—an epoch which requires a new category for its analysis?

I proposed the term 'exterminism' because, in my view, the second of these alternatives may be correct. I have rehearsed the argument recently, but without recourse to

the term, in my lecture *Beyond the Cold War:*
'The Cold War has become a habit, an addiction. But it is
a habit supported by very powerful material interests in each
bloc: the military-industrial and research establishments of
both sides, the security services and intelligence operations,
and the political servants of these interests. These interests
command a large (and growing) allocation of the skills and
resources of each society; they influence the direction of
each society's economic and social development; and it is in
the interest *of* those interests to increase that allocation
and to influence this direction even more.'

I don't mean to argue for an *identity* of process in the
United States and the Soviet Union, nor for a perfect
symmetry of forms. There are major divergencies, not only in
political forms and controls, but also as between the steady
expansionism of bureaucracy and the avarice of private
capital. I mean to stress, rather, the *reciprocal* and interactive character of the process. It is in the very nature of this
Cold War show that there must be two adversaries: and each
move by one must be matched by the other. This is the inner
dynamic of the Cold War which determines that its military
and security establishments are *self-reproducing.* Their
missiles summon forward our missiles which summon forward their missiles in turn. NATO's hawks feed the hawks
of the Warsaw bloc.

For the ideology of the Cold War is self-reproducing also.
That is, the military and the security service and their political
servants *need* the Cold War. They have a direct interest in
its continuance.

If we do require a new category to define this distinct
epoch of nuclear-confrontational history, yet it goes without
saying that this does not, by some gesture of a wand, mean
that all previous categories are dispensed with or all prior
historical forces cease to be operative. That may also be a
misunderstanding which my 'Notes' invited upon themselves.
Imperialisms and class struggles, nationalisms and confrontations between publics and bureaucracies, will all operate with
their customary vigour; they may continue to dominate this
historical episode or that. It will mean, rather, that a new,

featureless and threatening, figure has joined the *dramatis personae* of history, a figure which throws a more abrupt and darker shadow than any other. And that we are already within the shadow of that extreme danger. For as the shadow falls upon us, we are impelled to take on the role of that character ourselves.

Roy and Zhores Medvedev turn away from this mode of analysis. As Soviet patriots (albeit 'dissident' ones) they react rather strongly against any notion of co-responsibility by the superpowers for the current crisis or of 'symmetry' of any structural kind induced in the rival powers by three decades of confrontation. They offer a different analysis, of a historical character, in which Soviet militarisation is shown to be in reaction (sometimes *over*-reaction) to the military threat of NATO, and especially the USA.

I found their contribution to be in every respect illuminating, as well as positive and encouraging. I welcome especially the sense of solidarity with which they write, and the patience with which they explore disagreements. If I explore these disagreements further (and from the weak position of a greatly inferior knowledge of Soviet history and reality) it is because of the extreme importance of the issues, and the urgency with which the European and American peace movements await a discourse of genuine internationalism with wider sections of the Soviet public. And for this to take place we must first remove certain road-blocks and controls which the Medvedevs scarcely mention.

I learned much from the Medvedevs' essay and have few and insignificant disagreements with it. Yet it leaves much unsaid, and in doing so it could close off some lines of inquiry prematurely. The Medvedevs are viewing history as rational *causation*, whereas I am viewing the contemporary opposed militarist structures as historical *consequences;* so that some of our arguments are flying past each others' ears. Everything the Medvedevs say about the prior responsibility of 'the West' for militaristic pace-making may be true; yet the consequence of three decades of Soviet response to that may have been to enstructure militarism deeply in Soviet society also.

The Medvedevs argue that the Soviet Union has militarised itself reluctantly, defensively, that the Party remains in control of all organs of the state. Yet history is full of examples of the way in which deeper processes can override or co-opt such controls and intentions. It simply is not possible for a major economy to be inflected towards military priorities for some three decades (and more) without profound consequences in social, political and ideological life.

The Medvedevs argue that 'military-industrial-research interests in the Soviet Union. . . do not constitute a "state within the state" as they do in the United States, but remain a subordinate part of the state'. I am surprised they can argue with such confidence, in view of the opacity of Soviet state structures and the paucity of published information—which they are the first to acknowledge. 'Subordinate', in any case, to what? To a Party which itself must in some part represent these interests (to which some 15 per cent of the GNP is allocated) and some of whose leading executives are recruited from the military-industrial-security areas? There are some scraps of evidence known to me (many more weighty evidences must be known to the Medvedevs) which suggest that 'isomorphic' replication of militarist priorities is not unknown in Soviet life. Thus 'Boris Komarov', the Soviet ecologist, refers repeatedly to the ways in which 'defence' priorities can always over-rule the well-intended environmental regulations of Soviet authorities. The sad story of the pollution of Lake Baikal commenced when 'the Ministry of Defence needed new durable cord for heavy bomber tyres. Such things are referred to tersely as "strategic interests of the country" and are not subject for discussion even within the Council of Ministers. The immunity of the Baikal projects to any criticism is explained by these "strategic interests".' And recounting the story of the poisoning of wild life by PCB (polychlorinated biphenyls) he concludes that 'the secret of PCB, as might have been expected, was buried in one of the defence ministries. PCB was required for extra-strong insulation for military equipment: its composition and hazards were concealed for reasons of military secrecy: 'Here too "strategic interests" prevailed. In the most literal sense strategic interests pervade our whole being whether we want them or not'. And to all this 'Komarov' provides some lighter footnotes. He describes the wholesale slaughter of wild life by high- (and even low-) placed military, overriding every protective regulation: 'eagles, hobbies, kites, and other birds of prey are wiped out from military helicopters just for practice; Marshal Chuikov has even been known to sweep through whole areas with a column of all-terrain vehicles, field kitchens, etcetera, slaughtering every bird and beast in sight; polar bears have been hunted by helicopter; and so on.[3] It is all reminiscent of the safaris of British officers in Kenya or in the Indian princedoms, thirty or fifty years ago.

The Medvedevs will understand that I do not introduce this evidence with 'anti-Soviet' intent. I am simply insisting that one cannot divert huge resources to secretive and protected military areas without incurring huge social consequences; that the same consequences which are felt here in Britain at Stornoway or at West Wycombe are felt there at Baikal or at Kyzyl-Agach. When 'strategic interests of the country' are not even subject for discussion within the Council of Ministers, in what sense are these then 'a subordinate part of the state'? Is this not only too familiar to us in 'the free West'?

If polychlorinated biphenyls, protected by 'strategic interests', can poison the water and grass of the Soviet Union, I would think it probable also that similar toxic ideological compounds, also protected by 'strategic interests', will be poisoning or confusing the minds of the Soviet people, just as these poison minds in the West. The ideological PCBs commonly found on this side are those which offer partisan, alarmist, or directly nationalistic descriptions of reality—which justify each and every measure of militarisation in the name of 'deterrence' and the threat of the Other—which directly inhibit genuine international discourse, and which repress or inhibit critical reflection and discussion as threats to the 'security' of the state. One need not read very far in the literature on contemporary Soviet reality to learn

that such toxic compounds are widely dispersed, on that
side as on this.

This does not mean that we should look for structural
symmetries in the opposed superpowers. I have argued, not
for this, but for reciprocal and interactive modes of strategic
and ideological confrontation. If symmetry now, in the
1980s, begins to appear, this is consequence and not causation. We are entering upon extremely uneasy times, and we
ought not to refuse consideration of the possibility that one
of the options still open for a resolution of the political
problems of the Soviet Union is a military one. It is already
apparent that some sections of the ruling establishment there
are displaying anxiety lest the peace movement should infect
Soviet youth, but in a form critical of Soviet reality. In the
past few months there has been an assault upon 'pacifist'
tendencies weakening the 'heroic-patriotic' faith of Soviet
youth. Boris Pastukhov, a leader of the Comsomol, has
called for 'Undertaking with yet greater clarity of purpose
the military-patriotic upbringing, the moral, political, psychological and technical preparation of youth for service in the
ranks of the armed forces, to instil in young people courage,
the will and readiness to perform heroic deeds. . .'[4] This is
the moralistic and nationalist claptrap of all armed states.
But even if it is argued that these necessary ideological
measures are imposed upon Soviet authorities by the aggressive postures of the West in association with China, the
consequence must be nationalistic and militaristic indoctrina-
tion. And behind this claptrap, is it not possible to distinguish
the features of a distinct militarist lobby? Marshal Ogarkov,
the Soviet Chief of Staff, has recently published a book,
Always Ready to Defend the Fatherland, which advocates
the demands of the military in an unusually open way. He
advocates, like his NATO analogues, not only a massive
programme of weapons 'modernisation', but also advanced
preparations for switching 'the entire economy to a war
footing': 'In order to increase the military preparedness of
the country, today as never before it is necessary to co-
ordinate mobilisation and deployment of the armed forces
and the entire economy. . .' To achieve these objectives 'is

not possible without a stable centralised system of leadership of the country and the armed forces. . . an even greater
concentration of management'.[5]

This centralised management, this stable and concentrated
system of leadership of the-country-and-the-armed-forces,
looks rather like some kind of military junta to me. Because
Marshal Ogarkov has given a thought to this possibility it
does not mean that it will come about. But we have seen
already, in Poland, a military junta displace the Party in
power: and while this was a Polish solution arising from
Polish conditions, it establishes a new precedent nonetheless.
For the radical political weakness of the Soviet Union and of
every Warsaw Pact state is to be found in the weakness of
civil society; it is sixty-five years on from the Revolution,
and yet civil society in the Soviet Union has a sparse and
insecure presence, existing within the controls and by the
permission of the Party and the security police; and it is
precisely where civil society is weak that the military (in
alliance with other interests) can most swiftly enter in. It is
not just a question of force: it is a question of legitimacy.
Where no form of power is legitimated by civil accountability
and due and open process, then one form of power might
just as well give way to another. Each is as legitimate or as
illegitimate as the other.

I hope, profoundly, that the Medvedevs are right and that
my own fantasy is wrong. Yet for it to be proved wrong may
at least require that the possibility be steadily faced, so that
action may be taken to prevent it. And what disturbed me
most about the Medvedevs' brilliant essay was a sense that
the accumulation of absences and silences amounted even to
complacency. This is so far out of character in these two
indomitable and uncomplacent authors that I must be
wrong. Yet the sense lingered with me, especially at the
article's conclusion—in the section sub-headed 'The Responsibility of the Peace Movement'. And it turned out here that
this responsibility fell wholly, and without qualification,
upon the peace movements of NATO and of Western
European nations. The solution to the immediate crisis will
(it seems) be met by the pressure 'for unilateral nuclear

disarmament in Europe' but for 'Europe' it seems that we
should read 'Western Europe' and nothing whatsoever is said
about the need for any peace movement, or even reciprocal
strategy of agitation, in the East. So that while the Medvedevs' analysis is very much more rich and flexible than any
from apologists of the Soviet state, yet their conclusions are
pat and even orthodox.

Now this is a matter which, for our very survival, must be
honestly faced and openly argued out. For the Medvedevs,
in the first pages of their essay, suggest an immense Soviet
audience—an ordinary Soviet public, and also partisans of
socialist democracy like themselves, Soviet citizens who
attend to the work of the Western peace movement and who
share its concerns. Let us trust that this is so. It may even be
so. Yet something, somehow, has become skewed. For one
of the most remarkable facts of the past two-and-a-half years
has been the Soviet *absence* from the European peace movement. What Soviet citizens have taken in its discourse, or
been willing to engage, upon equal terms, in its councils?
A handful of doctors: Roy and Zhores Medvedev; that is all.
   No doubt a host of other Soviet citizens might wish to do
so but are inhibited by bureaucratic constraints. These constraints are not—or are not only—those imposed by the West.
They belong to the long-standing ideological self-blockade,
by Communist states, of their own citizenry: the Communist
international default. To examine, as rational causation, the
history of this default might give us a very different historical
answer to the question of co-responsibility for the Cold War
than does a history confined to the arms race. A history of
the arms race can be offered, as the Medvedevs offer it, in
terms of NATO action and Warsaw Pact reaction: this tends
then to the complacent conclusion that if NATO should halt
its provocative actions the Warsaw Pact will instantly cease
to react, and the peace-loving intentions of the Soviet Union
will then become plain to all mankind (except, perhaps, to
some Afghan tribesmen). But a history of the ideological
confrontation of the two blocs, which has contributed as
much as military measures to the adversary posture under-

pinning the Cold War, must result in more ambiguous conclusions. It has to be said, again and again, and in terms
which demand a Soviet response, that the repression of the
Prague Spring (1968) was as much the action of irresponsible
warmongers as was the NATO 'modernisation' decision of
12 December 1979. And if it is the responsibility of the
Western peace movement to contest with every resource the
latter decision, it is the responsibility of the Soviet people
also to contest the ideological and security structures which
poison the political discourse of Europe, enforce its division
into 'two camps', and legitimate the Communist international
default.

I will not attempt to sketch this alternative ideological
history here, although I have gestured towards it in *Beyond
the Cold War*. But the presence of this history, as consequence, is manifest in Europe today. By 'Communist international default' I mean the refusal of the Communist
apparatuses of the Soviet Union and of the Warsaw bloc to
permit direct international discourse between citizens or
groups, unregulated by their own security and ideological
controls; their insistence that all exchange, even between
peace movements, takes place upon their own favoured
ideological terrain; the radical insecurity which inhibits any
manifestation within the Warsaw bloc which might express
a critical view of any aspect of Soviet reality; and the very
damaging attempts to manipulate, or to divide, Western
democratic movements, including Western Communist
parties, trade unions and peace movements themselves, in
order to subordinate them to the diplomacies of the Soviet
state.

All this has a complex and bitter history. After 1945 there
was the severance of ten thousand strands of international
discourse, each severance causing confusion and pain. I can
recall that moment, when the frame-up of the Hungarian
Communist leader Laszlo Rajk was announced, and when we
opened our papers in surprise to discover that Konni Zilliacus
(the Labour Party's leading internationalist MP, expelled
from the PLP for his stubborn work for peace), Basil Davidson
and Claud Cockburn (two of the most able, internationally

expert journalists of the British left) had all been 'unmasked' as imperialist agents. And so it has gone on. Frame-ups and the unmasking of imperialist agents are less in fashion now. But the same arrogant authoritarianism, the same bureaucratic manipulation, and the same fear of any East-West discourse taking place outside the authorised forums and the permitted ideological terrain—all these remain in force.

The World Peace Council congeals some of that history and protracts it into the present. I am aware that many younger members of the European peace movement cannot understand the distaste with which some of us grey-headed ones regard that mendacious bureaucratic organisation and its national subsidiaries: these quasi-official state 'Peace Committees' appear to them as plausible places for international communication; and their efficiency as travel agents for visiting delegations eliminates many of the difficulties and costs of less structured exchanges. I will only say that some of us still active in the peace movement have had twenty-five or thirty years of experience of the WPC's manipulations and bad faith—a Council which, in all that time, has never found fault with a single Soviet action—and that the subject has become merely boring. It is an organisation whose function is to structure authorised East-West exchanges and to blockade all others. It is a satire upon any authentic internationalist discourse. The son of the traduced and executed Laszlo Rajk now runs a *samizdat* bookshop in Budapest. Any honest East-West discourse must hold a place open for him.

Let us propose this in a more positive way. The conditions which threaten us today—which throw the shadow of extermination upon us all—are military, political and ideological. For more than two years an influential peace movement has been developing, in Western Europe, Japan, Australia, the United States, from the spontaneous and democratic initiatives of the public. This has been contesting, in the first place, the menacing military and political dispositions of the NATO powers. What might give to this movement truly impressive strength—what might even bring some victory within reach—would be a junction between the Western peace movement and some congruent movement of opinion in the Soviet Union and in Eastern Europe.

This cannot come from travel and conference-promoting agencies subordinate to the *realpolitik* of the Warsaw Pact states. The present position is absurd. The orthodox Communist media, in the East, welcome and publicise the manifestations of the Western peace movements while at the same time censoring their demands and inhibiting an equivalent discourse in their own nations. If the articles or pamphlets of Bahro or Magri or Chomsky or my own *Beyond the Cold War* appear in Eastern Europe they will appear in *samizdat* and at the publishers' risk.

The Soviet state may not have co-equal responsibility for the thirty years of arms race, but it does have—and at this moment it has—co-responsibility for the continued ideological division of Europe, the Cold War. Europeans await, with increasing anxiety, the return of Soviet citizens to an international discourse: youth must be able to travel, writers to publish, peace movements to confer and to canvas alternative strategies, without attending upon some Office of Orthodoxy. It is not good enough that the gifted citizens of one of the greatest nations of the earth should cower secretively behind security barricades, and excuse themselves from all responsibility for this predicament with apologetic histories which always place the blame upon the shoulders of others.

We accept this blame: we in the West are contesting the policies of our own states. We ask the Soviet people to accept their responsibilities also: only their initiatives can begin to dismantle their own security and ideological barricades and repair the Communist international default. And the matter is urgent: the peace movement in the West, which anxiously awaits their response, cannot guarantee the continued vitality of its presence if that response fails to come. One cannot maintain the morale of a movement so inchoate and so moody without some signs of success, and one can imagine more than one scenario (a deterioration of the situation in Poland, a NATO adventure in Libya or the Middle East, a show trial of Czech 'dissidents' or a submarine disaster off Stornoway or in the Black Sea) which would check it or throw it into reverse.

Peace depends now and in the immediate future upon the élan and the continual enlargement of the democratic internationalism of the non-aligned peace movement. It depends upon the forging of a new internationalism, unmediated by state structures, between the citizenry West and East. The opportunity is open, now, and the response from Soviet citizens must begin to show itself before the end of 1982.[6] We must find ways to signal this urgently to the Soviet public in the coming months. There is no need, of course, to signal this to Roy and Zhores Medvedev: they are themselves evidence of the internationalism of Soviet citizens, and pledges that the junction between autonomous movements for peace and for socialist democracy, East and West, can still take place.

In conclusion, let us briefly consider relations between the Cold War, Europe, and the Third World. I have been criticised by several contributors for awarding such pre-eminence in my analysis to the fracture of power and of ideology through the heart of Europe as 'the central locus of the opposed exterminist thrusts': the place of origin of the Cold War and the place where its adversary postures are continually regenerated and refreshed. I am persuaded that I must take the criticism into account. It is not so much that I find my proposal to be wrong as that I am now unclear as to the proposal's status: I do not know what evidence would be required either to support it or to refute it.

It would be better if I stood the proposal on its head: *Europe, in the 1980s, is the weak link in the Cold War.* The question now is not whether Europe is the locus which generates the Cold War but whether Europe may not be the continent on which, as Erhard Eppler has said, the 'chain of armaments' might be struck through. Europe is now the locus of opportunity; and for this reason Europeans now carry a responsibility to the rest of the world—to the Third World in particular—to realise whatever opportunity allows.

Certainly Europe is menaced by particular military dispositions, by a density of weaponry, and by strategies which threaten a limited theatre war. But that is not all that has brought the new peace movements into being, as some North American observers may have supposed. There are also particular political and ideological conditions peculiar to Europe which make the fracture of its political culture seem increasingly arbitrary and insupportable. As direct conflicts of interest between the confronting blocs recede into insignificance in the heart of the continent, so congruent economic and cultural interests assert themselves. No 'global class struggle' divides the workers of Gdansk from those in Newcastle, or the peasantries of Hungary and Greece. The old ideological compulsions of the Cold War are losing their hold upon the rising generation. As impulses for socialist democracy or for civil rights find expression in the East so these can meet with a response in the peace and labour movements of the West. Increasingly it appears, in common-sense political perception, that the adversary structures of the armed blocs are all that are holding this confluence back. All this is a theme of my *Beyond the Cold War.*

To say that the Cold War is now perpetuated by its own self-reproducing inertia—that it is about itself—is perhaps a European perception. It is small comfort to those in El Salvador, Afghanistan, or Namibia. Yet it may be, within Europe's own context and conditions, true—as a perception which is challenging rather than complacent or Eurocentric. It is here that the chain might be struck through: but it is here also that new transformations, of the most radical and affirmative import for the rest of the world, might commence.

I am unwilling to predict what form these transformations might take, if the best case came about. I would predict only that we would have to devise new categories to explain them. In a general and loose sense I would agree with Halliday: socialist democracy, in some sense, might be the vocabulary of change in both worlds. But it would have to be more sharply anti-statist and libertarian than anything in the dominant Communist or Social Democratic traditions, or in Marxist theoretical orthodoxy: nothing less will be tough enough to meet the opposition, and maybe repression, of the opposed militarised states. It is likely also that (following

Bahro) it will be informed by an alert ecological consciousness since the congruent struggles, West and East, will be
founded upon the human ecological imperative. That being
so, it will shatter or transform or transcend the ritualised and
long-inert categories of 'Communism' and of 'Social Democracy', whatever historical legacy or detritus is left in the
institutions and forms of particular nations. It is not that the
Second International will make it up and enter a marriage
with the Third. New forces and new forms will replace
them both.

That is the best case, and the worst case remains at least
as probable. This best case is argued eloquently by Lucio
Magri,[7] with whom I express my solidarity and accord. I
welcome most especially his definition of the possible
relationship between the advanced and the underdeveloped
worlds. His definition of the matter is superb and I urge
readers to return to it again and again: 'Any new relationship with the Third World presupposes a qualitative change
in our own type of development. Such a change would have
to involve a reorientation of the European economies away
from the quantitative multiplication of goods for consumption
and export, and the wastage of natural resources that goes
with it, towards another style of development: one that was
sober in its consumption, exported technology and knowledge rather than commodities, sought a reduction in labour-
time performed, gave priority to improvements in the quality
of living.'

The arms race is a theft of resources from the Third World.
The export of arms, military infrastructures, and of militarist
ideologies (some of them disguised as Marxisms) from the
advanced world to the Third World is a way of distorting
social process, of aborting revolutions or of stifling their
potential at birth. This is not only an era of permanent
revolution but an era in which every revolution is screwed up
as every nation is dragged into the polarities of the Cold
War. If Europeans could strike through the chain of
armaments—and the diplomacies and ideologies that go
with it—and find a third way then in that moment the
possibility would open up of a new non-exploitative relation-

ship with the Third World, bringing material and cultural
reinforcements to the strategy of non-alignment and afford-
ing more space to Third World nations to pilot their own
course of development independently of either bloc.

I end with a confession of uncertainty. I will not fight for
the category of 'exterminism' provided that the problem it
indicates is not tidied away. We are at the end of an epoch,
when every old category begins to have a hollow sound, and
when we are groping in the dusk to discover the new. Some
of us must be content to offer unfinished 'Notes', or may
risk (as Bahro sometimes does) provocations and prophecies.
I distrust only those who (after Cambodia, after Solidarity
and Polish martial law) are satisfied with the old categories
and who offer to explain overmuch.

We are engaged in an international discourse of extraordinary complexity. We are trying to construct, out of the
collapse of earlier traditions, a new internationalist constituency and one capable of acting urgently and with effect.
We cannot write our recipes at leisure in the drawing-room
and pass them on to the servants' hall (although some try to
do that still). We must improvise our recipes as we sweat
before the kitchen fires. Even in Europe, to assemble that
internationalist constituency into a common peace movement—from so many nations, traditions, and from two
adversary blocs hung around with misrecognitions—requires
extraordinary skills. Intellectuals and communicators have
particular responsibilities and roles in putting that internationalism together in these early stages. They are the
couriers who must take the first messages across the frontiers
of ideologies. And they must be self-mobilised; they must
find their own routes; they cannot wait upon any High
Command of party or of peace movement to tell them what
to do. It is in this spirit that the editors and contributors
to this volume have acted, and I salute their work.

NOTES

1. My 'Notes on Exterminism, the Last Stage of Civilisation' first appeared in *New Left Review*, no. 121, May–June 1980, and were republished in *Zero Option* (Merlin Press, 1982), and *Beyond the Cold War* (Pantheon, New York, 1982).

2. Roy and Zhores Medvedev, 'The USSR and the Arms Race' in *Exterminism and Cold War* (Verso Editions/NLB, 1982), pp. 153–174; also published in *The Nation*, January 16, 1982.

3. 'Boris Komarov', *The Destruction of Nature in the Soviet Union* (London, 1980), pp. 7, 33–4, 77, 87–9. Zhores Medvedev, in a private communication, has persuaded me that there are serious reasons to doubt the authenticity of 'Komarov's' account. But the general trend of his evidence can be confirmed from other sources.

4. *Christian Science Monitor*, 11 March 1982.

5. *Guardian*, 12 April 1982.

6. Such a response did show itself, in the Moscow Group for the Establishment of Trust between the USSR and USA (and similar groups in provincial cities) in the summer of 1982. As I argue in other essays in this book, the tormented history of these groups and their repression by Soviet security organs, and the failure of any respondant 'thaw' in the East, were contributory factors in the (temporary?) defeat of the Western peace movement in its campaign against NATO modernisation.

7. In *Exterminism and Cold War*, pp. 117–134.

THE POLISH DEBATE*

The argument of your letter turns upon Poland; and, while your facts are often wrong and your quotations wrested out of context, some of your questions are fair. You are wholly wrong when you say that not a single 'unofficial person' from END travelled to Warsaw while Solidarity was overground. I trust that you will not expect me to name names or occasions. As it happens, one of the first British visitors to the Hotel Morski in Gdansk, early in September 1980, carried in his pocket a message of solidarity with Solidarity, which I had moved at a packed END public meeting in Newcastle-on-Tyne a few days before. This visitor, John Taylor—a temporarily unemployed WEA tutor travelling on his own savings and not, as *Trybuna Ludu* was subsequently to fulminate, a 'wealthy businessman'—moved in to Solidarity's Gdansk headquarters to help in any way he could (he assisted Solidarity to obtain some of their first printing equipment) until he was told by the Polish authorities to leave five months later. His account will be found in *Five Months with Solidarity* (Wildwood, 1981).

What John Taylor found was that Solidarity was pre-occupied, twenty-four hours a day, with its work as a union. 'Foreign affairs' or disarmament were not on its agenda, and (as you say) the matter of the Warsaw Pact was a question

---

* From the *Spectator*, 30 October 1982, responding to an 'Open Letter' to me by Timothy Garton Ash, *Spectator*, 21 August 1982.

too sensitive to add to that agenda. This was what other visitors, supporters of CND or END or Western peace movements, found in that first year: for example, Dennis McShane, *Solidarity* (Spokesman, 1981). (You will notice that I am only citing published and readily available sources.)

This 'self-limiting' (your own phrase) character of Solidarity's agenda was understood and respected by END. We never attempted to intervene, nor (unlike some Western cold warriors) to thrust our recipes upon them, and, despite the tenor of your argument, we never claimed Solidarity as a part of the 'peace movement'. Those of us who gave our public support to the movement did so as trade unionists and as supporters of civil rights, and without conditions. We have never said, '*if* you support the peace movement, we will support you'. It is true that we saw also in the Polish renewal, with its opening to more fluent communication with Western movements, a pre-figuration of a process that will blur the edges of the blocs, although the term 'objectively' (which provokes your scorn) is not mine but M. Balibar's. Despite all that has happened in the past ten months, I refuse to accept that this opening has been finally closed.

We did, however, with insufficient vigour, offer a public argument. This was that the right response by Western democracy to the Polish crisis was to relax military tension in Central Europe (in several statements we tried to disinter the bones of the Rapacki Plan), to stop leaning on the Eastern bloc with plans for Cruise and Pershing II, and to afford the Polish nation more space for autonomy. Our proposals met with little response within Poland, and we did not pretend that they did. In Solidarity's last open months more interest in this dialogue was shown. You state, with your habitual over-confidence, that Solidarity 'to the end scrupulously refrained from attacking any aspect of Poland's defence policy'. In fact the matter was debated, briefly, at Solidarity's last open Congress, when Bogdan Lis (who is now the underground leader of the Gdansk district) argued for a cut in the arms budget, disclaimed any particular criticism of either bloc, and concluded: 'We will always be against armaments, whether in the West or East.' (*Guardian*,

2 October 1981). An official Solidarity delegation took part in the huge Amsterdam peace demonstration, a few weeks before martial law shut the gates.

I don't think that the Western peace movements did enough to keep those gates open. But failure does not necessarily disprove an argument: it may only underline that forces are unequal. NATO also signally failed to keep them open. It is my view that Reagan, Weinberger and Thatcher, with their bluster and political capitalisation of the Polish crisis, did a great deal to thrust the gates shut. You disagree. You argue that 'the dramatic warnings addressed to the Kremlin by NATO and Western leaders' did a great deal to hold back (in December 1980) the half-million Warsaw Pact troops on Poland's frontiers. How do you know? These were not the only warnings addressed to the Kremlin: there were warnings also from the Yugoslav government, from the Italian Communist Party, from the Western peace movement. There was even a warning from E.P. Thompson (*Guardian*, letters, 11 December, 1980) that 'Soviet or Warsaw power action in Poland would have the most disastrous repercussions on the European peace movement'.

How do you or I know which warnings may have been attended to? The *Daily Telegraph*, in a remarkable editorial just over a year ago, attributed Soviet military restraint to the Soviet leaders' fear of alienating the peace movement. It is not a claim which we would ever make ourselves. But you wish to bully readers—and whatever Polish opinion you can reach—into believing that your answer must be the only right one. You say, with satisfaction, that you have met 'more supporters of Reagan in Warsaw than in West Berlin'. This may, in recent months, be true. If I must add 'alas!', and if I repeat that some Polish trade unionists and democrats have been looking to the 'wrong friends' in the West, this is part of a public and open argument which we, in the Western peace movement, are entitled to put. We do not present it as a Polish argument, but as our own. It is possible to admire the courage of Polish democrats, and to express unconditional solidarity with them in their democratic objectives, but at the same time to argue with them about

their analysis and their international alliances. Solidarity is
not a one-way road.

It is at this point that you pass over to misrepresentation.
You cite a half-sentence of mine in which I say that martial
law was 'a Polish solution', and go on indignantly to document the Soviet pressure brought upon the Jaruzelski regime.
I cannot conceive why you should suppose that I need
persuading of this. To say that Soviet pressure was mediated
through (and also partly shielded by) Jaruzelski is not an
'apologists' phrase': it is a plain statement of political fact.
I regard martial law as a condition of enthroned anarchy, and
a confession of total political bankruptcy: but if you want
to know the difference between Soviet intervention and this
present Polish interval, you need only ask a Czech. Nor is the
situation in Poland today to be regarded, even in the short
run, as a settled episode.

You also cite an article which I wrote in the *Times* five days
after martial law was proclaimed in which I said: 'General
Jaruzelski is a patriot: he has pledged himself to avoid bloodshed.' I have a problem here, in my technique as a writer. I
had always supposed that irony was an available resource of
English letters, from at least the time of Chaucer, and that
one might presume a reading public sensitive to its reception.
This assumption has betrayed me into many difficulties in
translation, and now I am finding that the privilege of irony
is refused by English readers also, who perhaps have been
bludgeoned into insensibility by the prose of *Private Eye*,
Auberon Waugh and the Militant Tendency (of Right or
Left).

If you read that article again with candour, and with
Professor I.A. Richard's four kinds of meaning in mind, you
will see that it commences with a long passage (including
your chosen citation) of bitter irony, mocking the conventional wisdom (even relief) with which some part of our
press (including the *Financial Times*) had received the news
of martial law. The conclusion which I reach, in the imme-
diately following paragraph, is that none of this wish-
fulfilling wisdom 'can survive even one week of martial law'.

You may defend that misrepresentation by a plea of generational insensibility to tone, but your next misrepresentation is indefensible. You cite me as writing, in *Exterminism and the Cold War*, that Solidarity had features (Catholicism, nationalism, etc.) 'which might wrinkle the nose of a purist', and you then proceed to offer this as a straight statement of my own wrinkled-nosed opinions. For pity's sake, permit me to place the citation in its context:

> Solidarity's life-cycle is one of the most remarkable and authentic examples of self-activity in history, and without doubt the most massive and purposive working-class movement in any advanced society since the Second World War. To be sure, it had certain features which might wrinkle the nose of a purist: it was nationalist, Catholic, predominantly male, and in its last months over-confident. Its internationalist perspectives were confined and confused. But my point, at this moment, is that an analysis of the contemporary crisis in terms of the global class struggle which cannot find any place for this astonishing episode of class struggle has somehow lost its way. Can the struggle have been between the wrong classes and in the wrong part of the globe?

I ask again—did you consciously misrepresent me, or has your generation lost the capacity to read? Surely it is not possible to read this paragraph as a whole without realising, first, that I am taking the mickey out of one or two Marxist grand theorists, and second, that it is an expression of profound humility before the historical experience of Solidarnosc? I am, after all, a historian of working-class movements, with one or two yardsticks in my memory, and my commitment to working-class movements and to trade unionism has been somewhat more long-lasting (and perhaps less suspect) than some of Solidarity's most vocal and self-advertising Western admirers.

I will allow that you do care, in earnest, about civil and trade union rights, and that you are as anxious about Poland's and Solidarity's future as I am now. I hope you are also concerned about these rights on this side of the Cold War divide: for example, in Turkey. But what would you have us do? We have conducted an open argument, both with official and with some 'dissident' voices in the East. We have given our advice that Europe has no future, except nuclear war, unless forces making for democracy and forces making for peace can recognise each other and learn to act together. We signalled that a military take-over in Poland would be 'a devastating defeat for peace'. And we, with Solidarity, suffered that political defeat. Defeat need not be final: it proves that our strategy is difficult (which we knew) but not that it is impossible.

It is not I but you, and a host of interpreters like you, who presume to speak for voiceless thousands in the East. What you do is select from various voices those 'dissident' voices which are locked into a hostility to their own Communist regimes so implacable that they view the entire globe in an inverted image, mistake Reagan for Tom Paine, and suppose that Western nuclear arms are, in some never-explained way, instruments of liberation. These often are honourable and selfless persons, who are entitled to their place in the European discourse. But you have no right to select these voices only, and to suppress the diversity of Eastern political conversation, silencing that intermediate discourse which is looking, between the two armed blocs, for a transcontinental third way.

In doing this, you help to confirm these persons in an ideological blindsight like your own. You help to bend against each other those very forces which, if acting in mutual solidarity, might liberate Europe from her bonds. And the rulers of both sides still stand in need of these rival bonding forces, of fear and ideological rancour, both for internal political control and to keep in their stations their client states. It was a little infelicitous in you to write, in the year of the 'Falklands Factor' and of the Victory Parade, that 'Brezhnev needs the bonding effect of militarism and nationalism a great deal more than Mrs Thatcher does'. Perhaps. But if the Soviet Union had elections and Gallup polls, I doubt whether the 'Afghanistan Factor' would show up so strongly.

What puzzles me most is why writers of your ideological persuasion so ardently *wish* independent peace movements in the East to fail. It is not only that they wish to show that the perspective of a third way is difficult, or to puncture my rhetoric. It is more than that. They have got themselves into an ideological lock in which it is necessary for the lesson of the ineluctable adversary posture of the two blocs to be repeatedly confirmed. It is as if, should nations or peoples begin to move out of this Manichaean framework and search for alternatives, then the entire globe would suffer an identity crisis. As it is doing now.

In this they resemble their opposite numbers, the guardians of ideological orthodoxy in *Izvestia* or *Rude Pravo*. It amuses me that the arguments of END are viewed with equal distaste in the Ministries of Defence on both sides. But now that independent and non-aligned peace movements are showing vitality in the East—and very certainly in East Germany and Hungary—is it not time for you to put your scorn on the ground (at least for a little while) and try to *help?*

WHAT KIND OF PARTNERSHIP?*

I hold the view that the Cold War is about itself: that is, the crisis in Europe is at the same time its own cause.

This is not an exercise in metaphysics. Let me explain it more clearly. It is easy to suppose that great military forces are assembled on both sides of Europe, and that missiles are deployed against each other, because there is some 'crisis' which these are intended to meet. But what if the militarisation of our continent is *itself* the crisis? We need look then for no ulterior cause.

Of course there are other causes, which historians examine, for the origin and development of this crisis. But these have contributed to a general *state of crisis* which has an existence and logic of its own. The Cold War has become a habit, an addiction, within European political culture. The reason why it continues, and is daily reinforced, is that it is easier for ruling groups, East and West, to surrender to its inertia and to adjust its 'balance' than to risk the possible 'instability' which might follow upon any radical challenge to its logic.

---

* A contribution to a panel discussion on 'The Actual Crisis in Europe: its Causes and Ways to Overcome It' in Athens on February 7th, 1984. This conference, hosted by the government-supported Greek peace organisation, KEADEA, brought together for the first time representatives of the official Peace Councils of the Warsaw Pact nations and of the non-aligned Western peace movements. Mr Zhukov, chairman of the Soviet Peace Committee, was a fellow-panellist and took offence at my remarks. But in the view of many delegates it was constructive to have a face-to-face exchange of this kind, and to bring into the open these controversial issues.

Let me illustrate this in another way. One major cause of the actual crisis in Europe (which we are too polite to mention) is the overwhelming military presence on both sides of our continent of forces which have long over-stayed the historical occasion for their arrival. This points to a simple remedy. Let us invite the Soviet Union and the United States, by mutual agreement, to dismantle their bases and withdraw their forces within their own borders once more. We might recommend this to the Stockholm Conference as a helpful 'confidence-building measure'.

Such a measure would bring World War II at last to an end. And, as a combatant in that war, I am now weary of it. If one had told any combatant in 1944 that, forty years later, American and Soviet forces would still be deployed on foreign territory, one would have met with utter disbelief.

This remedy may not be taken for a year or two, although Greece promises to teach Europe by example. But it is a proper and normal objective to set before us, and one which is in the best interests of the superpowers themselves. It might be called the 'Austrian solution' to Europe's crisis, which has served Austria well for a quarter of a century.

To present Europe's crisis in this way is to emphasise that it is two-sided. The repair of the torn tissues of our continent cannot take place on one side alone.

This does not mean that always and in each episode both sides are equally 'to blame'. That would be absurd. It is to point out that the rulers of both blocs stand in a reciprocal crisis-relationship to each other; that they both worship the same Goddess of 'balance'; that each Cold War impulse calls forth a response in the same kind from the other; and, above all, that the crisis is not only a crisis of weaponry but is also a crisis of adversary ideologies, and of trust, which, no less than nuclear missiles, threaten our common existence.

I see no point in allocating blame. That can be left to future historians if we are so fortunate as to have a future. If you wish for my view, it is that the United States and the NATO powers must be awarded the greatest blame for the escalation and technological refinement of nuclear weaponry. In the episode of NATO weapons 'modernisation' they are greatly to blame; and the present United States administration is adventurous, threatening, and bidding for military superiority. But in terms of ideological confrontation, and in the repression of transcontinental dialogue and citizens' communication, the Warsaw powers must be awarded the greater blame.

I need say little of the first question, since the unequivocal and continuing contestation by the Western peace movement of NATO missile deployment is common knowledge. But I wish to address the second, and more sensitive, question—and I hope that this conference will not avoid sensitive questions —in the attempt to disclose certain problems to the representatives of the Warsaw bloc who are welcome participants here.

There are very real difficulties in the relations between Western peace movements and Eastern Peace Councils which must be laid open. These are not both 'peace movements' of the same kind. The Western movements are loosely-structured alliances of voluntary popular associations, directly contesting the policies of their own governments and confronting the hostility of much of their own media. The Eastern Councils are quasi-official institutions, endorsed by their own governments and applauded in the official media.

Put in another way, the Western peace movements are popular movements primarily engaged in opposing Western militarism. The Eastern Councils are government-endorsed institutions—which are also primarily (sometimes exclusively) engaged in opposing Western militarism. That does not offer a relationship between equals. We, in the West, cannot regard it as a 'fair swap'.

Of course we recognise that Eastern Councils perform useful functions of communication and diplomacy (just as certain quasi-official institutions do in the West). We do not doubt that their members and supporters abhor the idea of nuclear war. We welcome occasions to meet with them. But we cannot acknowledge them as equal partners* in a trans-

---

* My phrase, 'equal partners', gave great offence to the official Peace Council representatives from the East. My argument about unequal political relations was mistaken for an attempt to put them down as

continental peace movement.

To accept them as equal partners could only be upon the premise that the threat of war arises wholly and entirely from the aggressive designs of Western imperialism; that no responsibility of any kind for Europe's crisis lies with the Soviet Union or the Warsaw bloc; that no public voices are needed in the East to advise or restrain their own governments or military; and that the Western peace movements are or ought to be auxiliaries to Soviet peace-loving diplomacy.

If we were to accept such premises, then our business in meeting together need only be to chant in unison anathemas against President Reagan and NATO's aggressive designs. But let it be quite clear that one consequence would follow. This would reduce the Western peace movement to an insignificant pro-Soviet rump, and would alienate that majority opinion which stands on the different premises of non-alignment.

This unequal relationship has already contributed to our present crisis and to the closure of the blocs against each other. For throughout the past four years the credibility of the Western peace movement, in the eyes of the Western public, has depended upon our assertion that, if we in the West refused Pershing and cruise, this would initiate a reciprocal process of disarmament.

We needed two things to vindicate this assertion and to swing the balance of opinion to our side. The first would have been an affirmative response by the Soviet Union to our request that it should, in advance of NATO deployment, dismantle a number of its superfluous SS-20s (for these SS-20s were the only good arguments which NATO had). The response to our request was silence. Warsaw Pact leaders are at one with the leaders of NATO in their abhorrence of any 'unilateral' measures. Yet I remain convinced that we could, together, have brought to a halt this whole insane auction of missiles, for a down-payment in advance of some 80 dismantled SS-20s.

---

national or even human inferiors. This was not, of course, my meaning. And I accept the suggestion of some fellow-delegates from the West that 'symmetrical' might be preferable to 'equal'.

No credible transcontinental peace movement can be founded on the premise that identical weapons are barbaric and aggressive, if in one bloc, but innocent and purely-defensive if in the other. That is to smuggle partisan ideology into our midst. It is time to turn our backs on this rubbish.

The second way in which our credibility would have been vindicated would have been if we could have pointed to a visible partner on the other side, entering into open dialogue with us, and willing to voice—not 'equal blame'—but public criticisms of the military measures of the Warsaw powers. Not only have we been unable to point to such a fellow partner, but, worse than this, we have noted with dismay the harrassment of independent voices and peace movements (not only, in outrageous ways, in NATO's favoured ally, Turkey) but also in the East. The symbolic significance of these episodes has still not been understood. Thousands in the Western peace movements stand appalled at the sight of a great and powerful nation which cannot tolerate the independent voices of a handful of people—let us cite the case of Dr Olga Medvedkova—who, whether right or wrong, are recognised by us as courageous partisans of peace and of dialogue.

It is because the Cold War crisis is composed equally of military and of ideological hostilities that these matters acquire such significance. Let me add this. It is untrue that any responsible persons in the Western peace movement wish to 'interfere' in the internal affairs of the Warsaw powers or wish to promote 'destabilisation' of these societies. We wish, not to 'revise' the frontiers of 'Yalta', but to throw these frontiers more open. We wish to enlarge in every way communication and informal exchanges between citizens— exchanges which the medical profession has to its honour pioneered.

We are calling for a 'thaw' in human relations between the blocs. We are calling for it now. The Western peace movement represents exactly such a thaw in the frozen ideological postures of the Cold War. We are waiting for a thaw in response.

Such a thaw need not wait upon the outcome of delibera-

tions at Geneva or at Stockholm. It does not require the
signature of statesmen upon treaties. It is in the power of the
citizens of Europe to commence a healing-process for themselves. May it not now be the turn of the East to commence
some ideological disarmament? We invite our friends from
the Warsaw bloc to consider with us how we may remove
certain restraints upon the traffic of persons and of ideas, so
as to advance 'detente from below', which will in turn lay
the foundations of trust upon which statesmen in future
will build.

I will give one example. I find that it was exactly four
years ago, to this very week, that I first wrote the preliminary
draft of an Appeal to rid the entire continent of Europe of
nuclear weapons and bases. This Appeal, when it had been
improved by many hands, became the European Nuclear
Disarmament Appeal (or 'Russell Appeal') which was signed
by tens of thousands across Europe, contributed to the rebirth of the European peace movement, and remains an
influential document in its discussions.

Yet—and it is difficult to credit this—so far as I am aware,
after the passage of four years, this little four-page document
has never been published in any freely-available form in the
press of any Warsaw power except in *samizdat!* I must
suppose that this is because certain ideological advisors found
that there were 'formulations' in the document which were
considered to be 'incorrect'. Tens of thousands of column
inches and of photographs in the Eastern press have been
devoted to the actions of the Western peace movement
against NATO missiles: the demonstrations, the Greenham
Common women's peace camp. But the proposals and the
strategies of influential sections of this movement are passed
over in silence.

Friends, how is it possible for there to be honest dialogue
between peace activists, East and West, if every word must
first pass through the fine-meshed sieve of an ideological
censor? How is it possible to talk of partnership unless, as a
matter of course, we undertake to publish in our na⸱·⸱ns
each others' strategies for peace? This is not a marginal
matter. I hope that this question of the exchange of un-

censored publications will be considered in our discussions.

Let me turn from difficulties to a great point of common agreement. Our discussions on this panel are subordinate to the great question before this conference: the furtherance of a Balkan nuclear-weapons-free zone. At a time when the two halves of Europe are closing their doors against each other, it is a privilege to be here, at the invitation of KEADEA, and to find one part of Europe where the door to peace is being held open.

Since this is a nation where one of the first and most bitter episodes of the Cold War was played out—an episode in which my own nation played a discreditable part—it is right that this nation should also be one of the first to heal old wounds. And, as my Bulgarian fellow-panellist will know, I have a personal reason for regarding this strategy of healing with pleasure. For it throws my mind back, once more, to the year 1944, when there was a spirit abroad in Europe which, for a brief moment, transcended ideological divisions and looked forward to a continent united in a democratic peace.

Nowhere was this spirit more heroically evinced than in the mountains of the Balkan peninsula. It is therefore right that it should be here that the vision should be reborn and that Europe's healing-process should begin. We, in the peace movement of West Europe, salute your initiative. In bringing together into one zone-of-peace nations from the Warsaw Pact, from NATO, and non-aligned Yugoslavia, you are offering to all Europe a paradigm of the possible future. Let this bring about a zone, not only rid of the nuisance of nuclear weapons, but also a zone in which the more fluent communication of persons and of ideas takes place—a zone of human repair.

THE TWO SIDES OF YALTA*

Dear Dr Săbata

You were kind enough to address an open letter to me as long ago as last April. If I have delayed a reply for so long it has been for two reasons.

The first is that your important and encouraging letter allowed for no response except the single word, *Yes.* But you would scarcely have thanked me if that had been all that I had sent back to you at Brno.

You argue (as many of us in the West have also argued) that 'what we really need is a joint strategy for transforming Europe into a single entity', But this can only come about from 'a democratic transformation', which will entail a process more radical than that which is usually implied by 'detente' or 'convergence'.

The change which you wish us to work for together would involve 'a convergence of a quite different type':

---

* *New Statesman*, April 4, 1984. The text of Dr Jaroslav Săbata's 'Open Letter' to me is in *Voices from Prague* (Palach Press END, 1983). Dr Săbata, a philosopher and psychologist, was a member of the Czech Communist Party Presidium during the Prague Spring of 1968. Expelled from the CP in 1971, he served five years imprisonment for 'subversion of the Republic' (his offence was to distribute leaflets in the 1971 elections advising citizens of their right not to vote). Released in 1976 he was one of the first signatories of the civil rights organisation, Charter 77, and one of its official spokespersons in 1978. Arrested at the end of 1978 for communicating with Polish KOR activists, he served a further twenty-seven months of imprisonment. He now lives in retirement at Brno.

a coming together in a convergent strategy of social and
political movements, traditional and less traditional, from
both halves of our divided continent. Its long-term political
strategy 'is the demand to *abolish* the undemocratic legacy
of the post-war social and political settlement, *end* the
division of Europe into two opposing systems and *unify* this
artificially divided continent'—in short, 'a democratic peace'.

As I have said, I can only reply 'yes' to this. Yet there was
a second reason why I have delayed my reply. Ever since I
received your letter a slow and predictable nightmare has
been unrolling before our eyes. I read your letter first last
June, just as an election returned to power in my country a
government truculently committed to deploying cruise
missiles here—and to libelling the British peace movement as
a witting or unwitting agency of Soviet interests.

From June until December the nightmare unrolled. Everything that we had warned against for more than three years
came to pass according to our worst predictions. The superpowers and their client states performed to perfection their
ascribed Cold War roles. The demonstrations of millions in
West Europe and North America were powerless to affect
the outcome. And, as we had also predicted, the Soviet
military responded to this in the same vocabulary of confrontation and 'balance', and instantly set in motion the
deployment of new missiles not only on Soviet territory but
also—as if mimicking NATO—on the territory of certain of
its client states in the Warsaw bloc.

Since the time that I received your letter the situation
has degenerated. The blocs have closed against each other.
And this has closed also the narrow political aperture through
which your perspective of 'a democratic peace' could be
glimpsed.

The beneficiaries of this closure are the security services
and the obsessional ideologists of both sides. It is a reciprocal
process with which we have long become familiar. Of course
the strengthening of the security state does not take place
on each side in exactly the same way. In the 'Free West' the
erosion of our liberties does not occur with one single all-
embracing decree from an all-wise Party Presidium, but in

little lapping waves like a rising tide: trials and threats under
the Official Secrets Acts, the deprivation of trade union
rights of employees in sensitive areas, increasing pressures
upon our civil servants and our media of communication.

You will perhaps find such examples to be trivial. It would
not be discreet to invite you to exchange examples of similar
precautions taken in your own country. Yet I draw attention
to these matters to illustrate another aspect of 'convergence'.
If, as you have written, the post-war history of our continent
is the history of its militarisation, then the rival antagonists,
like wrestlers locked in each others' nuclear arms, have been
growing more alike.

Even the vocabulary of the antagonists has a weary
similitude. For four years our NATO apologists have assured
us that cruise and Pershing missiles are enforced and
necessary measures of 'defence' against the expansionist
aspirations of the Soviet Union. And now I notice that your
own *Prace* (December 14th, 1983) has called on its readers
to support 'the enforced and necessary measures of the
CPCZ Central Committee Presidium and CSSR Government
against the hegemonist aspirations and intimidation which
the Reagan government and its armour-bearers in the offensive military NATO pact have called into being'.

The responsibility for this latest upthrust in the arms race
lies heavily (although not exclusively) with the NATO
powers. And NATO's apologists have, as always, sought to
justify their measures in the language of 'human rights'. And,
as usually happens, the consequence of the closure of the
blocs against each other is that further restrictions are
imposed upon the civil rights of citizens on both sides. We
have learned with dismay of measures taken against independent peace activists on your side of the world. And we
regard our own Cold Warriors as accomplices in this interactive process.

My response to you must therefore be somewhat tinged
with pessimism. You write that we now have the task of
formulating 'a common, universal, and all-embracing strategy
for the democratic transformation of Europe'. I agree. But,
with the new missiles now in place (and many many more

coming on after these) where does our strategy start?

Perhaps we might now suspend the argument about the missiles and seek to go *behind* the missiles and find out what is moving them there? What is the Cold War now about? From what structures and from what ideologies do these growing armouries arise?

The Western peace movement has for several years been so preoccupied with nuclear weaponry itself, and with its annihilating potential, that it has been mesmerised by this. We set outselves the task of halting certain new NATO systems; and although we have succeeded in arousing a peace consciousness of massive dimensions, we have failed in that task.

I do not think that it was wrong for us to be so pre-occupied. The weaponry itself, and the military options disclosed by the weapons, remain insanely dangerous. This understanding is a base-line for our thinking. But the pre-occupation with cruise and Pershing missiles allowed us to neglect ulterior political questions.

For even missiles have to be considered also in the light of political symbols. They are, of course, symbols of 'face' and of 'posture' in the superpower confrontation. But they have increasingly become symbols of internal political confrontations also, within both blocs and within nations.

At a certain stage it became necessary for cruise and Pershing to be imposed upon a reluctant West European public, not because of any evident 'Soviet threat', but in order to symbolise the 'unity of NATO' and the hegemony of United States military power over its European allies. And it became essential for ruling groups in these countries (above all in Britain and West Germany) to impose these missiles in order to inflict a public defeat upon their own domestic opposition: that is, the peace movement. In this symbolic sense these missiles have been aimed, not at you, but at us.

The Soviet counter-deployments now going ahead employ the same vocabulary of symbolism. Their missiles also are symbols of 'posture' towards NATO. And they are also symbols of the 'unity of the Warsaw powers', and loyal demonstrations and petitions in their support are intended to drown any questioning voices. So that in this symbolic sense the SS-21s, 22s or 23s are aimed in the first place not against NATO but against any strivings towards greater national autonomy by any East European nation. In this sense the missiles of both sides are like props which lean against each other, enforcing the increasingly-irrational division of our continent, lest (if the props were removed) we might fall into each others' arms.

The Cold War today is a habit passed down from the past; and it is a habit to which the governing elites, on both sides, have become addicted, since they sense that its continuance is necessary to justify and sustain their own purchase upon power. Lip-service is paid, and on both sides, to the desirable objective of the dismantling by mutual consent of both NATO and the Warsaw Pact. But if any actual step in this direction is detected, on either side, it is instantly denounced as 'destabilising', and as a blasphemy against that Great Sacred Cow which both East and West must bow down before and worship: the 'Balance'. It is before the Sacred Balance that we sacrifice our little liberties and burn, for the delight of her nostrils, an ever-growing tribute of our taxes.

This Sacred Cow was the first-born calf of another great Cow who was sometimes worshipped by the name of 'Yalta'. The name was never accurate, but we know very well what 'Yalta' is taken to mean today: it describes the post-war settlement which passed down the division of Europe as we find it at this day—a division not only geographic but also political and ideological. In short, 'Yalta' is reverenced or execrated as the Mama of 'Balance'.

The assent of the Soviet Union to the Helsinki agreement was purchased by the assent of the NATO powers to the finality of the settlement of the 'Yalta' frontiers. This concession was earnestly desired by ruling groups in the Warsaw bloc, who had been tormented for years by the rhetoric of John Foster Dulles and others, as to the 'roll-back' of Soviet power. And it was equally desired by certain of these rulers because they were aware that their own tenure upon power was uncertain.

From this a stereotype has grown up—that 'Yalta' is a settlement greatly desired by the rulers of the Warsaw bloc but only grudgingly acceded to by the rulers of NATO, for reasons of opportunism or in the interests of detente. And ideologists on your side of the world have done a great deal to give this stereotype credibility. The mere mention of the word is taken as a 'provocation'. And they insist, as a precondition of any discussion, that the inviolability of a particular historical adjustment of spheres of influence must also be extended to a pledge of the inviolability in perpetuity of the particular political systems now in being—but only in their half of Europe.

Anything less than this is, as you say, suspected as a 'call to arms'. In Western Europe far-reaching political changes are to be expected, and we have witnessed such changes, accomplished with maturity and with the minimum of bloodshed, in Portugal, Spain and Greece. But any change of a political order in your half of Europe—for example a change which offered to enlarge the potential of a democratic socialist society, as the Prague Spring promised to do—is ruled out of order as an outrage against Her Sacred Presence, the Balance.

However, I think that this stereotype is misleading. The true historical meaning of 'Yalta' is far more double-sided than it suggests. And if one digs a little beneath the rhetoric of the ideologists of NATO one discovers that they are no less fiercely committed to both 'Yalta' and the 'Balance' than are their Warsaw Pact analogues.

For the 'Yalta' settlement, in its fullest historical meaning, did not only license the Soviet military presence in East and Central Europe. It also licensed a very powerful hegemonic United States presence in Western Europe—a presence which has always dominated the councils of NATO and which has grown with each decade more dominant along with the growth in nuclear weapons systems.

The Soviet and American presences in Europe have of course been of a different order. If we leave aside the case of Greece (1945-50) the United States presence has not imposed regimes of its choice by military force. But while operating in a different mode and under different constraints, it has been an immensely powerful and distorting presence nonetheless.

It has by no means been a presence conducive to the advancement of human rights. It coexisted happily with totalitarian regimes in Portugal and Spain and with military regimes in Greece and Turkey. It is true that there were no American tanks in Madrid or Athens to prevent their peoples from liberating themselves from tyranny. We acknowledge this with relief, while at the same time noting that the same restraint has by no means been evident upon United States support for tyrannies in Latin America and Asia.

The United States military presence on our continent remains immensely strong, nearly forty years after the end of World War II. What is it doing here? How long does it have licence to remain? There are United States military, air and naval bases in Spain, Italy, Greece, Turkey, Norway, Holland, Belgium, Iceland and scores of bases and installations in West Germany and Britain. American warships (some armed with nuclear weapons) patrol the North Atlantic and Mediterranean waters. As I write, an American fleet is sailing up and down the coast of the Lebanon, and has been firing heavy salvos into the interior of that unhappy country. Cruise and Pershing missiles on our territory are owned and operated by United States personnel.

This is the other side of the 'Yalta' settlement. And it is jealously defended by the ideologues of NATO. One strategy which West European peace movements have been seeking to advance is that of staged disengagement on our continent, by means of nuclear-weapons-free zones: in the Baltic, the Balkans, or a zone or corridor in Central Europe.

Of course it can be said that such zones might only be 'symbolic'. But we prefer the symbolism of disengagement to the barbaric symbolism of missiles. And the symbolism might then be extended, to the progressive mutual withdrawal of conventional forces also—and thence to the more fluent movement of persons and ideas: the repair of the torn tissues of Europe.

What is remarkable is the hostility which has been evinced, from start to finish, to all such proposals by the leaders of the NATO powers. I suggest that this is because they are seen as a threat to the other side of 'Yalta': that is, to the iron premise that every part of Europe that is not to the East of the Yalta division must be drawn by all possible means within the military and diplomatic structures of United States hegemony.

This premise is also inviolable. Thus when the Swedish proposals for a nuclear-free corridor in Central Europe were introduced to the Stockholm Conference, Mr Alois Mertes, the West German Minister of State for Foreign Affairs, commented that such a corridor 'is not compatible with the indivisibility of the territory of the European-American alliance'. And a fellow West German official chided Sweden for failing to 'honour the vital security interests of the member states of the Atlantic alliance (*New York Times*, 21 January 1984).

The proposals for nuclear-free zones (which should entail reciprocal concessions from each bloc) can take their place in a European healing-process, and I commend them to you as a part of our common strategy. Yet, as you well know, something must be added to them, and this could be added now, in advance of any agreement between states. The healing of Europe does not have to wait for signatures inscribed in the Kremlin and the White House. As you have written, 'detente will not lead to the dissolution of the military-political blocs unless a political discourse is established, one that will "grow" into a new political bloc'. In short, the traffic of ideas and of persons can precede any treaty whatsoever, and the establishment of trust may be the necessary precondition for any treaty.

This is not to call for the 'revision' of the 'frontiers of Yalta'. It is a call to throw these frontiers open, and (wherever this is possible) to commence to act as if these arbitrary frontiers did not exist. What is preventing this? It is, first, that the rulers on both sides are the last people who are able to advance this healing-process, since their very function is ascribed to them by the rituals of the Cold War. And it is, second, the fear of unregulated social or intellectual change, and of possible 'destabilisation', which inhibits these rulers' breasts.

If NATO carries the major blame for the upwards armament auction, then we must award the prize to the rulers of the Warsaw Pact for their activity in the repression of transcontinental dialogue. I think that they do desire to achieve some nuclear disarmament, but at the same time they wish every instrument of ideological armament to remain in place. They might endorse a nuclear-free corridor in Central Europe, but they would hope that the corridor would be wide enough to prevent the two-way flow of ideas from running across it. They do not wish the causes of peace and of liberty to recognise each other and to search for a common convergence.

Yet even now, as this recognition is beginning to take place, our 'common strategy' remains indistinct. For 'Yalta' has two sides, and one side will not be unravelled unless we also unravel the other. If that Sacred Cow, the Balance, is preposterous in its military form, yet I fear that we must pay some deference to her in our political strategy. For whenever initiatives arise on either side, the rulers of the opposing bloc will try to turn these to their own advantage. So that, if we are to find a reciprocal common strategy, we must learn not only how to support the initiatives of each other but also how to refuse advantage to either bloc, even if this entails exercises of patience and self-restraint.

It was the failure to find this common strategy which contributed to the defeat (however temporary) of the two most powerful popular impulses on our continent in the past three years: those of Polish Solidarnosc and of the Western peace movement's resistance to NATO modernisation. These are both complex questions. I will only say that those NATO ideologues who celebrated the feats of Solidarnosc at the same time did their best to destroy it by seeking to harvest their own advantage and by hastening forward cruise and Pershing missiles. Even the French public, which generously contributed food and medicine to the Polish people, might have helped them more if they had—as a symbolic gesture towards the relief of East-West tension—dismantled some part of their own *force de frappe*. But there was no Western statesman, at any time, who suggested that Polish liberties were worthy of the price of one dismantled Western nuclear weapon.

This is a stern logic. But I think it a realistic one. Was it probable that the Soviet Union would permit its influence in Poland quietly to lapse at the same time as the American offensive military posture in West Germany was steadily *rising?* What we ought to have done, East and West, was to seize that moment to turn our political worlds upside-down in the effort to bring back onto the stage some new variant of Adam Rapacki's old plan, in which a demilitarised zone would take in, not only Poland, Czechoslovakia and the GDR, but West Germany as well. And only on some such precondition do I think it likely that your other desideratum —a peace treaty resolving the status of both Germanys—could come about. Is it not evident that the price of greater Polish autonomy must be some military concession from the West? Yet in 1981 scarcely a head in Poland, and few enough heads in the Western peace movement, were turned that way.

In 1983 the Western peace movements bruised their heels against the same inexorable logic. Throughout the year public opinion swayed in the balance. And what tipped the margin against us was not only the effective propaganda of our own governments but the superfluity of SS-20s. I am not dis-owning those sections of the Western peace movement which called for a 'unilateral' halt in Western deployment; on the contrary, I am convinced that only such unilateral initiatives will ever get a reciprocal process of disarmament going. Yet there must be a credible expectation that such a reciprocal process will ensue, and that measures of disarmament on one side will not simply be swallowed gratefully to enlarge the advantage of the other.

I remain convinced that if at any time before the autumn of 1983 the Soviet Union had responded to requests from the Western peace movement to commence to dismantle a number of its superfluous SS-20s, then the balance of opinion in the West would have halted NATO's deployments.

But, as we know, the Soviet rulers, looking across the heads of Europeans to their superpower antagonist, and preoccupied with 'face' and 'posture', would have 'nothing to do with unilateralism'. In this article of faith the worshippers of the Divine Balance have always been at one.

An influential part of Western opinion found our advocacy of disarmament to be 'one-sided' because they could not observe comparable movements in the East, capable of restraining Eastern militarism from turning the event to its own advantage. And this mistrust was fed by the evidence of the harassment of those independent movements and voices on your side which offered an open dialogue with us: harassment which has acquired a great symbolic significance. I believe that such forces exist, although the structures of power deny them visibility, and that they will grow in strength in the immediate future. And at the moment that a truly transcontinental peace movement becomes visible, then our objective of a 'democratic peace' will move from utopia into the world of practical possibility.

Both of these examples illustrate that a common strategy which seeks to heal the tissues of Europe cannot succeed unless it presses against the structures and ideologies of both blocs. It is necessary that I should make this explicit. For Mr George Shultz, the American Secretary of State, in his opening speech at the Stockholm Conference, has made his own intervention in our discussion. 'Let me be very clear,' he said. 'The United States does not recognize the legitimacy of the artificially-imposed division of Europe. This division is the essence of Europe's security and human rights problem and we all know it.' And he went on, in language which seemed to echo our own, to talk of 'an artificial barrier' which has 'cruelly divided this great continent—and indeed heartlessly divided one of its great nations.'

This was a mischievous speech. Coming only one month after the deployment of cruise and Pershing missiles, which have divided Europe even more cruelly and Germany more heartlessly, it was a speech of consummate hypocrisy, whose aim was to perpetuate the division of Europe. For, of course, the United States has little intention of doing anything more

than meddling, or 'stirring the pot', in Eastern Europe. And
even this is subordinate to the more important aim, foremost
in the minds of President Reagan and Mr Shultz, which is
stirring the pot of the United States elections.

The immediate effect of Mr Shultz's speech has been to
make more difficult the pursuit of our common strategy. The
speech might have been calculated to meddle in the affairs of
advocates of 'human rights' in the East, by pointing them
out to the attention of the security services as possible
friends of Western forces which may still cherish an appetite
to 'roll back Yalta'. At the same time the speech was received
by many in the Western peace movement with dismay. They
have been searching for a strategy to break down the blocs.
Now they fear that this could play into the hands of NATO's
propagandists.

Mr Shultz is trying to prise apart the forces making for 'a
democratic peace'. These forces have no part to play in the
prescribed rituals of the Cold War. But this reminds me that
while the United States is a great and—for some aspects of its
history—an honoured neighbour of Europe, it is not a European nation. And the people of Europe might find their way
better towards a healing-process without Mr Shultz's intervention. For the United States' presence in West Europe is
one half of the European problem.

It is now time that World War II was brought to an end.
Thirty-nine years of abnormal conditions and of the presence
of foreign troops upon our territories is long enough. Let
the goal of our common strategy be the withdrawal of all
United States and Soviet forces and bases back within their
own national frontiers.

This is the only realistic way in which 'Yalta' can be super-
ceded: not by its one-sided 'revision' (which will not happen)
but by removing military pressures on both sides at the same
time as the dividing frontiers are thrown more open. This will
not come about at once, all in a lump. There will be phases,
as new spaces, corridors or zones open up between the blocs;
as individual nations, East or West, loosen their bloc-bondage
and attain more autonomy; as the direct political discourse
for which you call begins to establish confidence. There will

be, at some point along the way, a place for Summit meetings and for conferences of European nations with a more serious agenda than the present Stockholm farce.

It will be an excessively difficult process. It is quite possible that Europe will blow up before we can succeed. At every stage one or the other bloc will try to turn events to its own advantage. If the United States should commence to withdraw its forces (as Mr Kissinger is now recommending) this might trigger off a compensating resurgence in West European militarism. If any East European nation sought to move into too close an association with the West, it might bring down upon itself a re-enactment of the events of 1968 which you will only too well remember. To achieve our common objective will require an unprecedented maturity in those popular movements, West and East, which seek to pace and to monitor the transition, and to limit the episodes of 'destabilisation'.

Yet this is not just one possible way forward. It is, I am convinced, the *only* way. The alternative is the convergence on collision-course of two vast over-armoured security states towards the probable terminus of nuclear war. We do not have an alternative. Either our civilisation will perish, or we must make the entire political world over anew. And our rulers will never do that for us.

If we can work together, if we can support each other, we have an outside chance of success. I do not know what we would then discover, on the other side of 'Yalta'. I do not think it would be some new Eurobloc. Distinct differences in socio-economic and political systems will remain. I would look forward to European diversity (and Russia is a part of Europe) not to bureaucratic 'unity': and to the deconstruction, on both sides, of certain forms of state power.

I agree with you on two essential matters. First, this new Europe of our imaginations could not possibly exist without a radical transformation in its relations with the Third World, which would in turn (as you have argued) assist in the transformation of that world itself. And, second, such a resolution would be profoundly in the interests of the people of the United States and the Soviet Union as well. It would relieve both nations from vast expenditures and occasions for confrontation. It would strengthen those forces contesting the militarisation of their own societies. And, rather than expelling their citizens from our continent, it would welcome them back as respected neighbours to our common discourse.

Jaroslav Săbata, I thank you again for writing. I fear that the events of the past two years have left me pessimistic. It is possible that Europe is already within the valley of the shadow of death. But this very crisis of the twin militarisms is arousing on every side forces of resistance, which might lead on towards the 'convergence of a quite different type' for which you call. And if the Western peace movement is dismayed, I can assure you that it is very far from being defeated. Such voices as your own give us new heart to continue in our common pursuit for a democratic peace.

Yours sincerely,
Edward Thompson

March 1984

THE LIBERATION OF PERUGIA

This appears to be the season for reminiscences of World War II, when every veteran is licensed to 'strip his sleeve and show his scars'. And since I have just returned from the Third Convention for European Nuclear Disarmament, which met in the beautiful city of Perugia, this is evidently the right moment for me to disclose my own part in the liberation of that city.

It is true that the Italian campaign, which preceded D-Day by more than a year, has fallen into some memory hole. But it is at least remembered in our media more often than those vast engagements on the Soviet front which had, for three years before D-Day, cost the lives of millions of soldiers and civilians. I may therefore assume that, while the Italian campaign is boring, it is not for some political reason unmentionable.

In one of his less happy flourishes Sir Winston Churchill described Italy as 'the soft underbelly of the Axis beast'. Soft it was not. Italy has a singularly rugged spine and the successive mountains and rivers provided barriers behind which the German armies could execute an orderly withdrawal while their well-disciplined rearguard inflicted, day after day, sharp casualties on the advancing Allied armies. It was a preposterous error to plant large motorised armies in the toe of Italy and then to fight, mile by mile, up the boot. It may be because the whole campaign was so misconceived that it is rarely mentioned.

In between very heavy set battles (Salerno, Anzio, the battles of Cassino, etc.) there was a ritual of cautious forward advance, of temporary check, and then of forward probing once again. Our tanks would go northwards up the roads until the leading tank hit a mine or was stopped by a blown-up bridge or came under fire. Then infantry and engineers were hurried forward to push back the German rearguard so that, in a day or two, the tanks could move on. The predictable casualties on each day's advance of this kind, along each road, would be the leading tank and some infantry and engineers. As well as whoever happened to get in the way of the incessant shelling which fell behind the lines—perhaps an ambulanceman or signalman, a padre, an old peasant and his donkey, a brigadier.

For reasons which will soon be clear I had to write a formal account of one episode in the liberation of Perugia, and this is how it starts:

> At approximately 18.30 hours on 19 June 1944 my troop was leading the advance into the village of Fontioeggi. When the leading tank, commanded by Sjt. S. started to enter the village, it was penetrated by armour-piercing shot from a gun sited up the road, and also engaged by enemy infantry weapons from houses on the left. After attempting to reverse, Sjt. S. ordered his crew to evacuate the tank, but was unable to get any member other than the gunner, Trooper W., out of the tank. . .

One remembers very much less, after forty years, than the writers of reminiscences pretend. What I can recall is this. My squadron of tanks had been sitting on top of a low hill several miles south-west of Perugia all day. A squadron is normally 15 tanks, but we were already depleted by losses and mechanical breakdowns.

We were a very visible target and we were being shelled (mainly by howitzers and mortars) the whole day. Ordinary shellfire didn't do much harm to a tank unless the shells scored a direct hit. But it was advisable for tank commanders to keep their heads inside the turrets. Every five minutes or so we moved around a few score yards on our little plateau, perhaps to unsettle the enemy gunners, perhaps to settle our own nerves.

It was a really hot day. The sun baked the armour of our tanks and, as we brewed up tea with a primus on the floor of the turret, we all got dozy. I distinctly recall that sense of drowsy diminished reality which comes with heat, exhaustion, and nervous tension protracted for so long that the nerves become unresponsive. I remember popping my head out of the turret from time to time to look at the towers of Perugia or at the state of the other tanks, even though (with a sniper in a nearby leafy tree) each time I did so invited entry into eternity. On one occasion a shell splinter made a dent in my tin helmet. But we were all so dozy that we seemed to have drifted to the edge of an unreal eternity already.

At approximately 18.30 hours, minus a few minutes, two of the remaining nine tanks were so hot that they refused to start and another two had had their tracks blown off by shellfire. So that when the order came to advance into Perugia there were only five working tanks left in the squadron, two of which were of my own troop.

The Squadron Leader ordered my troop to lead the advance. There followed a hesitant incident inside my own head. The standard rule-book procedure was this: in any advance, out of the three tanks in each troop, either the serjeant's or the corporal's tank would take the lead, and the lieutenant's tank (that is, my own) would take second place, from which middle position command was presumably best exercised.

But my corporal's tank was disabled, my troop was down to two, and the rule-book was vague about such eventualities. I therefore came up on the wireless and asked my Squadron Leader: 'Shall I lead?' There was no reply: either the Squadron Leader did not wish to reply or he had switched his set onto another frequency. I can recall a momentary chill of indecision. Then I leaned from the turret and signalled my serjeant to lead the advance.

I don't know whether I did this out of deference to the rule-book or because I was afraid. We all knew that the first tank down the road would probably be knocked out. It was because of this that I felt that I 'ought' to go first, although according to military rules the 'ought' probably went the other way. I had been placed at a point in the sequence of military decision at which I was momentarily endowed with the powers of life and death: to enhance the chances of life for some (including myself) and to diminish them for others.

We trundled down a long road into a suburb of Perugia at about ten or fifteen miles an hour. At the point where we started there were vineyards and gardens on each side of the road, but we were entering a built-up street with a bend at the bottom. As we approached the bend my serjeant's tank, some eighty yards ahead, jolted, rocked and stopped, a wisp of grey smoke hanging in the air. There was a roar of engines as it sought to reverse, and then it jolted and rocked once more. I saw the tank commander, Serjeant S., duck down into the turret. Then he leaped out, followed by the gunner, Trooper W. The two ran back to me, and the serjeant called out: 'I can't get the others out. I think they've had it.' 'Are you sure?' 'Quite sure. I called out to them. We got hit twice.'

I told my gunner to take command of my tank and I ran forward to the inert machine ahead. I remember my binoculars bumping against my chest as I ran. Jumping on the tank's back I peered into the darkness of the turret, my eyes half-blinded by the full Italian sun on the dusty white road. I called out and received no answer. I was being fired upon from a house nearby and it seemed impolitic to stay around.

I am still not clear why I made that little gesture. It was unwise to leave my own tank when it might itself come under fire. And I could scarcely have lugged a wounded man out of the tank while under small-arms fire. I suppose that the gesture was made, not only on an impulse of trying to bring some aid to my fellows, but also to assuage my own guilt at having been the instrument of sending them there.

That is all that I can recall about June 19th. The German rearguard evacuated the city in the small hours, and we entered Perugia on the 20th, passing the blackened carcass of my serjeant's tank as we went in. There were some cheering crowds in the city streets but my spirits were too heavy to be lifted. Compared with the spontaneous delight of the peasantry in many of the villages we had passed through, the welcome of the Perugia crowds seemed somewhat reserved. The city had been an administrative centre for Fascism—for police and lawyers, tax-collectors and rentiers, officers and ecclesiastics—and Perugia had been one of Mussolini's pets. There was a long anti-fascist tradition in the city—but perhaps the people were waiting to see how far 'liberation' would go?

The complement of a Sherman tank was five, so that three men had been left in that inert machine. I went back later on the 20th and inspected the tank, finding a pile of ashes, still moulding the shape of the lower half of a man, in the driver's seat. I talked with civilians in nearby houses, including a plucky nun in a convent just beside the tank. She had witnessed the whole episode from a window and had even, later that evening, run out into the street and called out to see if anyone was alive. Later she had seen a German soldier throw a hand-grenade into the turret, look inside, pour in petrol and set the tank on fire. I was satisfied beyond any doubt that the driver, co-driver and wireless-operator were all dead.

Army Records were not satisfied and the next-of-kin of the three men were informed that they were 'Missing, Believed Killed'. As their immediate commanding officer it became my duty to correspond with the next-of-kin over several months. Perhaps this is why, although I witnessed far more violent episodes, this small event at Perugia haunts me to this day as a symbol of the chances of war.

For the dead to be posted as 'Missing' is a protraction of the pain of bereavement. The imagination strains after impossible hopes of survival so that, as each hope is disallowed, the grief of bereavement is renewed time after time. 'He was our only child so you can see how we feel about it, if it is really true,' one father wrote to me. And the mother of another wrote:

> I know how busy you must be but we have received a very disquieting note, saying 'missing believed killed' and it has upset me again most terribly—surely if you know my darling is buried he cannot be 'missing'? Please forgive me—I am in the depths of despair

> and my mind is in torture. My darling boy saved his mother's
> thoughts until the last, his lovely cheering letters always assured his
> mother he was alright. . .

I was as callous as any young soldier had to be in order to
survive (my substitute for emotional responses took the form
of outbreaks of skin disease) but I could scarcely bear to read
these rather formal, self-effacing, ever-courteous letters:

> My brother was all I had in the world we had lived together the last
> ten years since losing our mother and I would like to know a few
> more details, if the spot where he is buried is marked or did an
> explosion make this impossible?

'Please did one of his friends pick some wild flowers and
place on his grave?' And always, whenever I sent the least
scrap of news, this was received with pitiful expressions of
gratitude from the kin of these troopers. They seemed to be
astonished to receive any attention from anyone in authority:
'Hope I am not asking too much of your time. . .', 'I am so
sorry to trouble you. . .',

> Will you try and do me a kindness and see that his personal belong-
> ings are sent back to me and if you really could get me a photo of
> his grave it would set my wife's mind at rest as she is greatly grieved. . .

With all the weight of my twenty years I did what I could
to offer comfort and to abbreviate the grief of my enquirers
by giving to these deaths a definite term. I remember these
letter-writers (whom I never met) better than I can how recall
the three dead troopers. Or, rather, these letters gave to the
soldiers a quite new and disquieting dimension. They could
no longer be defined only by rank and number and rôle and
by the humours and quiddities which they disclosed within
our small functional social group. I recall that I liked them
all, and (so far as I could know across the gap of army
rank) they none of them had any reason to dislike me. They
had shared in the resigned complicity of military life and had
joined in the repartee of ironies as we camped in the evenings

beside our tanks in the beautiful countryside of May and
June. But I did not tell their next-of-kin that, in the causal
sequence of command, I had directed them towards their
deaths—at that moment when I had beckoned forward the
serjeant's tank to take the lead, and had sentenced them,
instead of my own crew, to the consequence.

Why do I set this down now, forty years later, when the
Third Convention for European Nuclear Disarmament has
assembled in Perugia? I am aware that my petty episode of
warfare is so inconsequential that I could tack onto it whatever moral I might like.

What I will tack onto it is, first, that much of the experience of modern warfare is as personal and inconsequential
as that. All the wide-angle plural renderings which we see
on film or telly scarcely connect with any war veteran's
authentic experience. The individual moments of experience
are recycled as a collective subject, 'war', which is something
none of us knew much about.

'War' is a collective abstraction, a matter for romance or
for disgust. Post-war generations in Europe are preoccupied
with war in this abstract sense, and most thoughtful and
sensitive people are quite properly on the side of disgust.

What is sometimes overlooked is that the soldiers were
disgusted also, for good reasons. Did that large collective
noun, the army, have a collective purpose? Yes it did. It was
to finish the war and then go home. Did the individuals
comprising that collective share any personal aims? Yes they
did. These were to survive the war if possible, but the
'possible' included reservations as to fulfilling certain necessary
duties and loyalties as well as avoiding shame and self-
accusation.

These reservations were often large enough to cancel out
the possibility of personal survival. Some of my younger
friends, including feminist friends whose actions for peace
I greatly admire, suppose that there is a simple cause of war
in male structures and male aggro. This message is sometimes
associated with 'Greenham' and it met with fervent applause
from the youthful audience at the Labour Party's rally for

a Nuclear-Free Europe at Wembley on June 3rd, 1984.

It may be right that the younger generations should feel this to be so. If we have reached a point where the human species must refuse war, then we must draw upon our cultural resources. The antithetical poles of warfare and of nurture have often been expressed in art and poetic imagery in compelling sexual imagery: the opposition of Mars and the Madonna. A fragment in William Blake's notebook expresses it all:

> The sword sung on the barren heath
> The sickle in the fruitful field:
> The sword he sung a song of death,
> But could not make the sickle yield.

'Greenham' has drawn with effect upon this powerful symbolic inheritance.

In modern societies warfare has occasioned the sharpest dissociation, and often antiphony, of gender roles and alternative cultural forms, with consequences which have endured in time of peace and entered peace-time structures. These consequences may be contributory, yet they should not be confused with causes. For history (in my view) does not disclose segregated and antithetical gender cultures, but, rather, a plurality of emphases (class, racial, gender or occupational) within a unitary sum. And in any complex society the causes of war can never be explained by biological reductionism. The 'barren heath' and the 'fruitful field' lie intermingled with each other.

These are fascinating questions whose strict examination must lie within the disciplines of social history and social anthropology. The examination has scarcely yet been made, and feminists are right to propose the questions, although the good-hearted assertion of feminist feelings cannot substitute for the examination. The moods and the imperatives of the present may be admirable and necessary to our survival. But they cannot be smuggled back as universals into the interpretation of the past.

If we say, as some simplistic voices are saying now so

loudly that few dare to answer back, that there is something essentially male about war (all war, universal war), and that a feminist culture would never have sanctioned warfare, then we are smuggling in also the premise that 'war' (being male) has, always, in every historical eventuality, been wrong or disgusting or unnecessary, and that some non-violent feminist alternative was always available. I do not know that this is so, nor how it could ever be shown to be so.

Of course, more considered feminist analysis does not follow this simplistic biological explanation of the causes of war. But the view is very much around today. And it has arrived, through a feminist door, at the position of absolutist and universal pacifism. That is a respectable position, which is endorsed by some part of today's peace movement. But it is one which the majority of my generation in occupied Europe forty years ago considered and rejected. That generation comprised, as is usually the case, both sexes, and the women who served in the Resistance or in the Allied forces, whether in combatant roles in the Serbian mountains, the Warsaw ghetto, or with the French Maquis, or whether in sustained political and economic engagement in non-combatant rôles, would not thank their younger sisters today for accusing them of having been surrogate males.

I labour the point, although it is perhaps now of interest only to my own generation. The present time discloses quite different alternatives, and the imperative of resistance to nuclear weapons has become absolute. But because we endorse wholeheartedly the spirit of 'Greenham' are we therefore obliged to undertake a wholesale retrospective rehash of the past, including our own past, and disown our loyalties to those who, in a different age, decided differently and sealed the decision with their deaths?

In any case I cannot recall much evidence of male aggro in my own experience of war. On the contrary, the soldier (more often officer) who displayed martial *macho* was not only generally disliked but was also feared since he was likely to lead others into futile acts of theatre and unfunctional deaths. I would still prefer the old-fashioned diagnosis of the causes of war within the political economies

of states, the ambitions of ruling groups, and the irrationalisms of nationalisms and of ideologies: and, on that occasion,
of the Nazi and Fascist ideologies most of all. And (to give
back my argument to the care of more complex feminist
analysis) let it be noted that those Nazi ideologies and those
Fascist structures were as aggressively racist, martial and
masculine (albeit with substantial feminine cultural
complicity) as any in modern history.

Of course when the media recycle 'war experience' they do
not always give us wide-angle plural stuff. Sometimes
narrator or camera zoom in on a few rugged individuals.
The deception here is to show us 'war' in terms of individual
agency: these photogenic individuals displaying cunning or
heroism and thereby becoming the actors who 'won' the war.
For example, by breaking enemy codes at Bletchley.
    There may have been, in olden tymes, wars of that kind,
when the course of a battle was turned by the example
and exploits of—

> Harry the king, Bletchley and Exeter,
> Warwick and Talbot, Heseltine and Gloster. . .

Those times have long gone by, except perhaps in the low-
technology fighting of 'partisans'.
    Modern warfare is the ultimate negation of human agency.
Much of the killing in World War II was done at long-distance
between enemies who rarely ever saw each other. In World
War III they will never see each other at all, but only a blip
on a radar screen.
    What is decisive in modern warfare is military technology,
logistics, economic resources and so on. Beside these,
individual agency scarcely matters. And the chances of
survival or death are altogether casual and arbitrary. If
human purposive agency survives—but we are descending into
a technological determinism in which the matter is thrown
in doubt—then it is not in the 'war' but behind and before
the war, in the political culture of the warring states. If we
wish to be agents in the next war then we must be agents

now. At the moment when it starts all space for agency will have closed.

Another moral which I will draw from my episode is self-evident. The 'war' which contemporary resurrectionists on our media delight in showing is two-dimensional. It is quite flat. It leaves out the dimension of bereavement. This is always somewhere behind the camera crew, outside the margin of the book. The script has no place for the pain of the parents and lovers and kin.

Two generations of Europeans—those of my parents and my grandparents—had to endure this monstrous thing: the knowledge that their children, scarcely out of school, faced death at any time. They lived in fear of the postman, in fear of the newspaper, in fear of the radio news. I hold myself and my generation in Europe (although not in Asia, Latin America or Africa) to be greatly fortunate that we have never had to endure that kind of aching fear on behalf of our own.

To be sure, this is now a somewhat archaic reflection. For the Third World War, if it should come, will at least spare us this differential generational or gender suffering. Already in World War II the amazing technological refinements of gas-ovens and aerial bombing of cities were equalising all pain. Next time the babe in arms, the mother, the son and the grandparents will at least all go together.

Current suggestions that 'conventional' weapons are somehow more tolerable than nuclear weapons are also misleading. The conventional weapons of the first two world wars were hideous and their 'modernised' successors will be hideous in the extreme. Taboos against the massacre of non-combatants have already been broken beyond repair. And since as we are often told—nuclear weapons 'cannot be dis-invented' we can be quite sure that, in any battle between the blocs which starts with 'conventional' arms, the losing side will, at the point of defeat, summon the nukes back.

It follows that it is no longer sufficient to clamour for nuclear disarmament. If European nations should go to war then the distinction between the nuclear and the conventional will soon be lost. We must therefore enlarge our objectives.

We must work to disallow any kind of recourse to war.

We Europeans are packed into this small continent, our armouries overflowing with every modernised instrument of murder, while the two hostile blocs lie against each other as closely as lovers in a bed. The bland news presenters and the public images of politicians no longer deceive us. There is already a rising hysteria in Europe, like fog rising on a frosty evening from the culverts and drains. Let there be one lurch towards war, and the gods of the opposed ideologies will display a ferocity even more crazed than the ferocity of the gods of Iraq and Iran.

Certainly nuclear weapons are the most odious symbols of our predicament. They will remain prominent in our concerns. But the peace movement must now move beyond its obsession with these and become a movement for the making of European peace.

Perhaps only historians will appreciate how unlikely of achievement this objective is. European history has been marked at every stage by warfare, whether on this continent or whether exported to others, and the wars of this century have been as merciless and as indiscriminate as any and on the largest scale. Warfare has been a normal element in the polity of the clan, the city-state, the Roman empire, the cause of Christendom, the trading metropolis, the nation-state, the expansionist empire. At predictable intervals the young have been sent out to fight, and predictably they have been ready to go. War has been a normal function of all types of European society, the menace of war has been a normal instrument of diplomacy, and the expectation of war has been habitual within European culture.

It follows that a peace movement, if it is to *make* peace and not only make protest, must set itself an agenda which extends into every nook and cranny of our culture and our polity. It has to be an affirmative movement of an unprecedented kind.

If our movement is to make peace, and not only offer a rearguard resistance to the increment in the weapons of war, then it must address itself to the political and ideological conditions within which the next world war is maturing. It must learn the skills of communication across the blocs, where the lines of hostility are sharpest. It must concern itself not only with material disarmament but also with political and ideological disarmament.

That is why the questions of the division of Europe—and of the presence of foreign military forces and bases outside their own territory in both halves of Europe—must move forward in the peace movement's agenda. To say that there can be no prospect of peace until we overcome the division of Europe, to say that there must be some 'historic compromise' between the hostile polities and ideologies of the adversary blocs (and between the USA and USSR), is to reveal the actual size of our problem. Yet it is also to propose an objective more attainable than that of eliminating all 'male structures' from the world scene within two or three decades (which is all the extent of the reprieve which I judge to be left to us), or than that of removing all nuclear, chemical and biological weapons-systems on both sides while at the same time all the hostilities and structures of the Cold War itself are left intact.

It is entirely right that the millions who have been rousing themselves throughout the world in recent years should see themselves as a peace movement, as a movement of affirmation challenging the structures of the Cold War. Some Soviet ideologists, with their allies, have recently been attempting to re-baptise us as an 'anti-war movement'. But that will never be enough.

By an 'anti-war movement' they intend a movement which is limited in its agenda to matters of military posture and procurements only and from which all questions of ideology, polity and culture are excluded. That is, we are to meet together (the self-activating independent movements of the West and the official peace council diplomats of the East as equal partners) with an agenda which replicates the agendas of the arms-controllers and diplomats of the armed states.

We are permitted to run through this agenda: no first use, a test ban treaty, which missiles are to be controlled first and in which order, how an equable 'balance' may be

maintained. The agenda is so constructed that it generally
turns out that what must be demanded are Western concessions only, and since the Western military posture is
currently atrocious the Western peace movement is willing
to go along with that.

But when we attempt to extend the agenda from the
symptoms of militarism to its causes, when we propose
measures to overcome now (and not in some utopian
future) the arbitrary division of our continent, when we ask
to discuss together cooperation in a healing-process by means
of the opening of frontiers, increasing cultural and human
exchanges, and the disarmament of security services and
malevolent ideologists, we are instantly ruled out-of-order.

It is not only that we are told that all such questions are
'ideological intrusions' which have 'nothing in common'
with the purpose of the anti-war movement. We are told this
in menacing and bitterly-divisive tones. Mr Zhukov, the
Chairman of the Soviet Peace Committee, has been kind
enough to inform the readers of CND's monthly, *Sanity*,
that my object is to 'bury the peace movement'. He has also
recently in *Pravda* (March 11th) lampooned the arguments
of thousands in the Western peace movements as the products of 'US and NATO psychological war agencies'. It has
been insinuated that END and the Dutch Interchurch Peace
Council may be instruments of the CIA. Activists from
Western peace movements have been denied visas or have
been summarily expelled from East European countries.
All the foul and paranoid suggestions of conspiracy which
marked the Stalinist zenith have been deployed to create
divisions and to sow suspicions of treason within the Western
movement. In one secret briefing document of the Czechoslovak Communist Party (prepared before the Prague Peace
Assembly in 1983), my own name featured with that of
Enrico Berlinguer towards the top of a list of malign influences within the anti-war movement—which I take to be
a signal honour.

Another internal document of the Czechoslovak Party
commences: 'Imperialism recently attempts to weaken the
peace movement by infiltrating it with ideas, persons and

whole organisations whose clear aim is to break the peace movement, to prevent its unification, etc.' Since my own organisation, END, is (with the Russell Peace Foundation) especially singled out as an example, we must suppose that END, whose first Appeal in April 1980 for a nuclear-free Europe helped to initiate today's movements—an Appeal which was the direct precursor of the recent Convention in Perugia—was a prescient pre-emptive ploy by 'NATO psychological war agencies' to 'infiltrate' a movement which did not then exist.

I do not know how long it is possible to continue to sit down in the same room with people who are guilty of bad faith, libel and the pollution of political relations, and to pretend that nothing is going on. I try to be patient still. I try to remember that these people are only bureaucrats in the service of armed states, and if they are not better then at least they are no worse than the bureaucrats of NATO. They are doing the job they are paid to do. This job is to try to co-opt the Western peace movement as an auxiliary to Soviet diplomacy just as the job of their NATO analogues is to try to co-opt Solidarnosc and human rights movements in the East as auxiliaries of the 'Free West'.

But they have not been, in the past year or two, the kind of functionaries who can help us to make peace. They have often been, precisely, the emissaries of ideology. It is easier to talk with any Soviet or Czech citizen—with scientists, musicians, teachers or even with diplomats—about the real problems of overcoming bloc division than it has been to talk with some members of these 'peace councils'.

For this has not been their office. Their office has been to write agendas which disallow the discussion of these problems as 'ideological intrusions'. Their office has been to present Warsaw bloc policies as, on every occasion, the most perfect and peace-loving known to history, and to demand their endorsement by all. Their office has demanded that they and they alone must be the channel for relations between Western peace movements and their own peoples, and if unstructured dialogue takes place with 'unofficial' voices then their legitimacy is called in question. Their function has been not to open dialogue but to police it and place it under Party controls.

Perhaps the recent Perugia Convention has shown the first signs of cracks in this old Stalinist mould, and of an entry at last into genuine dialogue with the West. It must be as difficult for Warsaw bloc bureaucrats to break with the forty-or-moreyear-old habits of political manipulation as it would be for their NATO analogues. And yet, if the Cold War and the division of Europe are ever to be brought to an end, then at some point the bureaucracies of both sides must be persuaded to be consenting parties.

It is not possible that some of these men and women, on both sides, do not know the gravity of the predicament into which the blocs have become locked. They must suspect that the question of *making* peace, of an 'historic compromise'* between the blocs, is the only alternative to terminal nuclear war. One or two of them may even suspect, when they consider our divided continent, that they are themselves a part of the problem.

If this understanding is now stirring in some minds, and if we are seeing the first evidence of a genuine response within orthodox Communist ideology to the pressures of the Western peace movement, then the East-West exchanges at the Perugia Convention may be counted a small success. As for the Western peace movement's own resistance to NATO's formidable militarisation, this is already in hand and it will grow in strength. We require no instructions on these matters from the officers of the East.

I have strayed far from my theme, and Europe herself has come a long way since that day, in June 1944, when I drowsed inside my tank on the outskirts of Perugia. It is not easy to join into a single theme those episodes from the last war and the strategies for preventing another. If these things sometimes run together in my mind, yet I cannot expect the post-war generations to understand.

---

* The phrase is that of George Konrad, the independent-minded Hungarian novelist, in his *Antipolitics* (Quartet Books).

Revulsion against war among the young is a necessary moment in our culture if our species is to pass from its pre-history of barbarism to the first ledges of civilisation. Yet the revulsion extends also to the past, where it engulfs my twenty-year-old self and my fellow soldiers as we trundled in our tanks down the road to Fontioeggi. Because we were fighting-men we must be objects of pity or disgust. It is un-necessary to ask what were our views of war nor what we supposed we were fighting about. We must either have been victims or else doing our *macho* thing.

But I do not think that we were either. We had a certain hardness towards ourselves and we had little self-pity. We were disgusted by war but we assented to its political necessity, a necessity which might—although we hoped most ardently that it would not—entail our own deaths. That is why I see—although the post-war generations cannot and perhaps should not see—the anti-Fascist alliance of World War II as having some political affinity with the peace movement of today.

It may seem absurd to see those Allied armies, the Resist-ance movement in the mountains and the cities, or the 'home front' where the women and the old laboured in munitions works and were bombed and bereaved, as precursors of today's peace activists. It is easier to see the victims of Belsen and of Auschwitz as precursors of the German peace move-ment, as indeed in some sense they were.

Yet the sense of some affinity persists. Then as now there was an active democratic temper throughout Europe. There was a submission of self to a collective good. Then as now there was a purposive alliance of resistance to power, a 'popular front' which had not yet been disfigured by bad faith. And there was also an authentic mood of international-ism which touched the peasants in the Umbrian villages and the troopers in our tanks.

The division of Europe (for which I hold the rulers on both sides responsible) was a betrayal of all this: of demo-cracy, of internationalism, of personal sacrifice. It turned those famous victories into a pile of shit. In 1944 all of Europe, from the Urals to the Atlantic, was moved by a consensual expectation of a democratic and peaceful post-war continent. We supposed that the old gangs of money, privilege and militarism would go. Most of us supposed that the nations of West and Southern Europe would conduct their anti-Fascist alliances towards some form of socialism. Most of us (including many of the Communists of those countries) supposed that the nations of Eastern Europe would be governed by some form of authentic socialist popular front. We all supposed that the people of the Soviet Union (before whose measureless sacrifices we felt humility) and the people of the rest of Europe would cohabit on the same continent agreeably as good neighbours. It was brave rhetoric, and we bought it, and some bought it with their lives.

That is why I return to 1944, before Europe was struck into two halves. I feel a distinction must be made between the long casualty-lists of World War I and of World War II. I can only see the dead of the First World War as victims, futile losses in the ledgers of rival imperialisms. But I hold the now-unfashionable view that the last war was, for the Allied armies and the Resistance, an anti-Fascist war, not only in rhetoric but also in the intentions of the dead.

So long as Europe remains divided, so long as hostile militarisms occupy both halves, those intentions are being violated. It is not their past credulity but our present inaction which reduces those intentions to futility. My fellow soldiers who were burned in that tank were not ardent politicians. But they were democrats and anti-Fascists. They knew what they fought for, and it was not for the division of Europe, nor was it for the domination of our continent by two arrogant superpowers.

Nor was this the spirit which animated the freshly-risen democracy in Perugia in 1944 and 1945, and which still can be felt in that well-governed Communist municipality today. The spirit which breathed through the *Corriere di Perugia*, the organ of the Umbrian Committee of National Liberation which was founded within a month of the city's liberation, was that of the popular front and of democratic self-government ('l'autogoverno democratico'). It was edited by Aldo Capitini, a leader of the local Resistance who was committed to the methods of non-violence. His editorial celebrating the end of World War II (7 May 1945) is headed 'Mondo Aperto': Open World. The greatest war known in history must now give rise to the greatest and most complex peace, with nations subordinating their sovereignty within federal institutions and with a developing internationalist culture informed by 'l'anima aperta', an open spirit.

We have to return to that time, before the division of our continent, and search for that 'Mondo Aperto' once again. If the Convention at Perugia did something to help this healing-process on, then it will have done more than place wild flowers on those distant anti-Fascist graves. It will have liberated the intentions of the dead.

RETROSPECT, 1944-1950

OVERTURE TO CASSINO

At 0159 hours the Objective lay unconscious under an obscured moon. Dew settled imperceptibly, glistening on the folded flowers, christening the foreheads of the German linesmen who groped along the ditches among wild rose. Occasionally a shell stalked in solitary trajectory over the valley, scratching a spark from the mule-tracks supplying the Mountain. A dog unkennelled many weeks before, when the farm had crushed the head of his peasant master, called back into the echoing voices of the gun, hearing perhaps the edicts of his god, a red-eyed terrible god with scarred ears and long yellow fangs.

The River carried away to a warm sea the last snow from the Mountain. On the Allied maps it was marked in coloured china-graph as BLUE. By day it was brown with a tinge of yellow clay; by moonlight, the colour of unpolished steel. This night it was the colour of nothing, going down a long way.

H hour was set for 0300 hours. The preliminary barrage was due to start softening up the Objective at H hour minus 60 minutes. This was 0159 hours, H hour minus 61 minutes. One minute to two.

Telephones were ringing in the gun batteries. 'Time is now 0159 hours.' '0159 hours.' The officers looked at the second hands on their watches.

As a matter of fact it was not one minute to two. Time had been set by the Corps Commander's watch, and the

Corps Commander's watch was half a minute fast.

But what difference did this make to the round earth, turning through its alternate cloaks of light and shadow, a point of matter in the path of eternity? Could any conceit of men alter its fixed relations to the constellations and the void?

What difference did it make to the Objective, that man-made abstraction, made up of clustering vineyards, shell-pocked farmhouses, sand-banked embrasures, wild briar, ripening cherries?

What did it matter to the Mountain, eyeless at night, but open-lidded and vigilant by day?

What difference to the German sentries, enclosed in watching darkness, impatiently awaiting another pattern imposed on the rotating earth, the pattern of reliefs scrawled on the guard commander's pad?

What difference to the dog, crazy, carrion from the battle-field in his belly, his ribs like spokes, all time topsy-turvey since his master was killed?

Perhaps it made a difference to the Corps Commander, tapping a cigarette on his wrist, glancing once again at the map? No, it made no difference to him. He had named the Objective. He had assembled his divisions. He had helped to shape the will of this thing, crouched and purposeful, red-eyed in the night. Its will was no longer his will nor any part of the will of his staff. This will must now work itself out, and could be countermanded no more than the rolling earth.

Certainly it made no difference to the bridging parties or to the infantry, lying with blackened faces on the Allied side of the River. Nothing made any difference to them. Ahead of them lay only darkness and time to be endured. If the imagination crossed the darkness and boarded England again, returning to the drowsy civilian world of the wish, yet the body lay in peril and did not respond.

The Objective was named on the maps LAUNDRY. The General's ADC had suggested the name because the troops had a popular song about hanging washing on another German line. The General had been delighted. It was a good thing to have some humour on a party like this.

Oh certainly it makes no difference to the infantry. How can anything matter to the infantry tonight?

It is 0159 hours. This is the military way of saying it is nearly two o'clock in the morning. A bad time to be about and lying in wet grass, unless you're a romantic poet or are courting.

Of course, a romantic poet might make something of the scene. Up and down the valley, in copse, tank harbour, by the side of camouflaged dug-outs, the nightingales are singing. The German sentries can hear them, so can the dog, so can the Corps Commander: there is no-one in the valley who can't hear two or three. The air is bright with their flourishes of colour, their necklaces of vibrating song. Surely there is something here to take the minds of the infantry away from their predicament?

> Now more than ever seems it rich to die,
> To cease upon the midnight with no pain,
> While thou art pouring forth thy soul abroad
> In such an ecstacy!

But then the nightingales in this valley are not exactly ecstatic. Nightingales sing very often because they are disturbed, frightened, or angry. These nightingales are both angry and frightened because of the occasional gun which is harrassing the mule-tracks on the Mountain. Every time the gun barks the whole valley rolls around with noise. Then all the nightingales start singing together.

We might as well forget about the nightingales. They belong to an altogether different pattern. The Corps Commander would agree that they don't come into the picture.

There are thousands of patterns imposed upon this earth of ours. There are the swerving revolutions of the planet, the pattern of day and night. There is the pattern of the seasons, of luxuriating foliage, drought, fog, black frost.

There are the man-made patterns, fashioned in the image of productive society, measuring into neat anthropomorphic divisions the curved crust of the earth and the involuntary cycles of the stars. There is the pattern of months, aeons, seconds, dates, light-years. Of milking-time, opening-time, hay harvest and Christmas. The patterns which regulate activity and mark mortality and change.

There are the patterns imposed on space. Milestones, orchards, cities and continents, avenues, inches, farms. Boundaries of ownership, government, taxation. Just and unjust patterns, marked out with hedges, rulers, frontier-posts.

Tonight we are not interested in any of these patterns. Men have invented new patterns which have nothing to do with any of these. There is a new measuring-rod for time. It has a large nick in the middle called H hour. It doesn't matter any more if it is dawn or harvest-time or noon. If you don't know the new pattern the best chronometer will be of no more use to you than a sundial at midnight. The only thing of importance is the position on the measuring-rod and the distance from the large nick.

And there is a new way of measuring space. Across the familiar lines of farms and villas and contours new lines have been drawn in coloured pencil on the maps. The Roman road has become an axis of advance. Those vineyards have become a forward concentration area. Streams and lanes have become report-lines and company objectives.

And in these new definitions of time and space a new force is about to be set loose. This force isn't mentioned in the orders nor has it been given any code-name. But it is here already, crouched beneath the mountains, and there are few who don't sense its presence. It is a consequence of men's actions, but it has a will of its own, independent of any men. H hour is the proclamation of the reign of this will.

This is the Italian theatre of war. It was described as such by the precise voice of the BBC announcer on yesterday's news.

What is a theatre of war?

What sort of a show are we going to see? The overture is about to be played. There is a rustling and coughing among the audience. The tank crews gather in groups and look expectantly around at the hills. The Corps Commander climbs down from his vehicle and raises his cane like a baton.

Quietly the sappers file out to lift the minefields on this side of the River. There is a luminous glint as an officer checks his bearings on a compass.

Will there be a hero and a villain? Perhaps it will be a melodrama? Or a long and boring history?

The air is stained with a surplus of human emotion. The officer stands with a watch in his hand. He calls out the seconds—'Fourteen. . . thirteen. . . twelve. . . eleven.' The gunners stand by the breech with numb faces.

What are they all expecting? The moment hangs poised above them like a powerful lens, revealing hairline cracks and fissures in their hearts. Inside the wrist-watch the slight steel regulator rocks, exchanging time future into time past. Soon it will process H hour also, without faltering in its metallic progress. Inside the men the knocking, fractured regulators are more fallible. It does not matter if you have not yet been born. You will be marked by this moment more deeply than you will know.

The harrassing fire stops. The dog leaves off barking. Even the nightingales are silent.

And for one moment beauty intervenes and supercedes all other patterns. The moon sails serenely from the clouds and looks down from castellated walls and spacious moats. She pleads with an even voice for the whole valley. In the coppices the gunners seem suddenly to be standing knee-deep in green water, and the shadows of moving leaves dart like fish among them. The flat pale light comments quietly, urbanely, on the scene, and men glance at each other's faces and relax. The German linesmen are aware of the scent of wild rose and of the bruised grasses at their feet. The moment is postponed: the moon has intervened for humanity.

The clouds reject the moon. Their shadows cross obliquely the valley. As the last cusp of the moon vanishes men under-stand at last their mortality. The moon neither pleads nor regrets. From her craters and dried seas she reflects equally the light of the sun and the prayers of men. Now that she has gone the night is deeper than before.

Men are alone in the roofless valley. Only the will they

have created keeps them company. They sense it waiting
expectantly in the deeper darkness left by the moon's
departure.

There are four seconds left. Tell me, before they begin.
Who are the characters in this play? Will it be an allegory,
with Fate, Despair, Law, Chance? Or could they be men?

There is activity, decision. The gunners stand back a little
from the breech, they take hold of the next round of
ammunition. The officer raises his hand.

The Corps Commander throws away his unsmoked cigarette. He goes into the command vehicle and shuts the door.

Above all, tell me: *Who wrote the play?*

The German linesmen start and look up with terror at the
southern hills, outlined in silent and continuous white flame.
Over no-man's land, the River, the mine-fields, there is a
whirling of huge baffled wings, barguests, strange harmonics.
Twelve hundred guns say grace.

I cannot hear an answer. The ear-drums of my consciousness are stunned. O Christ be merciful now that we are
encircled by gods! Hear their astounding voices! See them,
with their red eyes, their scarred ears, their terrible incisors
of flame!

An army is an organism in the same way as a centipede, an
armadillo or a capitalist state is an organism, and is subject
in similar ways to laws of growth and change. It has a blood-
stream which branches into many little veins, an intricate
nervous system, controlled actions and defensive reflexes,
defensive armour and a striking arm. It has moments of fear
and exultation and moods of dark depression. This interfusion of sense and emotion is called morale. Also, like
some other organisms, it has a will.

The general will of the army became know to the officers
in the week before the battle in many order-groups and after-
dinner discussions; and, by more devious routes, to the other
ranks and to the German General Staff. For many days staff
officers, hurrying from room to room, calculating figures
and times, had fought out the battle in a hundred ways. They
had laid the creeping barrage and ferried the infantry. They

had brought up bridging material and bombed railheads. With steaming mugs of tea on their desks they had annihilated enemy brigades.

The will was first defined by the Army Commander in a top secret conference. He ran his finger along the enemy positions overlaid on his maps and explained that he would blow the enemies out of their holes in the ground and if they were still alive he would shoot them before they could get away. *We will destroy the enemy*, he said.

Confirming to this overall objective, other objectives were set for the horizons of smaller units. The Divisional Commander poked with his cane at a sand-table and said: *In brief, gentlemen, we will encircle the enemy on the mountain —here—joining up with other troops who will come round from the north-east—here. We will destroy the enemy on the mountain—box him in and hammer him—and then. . .*

The colonel of one of the infantry assault battalions told his officers: *We will cross the river at this point at H Hour. Let's hope the gunners do their stuff. Then we'll advance to this point, and you, John, will patrol forward and mop up the enemy on that spot-height. They haven't given us much time, so. . .*

On the day before the battle a squadron leader took his troop officers up a small hill overlooking the valley: *Well here it is. Keep your head down, Peter. That's where the sappers will put the bridge. We'll be in support of the leading battalion behind that little ridge by first light. Order—second troop, H.Q., third, fourth, first. O.K.? Now take a good look. Don't flash your glasses.*

The valley was full of green leaf, chopped-off trees, miniature white houses. The river coiled across in front, the colour of a watch-spring among the grass. No-one could be seen. Only a distant fist of dust suggested a vehicle moving behind a farm.

At length the squadron leader said: *All right? Now get back and put your troops in the picture. I want every man to know as much about the battle as I do.*

So the will of the army became communicated to all the parts of the organism. Engineers, gunners, military police, recovery sections, signalmen and forward dressing-stations all formed wills corresponding as exactly as possible to the general will of the army.

The smallest cell of the organism was man, the fighting soldier: the Canadians, French legionaries, Polish refugees, London busmen, Indian mercenaries and peasants, negro cotton workers and New Zealand farmers who made up the stuff of the allied armies. Just as the best fighting units were supposed to be those whose reflexes had been conditioned by training and experience to unhesitating obedience to the general will, so in war all particular wills, of Methodist or Sikh, of anarchist, father or hypocrite, were supposed to be suppressed in their duties as fighting men, merging identity in the will of the army. It did not matter what private passions rubbed under the cuffs of the uniform. No margin of error could be allowed for the squabbles of an individual's conscience.

All of that was irrelevant. Its sum and average only was of interest to the staff and was noted under the heading of 'morale'. If there were miscalculations in their plan it would be for different causes, since, as they well knew, the enemy also possessed an organic and contrary will. And accident stood ready to intervene against them both, and to override with arbitrary will all other wills.

For nearly one hour the gunners have been imposing a blood-stained pattern upon the complex of flowering soil, flesh, plaster-work and military equipment which makes up the Objective.

It is now H Hour minus ten minutes.

The engineers have already started their work. They have cleared a passage through our own minefields down to the river. They have brought bridging materials and smoke canisters close to the southern bank. Now they are bulldozing a track for the tanks towards the river, and marking it with white tape.

At H Hour minus eight minutes every gun in the area will abandon its particular target and concentrate on the north bank of the river, clawing for the flesh of the enemies in the foremost series of holes.

All at once there is a pause. Intense silence. The silence is worse than any climax, and the singing ears beg for the barrage to come back.

The infantry lie close to the south bank, waiting. They press against the ground. Only the thickness of their battle-dress is between the careering juice of their hearts and the cold swab of the earth.

They have left behind them all customary human identity. Their faces are smeared with black mud. Leaves and grasses are stuck into the netting on their tin helmets. They have cut off their badges and signs and burned all papers. Only their identity disks, stamped with name and army number, link their bodies with the files of army records.

Wheels turn, the smoking ends of guns come down, and now it is H Hour minus eight. In front of the infantry, across the space of a few yards of soil and stream, the earth roars upwards in spires of dust and flame. The wind of the passing shells brushes their faces. They can hear overhead the shells pushing and tumbling as they fall through the air, and the whining descant of the towering howitzers. It is as if the sky is an earphone clamped on the ear of the valley, an earphone full of giant atmospherics and heterodyning frequencies.

The waiting soldiers press closer to the waiting swab of the earth. The hard ground nudges their thigh bones and creases the pattern of cloth into the skin. The imagination refuses to cross the yards and minutes ahead. In eight minutes or seven or four (their memories tell them) they must stand erect and walk into that flame-lit darkness. But the senses refuse admission to the messages of memory. The dew alone seems permanent and the scent of crushed grasses. The moment is all that is real, for ever and ever, and it is savoured outside of time.

Others don't notice the guns. Later, if they survive, they won't recollect them. One is dry-cleaning his rifle for a last time. Another ransacks his memory for his orders, and finds that it is blank, like a child just before a public recitation. Another feels in his pocket to see if his cigarettes are still there, and wonders if he will have to wait until dawn before he can light up.

At H Hour minus two minutes the barrage will lift two hundred yards so that the infantry can cross to the north bank under its protection. It is lifting now. An officer taps the nearest men and stands up. He is the one who had forgotten his orders. Now that he is moving everything is remembered.

One of the guns has been falling short and its shells have been bursting behind the infantry. Now it lifts its range two hundred yards.

The first shell falls ten yards from the officer. A man cries out. Clots of mud sting their faces. It is too dark to see where the injured man is; the flash has dazed their night-sight. The officer turns back and hesitates. Someone mutters *Jack* and someone else *Got it pretty bad*. Then the officer calls his men and they run towards the river, carrying with them their canvas boats.

The second shell from this gun bursts harmlessly, but the third reaches out further and claws through the centre of the main bridging party. The major in charge of this is known as a madman, brilliant survivor of a hundred operations, confident of success in this. He is killed outright and several of his officers and men are killed or wounded—more than one would expect from a single high-explosive shell. The field telephone is already cut and now a splinter pierces the wireless-set and lodges in the operator's throat. A smoke canister is also set alight, sending thick sulphurous fumes over the area where some of the infantry are crossing. A competent and experienced lieutenant is left in command, but it will be some time before he finds this out. At the moment he is choking in the smoke, looking for the major. Nor has he yet discovered that his friend, the officer next in seniority to the major, is lying downwind from the smoke-canister with a wound in his back.

At H Hour plus eight minutes, if the crossing is a success, the barrage will lift another two hundred yards and support the infantry forward to their next objective. Then the engineers must throw the Bailey bridge across the river. This has all been carefully and exactly described in the Intention and Method paragraphs of the orders. It is the will of the General, of the dead major, of the organism.

It is now H Hour plus eight minutes. We have reached that nick in the new measuring-rule and now we have passed it.

Why has the barrage not lifted yet?

What has happened to the infantry?

On a sand-table it is simple. The General points with his cane. This is a farm, a coppice, a track. On the air photographs there are flat hills and round trees with shadows. On the map the suspected enemy positions are overlaid in sepia. All that is quite simple. From the Observation Points overlooking the valley it is possible in daylight to make out the objectives, the deep lanes, the unsown cornland. The distances seem very small.

Now there is no light except when magnesium starshells hang from their parachutes and swing in the sky. Shadows lunge like threats. Darkness again. Lifted faces, grey-white, blue-grey, white. Bushes which crouch.

You can hardly call it a bloody river, John. A chap could get across it in three damn good jumps.

Black as ice in the polar night, swift and deep. Narrow here, with high banks. The colour of steel under swinging magnesium arc-lights, more tangible and viscous than water ought to be.

I am across the river on the far bank, panting in grass.

A shell spawns near my boat. I'm closed in the steel grapple of the water, and I, and I.

I touch the bottom and rise gently. I'm weighed down by my ammunition pouches and the sling-swivel of my rifle has caught in my belt.

I'm hunched on the bank, waiting to cross. I watch the officer for the signal.

The organism is trying to jump the river. All its bragging strength and will-power is bent against this strip of water. The river is a tank-trap, a thorn-fraught barrier. It is fertility to the fruiting valley, the spine of abundance, nourished by the tribute of the mountains. The parish of frogs, giving

with abandon earth's richest fluid, source for the flourishing
handwriting of gladioli and vine on the parchment of summer.

Time enters a new pattern and space a new element. It is
neither dawn nor midnight, twilight nor noon. Five swinging
suns sway in the sky. Red comets shed their tails.

I'm bent double, camel-walking by firelight through a field
of unsown corn. I see no enemies. Shells crop the banks of
the river behind, but here it is quiet. The barrage must have
blown the enemies from their holes. They've fled. I tread on
a flower with three delicate stalks. They give way expectantly.
The canister climbs to shoulder-height and carves into flame
and grapeshot. Another moon foals out of the night, but the
open eyes of the soldier lying in the minefield do not flinch.

*How d'ye like the party, Jim? Its a fucking shame the old
bugger isn't here himself for the reception.*

German mortars are already crunching their jaws in the
little bridgehead. Bigger guns join them. They show great
interest in the flaring smoke canister and bridging materials.
They guess the will of the dead major to bridge the river at
this point. They make it impossible for anyone to stand in
the area for more than a few seconds.

I'm commanding a platoon. It is my first set battle. My
platoon crossed the river in the first wave. Now yellow smoke
blows around me and I've lost my men. I call out but there's
no answer. I hurry forward. The black river opens suddenly
in front of me. I turn around and run through the smoke,
still looking for my men. I stumble over a man lying in the
grass. I shake him and ask him which platoon he belongs to.
I try to pull him to his feet. I don't recognise the man. How
can I tell which platoon he's from if he has no face?

To the left small-arms fire breaks out. Machine-guns speak
in a hurry, out of breath, words tripping on their tongues.
All life with feathers or fur is fleeing this patch of earth.
The dog, hiding in a cellar, pants and salivates. Dazzled and
concussed, all the grace of undulating flight departed, finches
bolt from bush to bush. They fly into trees and walls like
moths. The lizards hide beneath the rocks. Only the insects
and the men are active. A shell uproots an ant-hill. The sand
seethes with bustling refugees, lugging their larvae over

mountains and down ravines.

I'm safely across the river. My cigarettes are dry. I can feel them in my pocket. I was at Alamein, Mareth, Salerno. I'm a private and I'm still alive. I hang back, a shade behind the others, watching at every step for cover. Like an early astronomer I can dimly make out some reason in war's firmament. I see a cluster of short flashes outlining the section of the hill up which we're running. Those are the ones to watch out for. Mortars. I throw myself into the ditch which I've been following. I'm a prophet. I move with more freedom than my comrades in this weather since I act in accord with its compulsive laws. The shells shut their teeth all around me, but I am safe. My friends were still running when the shells fell among them. How could I warn them? No-one will take orders from me. I'm a private and I'm still alive.

The General is waiting to cross the river as soon as the bridgehead is soundly established. He felt an impulse a few minutes ago to cross with the first wave of troops. But he's a nerve-centre of the organism and must not be unnecessarily exposed. Nor could he project his will into that flamelit valley without command vehicles, wireless sets, field telephones, scout-cars and jeeps. He stands on a shoulder of ground a thousand yards from the river. Several minutes have passed since the first wave went in. Sometimes in the light of flares the General can see groups of tiny men detach themselves from the river bank and run towards ditches and lanes. Shells are sprouting thickly by the crossings, and he can see flashes and puffs of smoke near the running men. Occasionally a shell falls in the water, sending up a spout as if a toy whale were blowing.

The moon breaks free of clouds once more before falling behind the mountain. In the sky are long cliffs and beaches, wide silver estuaries, uncharted dark oceans pointed with sad swiftly-travelling stars. The General sees a mumbling hedge of smoke smudging the river's edge and he curses. The enemy mortars and shells are considered in the plan. A margin of life has been calculated for this phase of the battle, a sum has already been totted up and subtracted from the battalions. But this smoke is contrary to the will. *Some bloody idiot has set off one of those smoke-canisters,* he remarks to no-one in particular. *Remind me to find out who the bloody man was.*

My battalion is being cut to pieces. I saw the boat in which one of my company commanders was crossing receive a direct hit. I'll think about that later. In three minutes time we must be on the line of the first ridge. Lunacy! They always time these things wrong, I suppose they thought that we'd just stand up and walk there. Well, it will have to be fifteen minutes now. *Where the hell is that bloody runner?* Operator off-net, lost touch with brigade. Have to signal with Verey lights when we get up there. When we get there. Where has A Company got to? Surely *some* of A Company is left? They caught it in the minefield I think. Will that be them up to the left? There's a brisk battle up there. Yes, they've got the Brens in action. Good lads. How the Jerries got through that stonking I don't know. Have to winkle them out one by one. *Got through yet, operator?* We'll make for that broken tree and send out the runners again. *Operator, how the* DEVIL *d'you think you'll get through if you fling y'self on the ground every time one of those goes over, eh?* Hello, there go the mortars again. Why the hell don't the gunners do something about them? Oh my poor battalion! These beggars are going to come pretty close. I'd better get down. You can hear them all the way. Either it has your name on it or it hasn't. I'd better get down. But the men are getting windy. It's my duty to stand on my feet. Christ they're coming right for us! GET DOW. . .

Now I'm on the move I feel better. Movement warms the stomach. I'm a section leader and I know my job. I've lost touch with my platoon commander, but to the right and left I know there are other men from the company. We have to follow the line of this farm track. One of my section copped it in the minefield but the others are following. A Spandau suddenly clatters only fifty yards ahead, fluently breeding metal into the night. We drop. It preaches into the darkness in formal phrases, easily, without emphasis. Metal slugs spin from the turf above my head. I look over a bank cautiously and spot the position of the machine-gun from a sprinting tracer. I gather my section round me, waving to them to keep down. I'm enclosed in the circle of my purpose, forgetting the battle all around. I've met this situation before. I've lost sight of my platoon's objective, and must now select my own. The army calls this initiative. I recall the will of the organism and make my own will conform to it as closely as I can. I give my orders softly. The men's faces are screwed up in anxious concentration. Since it is I who am giving orders and not some la-di-da officer they feel a sudden comradeship, as if they had assumed personal responsibility for the battle. They respect my judgment, they nod and say O.K. One of them asks about a signal. They breathe the fullness of this momentary rest, lying on their backs in the grass. Number One and Number Two on the Bren will engage the Spandau from the front. I'll take the rest of the section round, right-flanking, and destroy the machine-gun post with grenades. Number One accepts his responsibility with gravity. He must beware of firing on us as we close with the objective. He forgets the child which discipline and uniform have made of him, and he becomes a man again, a civilian, a craftsman with self-confidence. I know that I can trust him. I lead off into the darkness, watching the night with every sense alert. My finger takes the first pressure on the trigger of my tommy-gun, a grenade is hooked by its firing-lever to the front of my belt, safety-pin half withdrawn. Half-way to the objective a flare breaks open the sky and as I drop a bullet bangs like a fist into my shin. I lie still for a long time, feeling no pain. But I can't use my leg and a sticky patch spreads on my trousers. I crawl to a ditch and send a man back to bring on the Bren gunners. Number One must now take over command. I don't want to be left alone. I think I should keep my section together. The pain begins to grow. I don't want to be left in the night alone. My messenger crosses without warning into the view of the Bren gunners. His black hurrying figure with canted rifle is that of an attacking enemy. The gunners shoot him through the head. For a long time they watch the darkness. They don't know that its their friend who lies above them.

The red-eyed beast is loosed and neither the German Corps Commander nor the British General can control its will nor define it within any limits. Eight minutes have passed since H Hour. The infantry should have reached the first ridge and the barrage should lift two hundred yards and support them to the next. Then the sappers can get on with their bridging work. The General still has no information. The flares are less frequent now. Intersecting lines of tracer indicate the points of the fiercest fighting. Every now and then a Bofors gun fires four large tracer rounds, speeding up the valley to show the infantry the axis of the attack. The signals officer gets through to the infantry brigadier and the General speaks to him. The brigadier is anxious and irritable. *I'm sorry, General, I haven't had a word from James since he crossed. Yes, I'm trying. He just went into the night. Yes, I'm through to David. He had a bad crossing. No, he's not on 'Brown' yet. He's having some bother with Spandaus on the right—point one-sixty, about fifty or sixty yards from the crossing. General, can you tell the gunners to get their fingers out and do something about those mortars behind the first ridge? Yes, I KNOW, but will YOU tell them that?*

I've never been in action before. This isn't what I expected. I've seen none of the enemies yet, but already several of my mates have been left lying in the grass. It was a great do yesterday when we saw all those guns and tanks moving up. And then the bombers going over, squadron after squadron, bombing railheads and bridges the officer said. I was going to win a medal, saving the Sergeant. 'What, you?' he was going to say, lying there with his leg blown off. 'Yes, me, sarge,' I said. 'But you! And after I put you on a charge. . .' I waved my hand. 'Forget it, sarge,' I said, 'I don't bear no ill will. I'll see you out of this lot.' Then the Nazis coming, twenty, thirty, swastikas and great helmets like the flicks, and me picking them off, got him, got him, got him. Dragging in the sergeant and then collapsing with loss of blood, all the officers gathering round, that little runt our platoon officer ran away perhaps and the Colonel saying to him, 'Look at this lad, you ought to be ashamed. He's an example to all of you.' And then, to me: 'I'll put you in for it straight away, young fellow. An immediate V.C.' And me: 'Oh no, sir. I just done my duty.' This isn't like that at all. How few we seem—pygmies against giant trees and the jumping shadows of bushes. I'd run and hide in a ditch only I'm most afraid now of being lost in this hostile immensity. My section is alone. Perhaps we're trapped behind the enemy lines? I can see none of the others who were crouched like us on the other side of the river. Perhaps we mistook the order? Perhaps no-one else has crossed? When the flares go up we freeze motionless in the shadows and the sergeant whispers to me to keep my face to the ground. But there is nowhere to hide. The great eye of flame searches me out and all the guns in the valley turn and look at me. When the eye shuts we hurry on up the field. I drop as metal whines past and then I've lost them. They've gone on ahead. I'm alone. There they are again. I recognise the stocky shape of the sergeant, I run after him and catch at the cuff of his denims. He starts and turns savagely on me. We freeze as the eye again opens its lids. A white form pounds me in the chest, batters at my face. The spirit of night beats against me, claws and strikes at my eyes. I scream. The eye slowly closes. I'm still screaming. The sergeant curses as I grip his arm. He swings his rifle-butt into my face and shakes me off. He goes off, leaving me alone on the ground with a broken jaw-bone. A white owl with a broken wing keeps me company.

What's happening on the ridge two hundred yards from the river? In vineyard, dead ground, re-entrant, deep-sunk lane? How goes the day for England? Where are my proud battalions? Where does my friend lie tonight?

Close quarters now. This blood-stained interval of ground the weather of shell-fire doesn't touch. The noisy correspondence here passes between men on the ground: sprinting epistle of Spandau: matter-of-fact comment of rifles: caesura: juddering Bren gun, repeating again and again the same brief phrase: punctuation of grenades, colon, colon, full stop.

Where is my man, O where is my love in Italy? I wake and stare as the wind hunts through the eaves. Was it in my dreams that I heard that cry? Now I can see him clearly. His face is white and flame-lit. He stares at me strangely. I gasp and rise in the bed, reaching out my arms. He makes no sign of recognition.

Men are fixing bayonets. Out of the scabbard of custom they draw the primitive steel, first cousin to the assegai, great-grand-child of the murderous flint. Civilisation moves on through its contradictions as it has always done, its feet slipping in the infantry's blood. You with your sophisticated poise, you with your perfumed skin and stained nails, you with your armoury of abstractions, you were created by long sharp tools and the spurting of blood.

I trip on a root. I fling my rifle to my side and skid forwards on my face. Grit scores my teeth, I smell wood violets against my face.

I move silently up the lines of vine, fostered from stunted roots. As I duck my head under the tendons I feel the cobwebs peel onto my face. A spider runs down my cheekbone and across my neck.

I crouch behind a shattered ox-cart and peer carefully through the shafts. I've taken the pin from a grenade, my arm curves behind me, I feel the spring of the firing-lever nudge the palm of my hand. I see movement. I hurl the grenade forward and fall on my face. The grenade curves in the air and lies smoking on the ground. It rolls back down the bank towards me. I press my face into the earth and count the seconds.

I'm running blindly in darkness, my bayonet at the ready. I stumble and recover myself. I remember the loud-mouthed instructor at the battle-school in England. We leap a ditch and lunge at swinging sandbags. He tells us to imagine the blade sinking in an enemy's belly, a moment of resistance, then it breaks through the cloth and skin and runs easily in. IN! OUT! ON GUARD! REMEMBER SINGAPORE! IN! CHURN-UP-HIS-GUTS! OUT! But now its dark and I'm running alone. The faster I run the less chance I have of getting hit. Time to think of hundreds of things. Wonder if I'll live to see the dawn. The Corporal is dead, wonder who will play left-half in the team now. A Spandau fires in my direction at a level with my belt but I don't swerve. I play left-back in the team. I don't think very quickly in a game, but I can boot it right up the field. Its better now that I'm running, I don't even know that I'm windy. I feel like shouting and killing. I'm close to that Spandau now, eyes show for white instants, shapes move. I'm a heavy man and my boots pound the ground. I remember the great pistons of the engines passing our back-yard.

A red Verey light soars up to the right. A green. Green over red—that must be point one-sixty where that Spandau nest was. There are Englishmen on that hillock, C Company has reached its first objective. But there is still firing from that quarter. Matter-of-fact statement, fluent self-expression, full stop. The bullets stop only when they meet life, in tree-bark, flesh or turf. When they meet rock or steel they ricochet far into the darkness. They complain over the General's head, and spin listlessly into the further ground where the tank crews are waiting for the dawn. Is this a counter-attack already, men wrestling for these deep dug-outs, disputing for possession of these open graves? The General feels his command slipping from him. His reputation twists in the air like a tossed coin, and however loud he calls he can't determine on which face it will fall. He gives un-necessary fussy orders. He interferes with the serious-faced signallers. Under his breath he curses the colonel of the assault battalion, who lies wounded where the mortar bombs are still falling.

I'm a doctor. I crossed the river two minutes after H Hour, or whatever they call it. I've got two orderlies with me. And the padre, of course. He needn't have crossed tonight but he felt that his presence might comfort the men. Only morphia will comfort these men. But I can make use of his help. Hey what a strange business this is! All around me men are making history. That is, they're cutting slices off each other's flesh. In their surgery they employ all the instruments of industrial civilisation—engines, precision tools, cunning techniques, the disciplines of science. Then they blindfold each other with darkness and distance and set about their haphazard butchery. And me? I'm sent on afterwards to patch up what they've done. You suppose I have an operating theatre, white-masked assistants, sterilised instruments, anaesthetics, drugs? Hands, I've got my hands and my skill and whatever I can carry across a river in a canvas boat: tongs, a little morphia, bandages, splints. I might be wrapping up parcels. This chap's eye hangs from its socket, but he's walking; he understands what I say and he answers in a controlled voice. Such cases aren't described in the textbooks. I see I must call in a specialist, I must hold a consultation. *Padre, hold the end of this bandage while I bind the eye.* He's not a serious case, he can still walk, and if his heart doesn't stop with delayed shock he'll live. This man hasn't a scratch on his skin. He's concussed and blood trickles from his ears. His face is black from blast and some of his clothes are torn off. I prescribe for him warm sheets, a carefully-watched temperature chart, absolute silence and rest, a special diet. And this man, with a bullet through his lung and blood in his mouth? Ah, I'm experienced in this: in this I'm my own specialist. Morphia in his arm, a greatcoat over him, lay him gently in the dew under the vines. All this exertion, all this expense of technology to kill a man! But a man is so easy to kill. If he falls to the pavement from a high window he's done for. Or drive a nail into his head. To make him live, now that's a different matter. You must know a great deal about a man's body before you can heal it. To kill him you need only pick up a stone.

Communications between headquarters and the men on the further bank of the river are now altogether deranged. A tiny bridgehead is established. But there is no bridge, and the river, like the blade of an axe, has cut the limb from the body. The will of the red-eyed god has supervened over all other wills. The infantry are atomised. Each individual obeys a logic or necessity of his own; he follows a personal objective, thrust upon him by his past, his beliefs, his environment of darkness and of flame. Now the impetus of the organism, morale, is spent like a wave among the porous sands of the German defences, and is no longer renewed from any common source. Only here and there the spirit flares up, renewed from private reserves. Here a man governed in his

actions by habit, discipline, training. Here a man struggling
to maintain a high position in his own self-esteem. Here an
officer determined to uphold the prestige of his caste, feeling
a possessive responsibility for the course of the battle. Here
a man who has suffused the battle with his own desires and
intentions, whose personal objective is to bring the battle's
outcome into conformity with the objectives of a class, a
nation, an anti-fascist war.

Morphia! Isn't there any morphia left? What an im-
pertinence to speak of souls, what insolence of the padre to
speak of a god! His god of peace and love slunk away from
the valley more than two hours back, ears couched, tail
curved to touch his belly. What use is his training now, the
conversations in a seminary around a scrubbed refectory
table? Better if he'd had a week's training in the ways of
repairing flesh: not First Aid, simple fractures, flesh wounds,
but the business of real life, complex violations, tormented
and pulped-up flesh. His eyes betray his own sense of impotence. I'll admit that the lad has courage. He doesn't pay
much attention to the shells, his hand is steady. I think I
must move my hospital to a better position, I'll have a good
enough practice wherever I go. What I need is morphia,
bandages, morphia. The lung case is dying, drowning in his
own blood. The padre kneels and takes his hand. He suggests
to the man that they should pray. What an idiot the man is!
Leave the poor bugger in peace, he needs a blood-transfusion
and I can't give it. In a whisper the man begins, *Father which
art in Heav'n hallowed be. . .* What does hallowed mean,
anyway? Hallowe'en. Pumpkins lighted with candles, spooks,
skulls lighted with flares. This animal, man, what a splendid
contraption his body is! If there's one sign of sanity in
manic history it's that the body of his mate, woman, is not
in this part of the valley tonight. *Tha will be done on earth
as it is'n heaven. . .* Branching veins, tender valves, glands,
interfusion of nerves, the digestive tract, the pumping heart;
the delicate accurate hands, shaping tools, changing and
ordering matter, changing man himself. . . .*This daya daily
bread. . .* His brain, controlling his hands, learning in turn
from them; the soil blossoming into consciousness, knowing

reality in order to change it, able to comprehend the planets and the larvae of ants, able to fill this valley with flame. *For thine is a kingdom, power an a glory, was in the beginnin' is now'n ever shall be world-without-end amen.* A flare lights up the vineyard, my flourishing practice, the kneeling padre, the ash-white face and the bubbles of blood on the lips of the dying man. I glance quickly at my patient— have I misjudged his case? No, there's nothing to be done. But what is that expression in the man's eyes? He holds the padre's hand and watches him with courteous compassion. He is only praying to save the young man's feelings. The padre can see this also. Ahead of us the clatter of small-arms rises to a crescendo. The padre stands up and walks towards the ridge. I call after him. Idiot! I need your help, your hands. How the flesh of these men is torn! He goes, I won't see him again. O my god, why have you left me like this? Man of woman born, animal out of tall animal thrown, I need your brain, your hands.

The dying man is speaking. I drop my work and step quickly across. He breathes irregularly, in great gasps between pauses: if he starts to cough he will choke. If I were to cover him with ten greatcoats he wouldn't keep warm. I lean over him, and he whispers with great difficulty: *How is it going? You'll be all right,* I say. *We'll have to get you back on a stretcher but you should be all right. The battle,* he asks, *how is it going?* Well, Christ of mercy, what a question to ask! I say it's going well. But what a question! Of course it's a success. I've never seen so much slicing of erect and contemplative flesh. But *how* it is going, what the objectives are, what the result of it all will be—that's a fair problem to occupy the deliriums of a dying man.

If history is made by murder, what great histories are being made tonight. Now the battle moves towards its fulfilment, men shed the fragile acquisitions of civilisation and fight hand-to-hand, in fury and in panic. They move as if isolated, underwater or in primitive forests. Teeth sink into skin. Men sway in the arms of strangers: they strike for the sensitive points, neck, temples and eyes, base of spine, genitals. My

love in Italy embraces another body: they howl and wrestle
above an open grave. Man's spine arches, his arms lengthen,
his forehead recedes. Ha, this is a success! He will soon have
fur and a tail! And yet it is what is human about him, his
consciousness and conditioned will, which roots him to the
battlefield. What other animal would endure so long a night?

It is now H Hour plus twelve minutes. Why hasn't the
barrage moved on yet? What has happened to the infantry?

Few of them remember what is their objective. None of
them know how the battle is going. They give no thought to
history and they have lost count of time. These twelve
minutes have severed them from the past, and this new
pattern seems to stretch out in all dimensions and to en-
compass them for ever. Time-future and time-past have been
exchanged into an everlasting now in which the anguished
consciousness throbs until time-never falls.

Coda

He lies by star-of-bethlehem and rose
Beside the track, among the terraced hills,
Where broom in flower flings a yellow sash.

Save some in England all of Europe knows
So I'll not tell you how a dead man smells
Nor what five days of sun can do to flesh.

Come, gentle officers of burial,
And do not leave him here where strangers roam:
Sweet diesel, solemnise his funeral,
Grave bulldozer, dig deep his resting-room.

Monte Grande, May 1944.

CASOLA VALSENIO: THE CAT

I'm sure no love of ours had kept her there
After her master left. She hid herself from sight
By day. She seemed to know that men had ceased to care
For company. So she patrolled, like us, at night,
And often in the dark we started up in fright,
Thinking she was the enemy inside our wire.
But still we let her be, until she tripped a flare,
And spent its light, and showed the Germans where we were.

I ordered that the cat be shot. 'There is no time
In war to exhaust one's heart on animals,' I said.
'What is a shell-torn forest to one shattered home?
'This wretched cat before a human life?' I said.
'The longer that she lives the sooner we'll be dead.
'Besides, she'll serve to give your marksmanship a check.'
So we waited. And the next time that she came
A man fired, wounding the creature in the neck.

She cried and all night wandered crying in the snow.
Her blood thawed crimson patches in the bitter white.
And still we heard her weakening below
Until the soldiers' faces wasted into white
And misting pity misinformed the sentries' sight,
Because of her complaint who wandered to and fro
And was distressed by forces which she could not know
And in her time of dying had no place to go.

War, when a soldier dies, his comrades turn away
Their eyes and shut their hearts. There is no man who'd dare
Consider on the thing and still maintain the day.
It is set by for remembering in a future year.
And so it was this sorrow entered unaware
And vanquished us. And we were half-ashamed to show
Such pity for a creature we set out to slay.
She was the waste of Europe, crying in the snow.

Grassina, February 1945.

APPROACH MARCH, LAST OFFENSIVE

May this offensive mean some end at last!
Time and again the fascists have been beaten back
And our avenging armies, growing in might,
Have battled down converging roads, until it seems
The end has grown remote with our civilian dreams
And we'll be everlastingly condemned to fight.
And yet this evening, watching my division spreading past—
A vast armoured city moving on tracks—

I triumph in our strength. The convoy lights
Outstare the stars, and like a never-ending stream
Of evidence for final victory, the bragging tanks
Make powder of the road. Burnt fumes and dust
Become a fragrance to us, and we give our thanks
For these abundant means since end they must.

Cesana, April 1945.

DRAVA BRIDGE*

How many armies there were in that corner of Europe I
wouldn't like to say. If you took one hand from each man in
my tank crew, you still wouldn't have enough fingers to
count the nations whose children limped and fled in panic,
fought for bread and lost the will to live in this rich, well-
watered pocket of land.

No man was more than a moment of consuming grief,
and few were more than the pain in their reiterating feet.
None of them knew where the roads they were marching
ended, any more than they understood the forces which had
taken them to the white battlefields of the Ukraine and to
jagged Montenegro. You will not find their names in history,
although they were the soil that was tilled and harrowed and
in which great factions grew. You will never find their graves.

Our army had been laid on the wide anvil of the desert and
fashioned by the hammer of the sun. And then the way up
Italy, back in Europe again, but whether we came from
Durham or Mile End there was nothing in the country for
an Englishman to understand. The way the land was watered
was all wrong. The streams were abrupt ugly gashes the
width of a small Bailey bridge, and they dried when the
autumn cloudbanks ceased to curse. The big rivers stood
still and smelled. Whenever we made our bivvies it was in an

---

* *Our Time*, December 1945.

olive-grove or perhaps a vineyard with the leaves tired and yellowing and all the roadside muffled thickly in dust so that a hurrying donkey-cart looked like a Roman legion on the march and the skivvy of a startled lizard left a sullen puff like rifle-smoke in the air. I can remember no trees taller than our aerials except for the cypresses in the cemeteries.

That was before we reached this place. When we drove up to the mountains it was like coming to the gates of hell. I don't say that for effect. It was like coming to the gates of hell. The mountains stood up erect from the plain with black scarred faces. The sky was sagging with impending thunder and black, so that it seemed that some great tank was burning behind the mountains and belching a volume of coarse diesel fumes. And when the lightning at length came it was as if the flames had found the ammunition racks and flushed the cordite into a short white gasp, while overhead heavy guns argued our destiny. It seemed to us that there could be no way through when we were in the pass. It was like looking up the barrel of a gun when someone puts a round in and shuts the breech.

When we came out of the pass it took us some moments to understand. This was when we first began to believe that the war had ended. Here were young green oak trees and beech woods. Here the grass was as green as an English water-meadow and the streams were clear and continually making laughter. Here were clean white villages and cattle swaying a loaded bag of milk. This was surely the richest plateau in Europe, where men might trail their fingers in the fertile earth and multiply their wealth, and we might find rest from soldiering. It was like coming out of a long spell of action, and laying your cheek into the earth and smelling the roots of grasses before you are asleep.

The perspectives of time and prejudice, experience and space, could not focus these people in our understanding. For us they were the newsprint, the digits and the symbols, caught like paper in a blast furnace, and now the flakes of dissolving ash seized and thrown outwards by the hurrying tempests of heated air. Some would have been satisfied with statistics and the mathematics of Fascist oppression and defeat. Certainly it might be said that they had once been Greeks, Germans, Cossacks, Slovenes, Poles. Or that they were plague-carriers. Or a migrant body of the creature man, dying in Central Europe for want of bread. Or a transport problem. Or pregnant widows and orphaned sons and divided lovers. Or Fascists and slaveworkers, peasants and traitors. Or, more simply, the human cud which was all that remained of the German armies, slobbering from the dead but still warm jaws of the Fascist war.

No man was more than an instant of returning pain, and few were more than wastes in a desert where all green strivings had withered into apathy. Their skies were grey and overcast with continual hunger, and their horizons numb with the enclosing monotony of defeat. They were the husks of the people of Europe, and their spirits had been threshed and ground in war. Only the winds which blew them were still man-made winds—the winds of propaganda and man-made panic, the curses of their officers, a voice on the radio saying:

The Bolsheviks, the Bolsheviks! You must move west, or the Bolsheviks will take from you all we have left to you—life!

Carrying the load of melting snowfields, the Drava runs swift and deep, yellow and sinewy as the arm of a Chinese peasant. Sometimes the forests lean over from the mountain-sides and look down steep cliffs at the churn of water. Sometimes the land collapses like cloth in leisurely folds of wheatscape on either side. Occasionally a wooden bridge crosses the stream, its supporting posts tugging like oarsmen against the heavy water.

Somewhere to the East we knew there were the landscapes of the Danube. There rolled the cornlands of Hungary. Somewhere to the East was the Red Army, advancing with its burden of grief and anger, each individual soldier carrying with his rifle his visions of blackened and wasted labour, each peasant carrying like a cast in his eye the memory of Fascist abuse and of Russian dead.

Up from the South and in amongst us thrust the partisans —Yugoslavs and Italians, men whose only nationality was hate for Fascism, whose only profession was belief in man. Their conversation was resistance, their tongues were the implements of war, their currency was blood.

Ah! Our comrades! Our allies in the war for Freedom! We have met at last comrades, we have won our 20 years' war with the beast! This is a day for laughter! This is a day to kill Fascists!

I ask you to consider—how could we understand the humours of these ragged men? We who had fought a concise and methodical war in the parched throat of Italy—we had only been puzzled and dismayed by the random selection death made from our company. How could we understand these ragged peasants, who walked in the dawn of a new world as if each step they took was an oath affirming human victory? How could we return their generous salutations?

So we stood on the wooden bridges, watching the Drava hurrying the snowfields off to Hungary, seeing only the misery and the pity as the chaff of the richest granaries of Europe blew past us down the roads. Wherever we walked we saw the litter of their discarded arms. Only the grey-blue of their tattered uniforms startled at times in us the reflex 'enemy', already dulled and echoing in a week of dividing experience. Certainly it might be said that they were Croat conscripts marching in tight formation, while behind them their officers rode and cracked their whips and cursed them into panic, and behind again, there followed their women-folk and children, white with the indignity of twenty centuries of war.

But there were no men and women left among them, and not one of them was any more than a moment of consuming grief.

And so, when the order came, we who had come from the desert and Mile End held the bridge against these man-made winds—not in the pride of our conviction but in the resignation of our uniform. These men were no more a transport problem, but the terms of a military agreement, signed in an hotel lounge. They were the prisoners of our allies. They were the wages of the partisans, thrusting up from their fierce majestic frontier, laughing at the victory of man. They must not cross the River Drava which marked the division of our separate military zones.

This was surely the richest plateau in Europe where men might stretch out their arms and multiply their wealth, and we might find rest from soldiering. Here the grass flowered into butter and the woods exclaimed with birds. Here on the Drava bridge we marked in crooked rolls of dannatt wire the signature of a treaty signed in an hotel lounge. And panic blew the chaff of Europe against this wire, and on the further bank of the Drava there gathered the abandoned implements of Nazi power. I am speaking of men and women. I am telling you about the cud of war.

And some cast their bodies into the churning water and swam to the West, away from the figures of speech imitated in the moving coil of a headphone and the curses of officers crazed with fear. And after a thousand separate reflexes of physical anguish, their bodies swelled the load of sand and brushwood, and were swept down to the Danube valley where the Red Army camped among its memories of the black Ukraine.

A man crawled up the wooden planking of the bridge and faced us through the wire. He spoke to us in Greek or German or Croat, but the words we heard were the soft welling of blood from the wounds in his chest and the silent footsteps of annihilation in his eyes.

The partisans thrust up the bridge, affirming victory with striding oaths, knocking the oaken scaffold with their conquering boots. How could we understand the sacred anger of these ragged men?

We stood in the resignation of our uniform, pointing hostility at them with our levelled arms, listening to the wounds of the man at our feet.

'He is our prisoner,' said the partisans. 'Why do you

threaten us? We will take him back with us to the East bank of the Drava River.'

'He is wounded,' we said. 'We will send the man to hospital.'

'He is a Fascist. He is an officer of the Ustasha.'

'He is dying. He is an orphaned son.'

'He is a target for our justice. He is vermin. He is a stain on the history of man.'

'He is a son of woman.'

'He is a Fascist, condemned by his own men, the men he whipped to jagged Montenegro and the battlefields of the Ukraine. Pah! He is not worth this spit I toss into the yellow Drava.'

'And his men?'

'They are peasants, the chaff of history. We will make them into citizens.'

'And this man?'

'This is no longer a man. He has spent his human rights.'

'He is wounded,' we said. 'The war is over.'

'The victory is beginning,' they said. 'This is a day for killing Fascists. This is a day for laughter, my friends.'

Twelve standing oarsmen thrust us upstream, against the weight of glaciers at the river's source. On either side of our scaffolding collapsed the lawns of germinating bread, and the green abundance of cultivated earth. None of us knew who had built the bridge, nor had any of us been born in this pocket of land. None of us had chosen to come to this place, nor to leave our homes in Durham or Belgrade. Around us we felt the watching peace of the land, and overhanging us we knew the dome of time.

We did not know the name of the wounded man and you will never find his grave. We did not know what chance of character, and influence of upbringing and thrust of history had fused to lay him at our feet. He lay between us, marking the frontiers of our allied faiths. It might be said that he was an officer of the Ustasha, remembering a past of crimes; or that he was the son thrown of a mother, aching to achieve the promise in his seed; or a wounded body, an instant of

pain studding eternity; or a fraction of consciousness, laid
on the wooden planks of the Drava Bridge, reflecting in the
terms of his spirit the yellow water and the rich crust of a
planet and the over-arching sky.

And so we debated whether this receptive lens of life
should be shattered on the Drava Bridge or whether it should
watch over the passing of another twenty years. And the
issues that we argued were man-made issues, the colours of
our uniforms and the signature of a treaty, scrawled across a
bridge in dannatt wire; but interwoven with our words was
the curse of twenty centuries of war.

'He is a Fascist,' said the ragged peasants. 'He will breed
more vermin in the world.'

'He is a wounded man,' we said.

'He lies on our side of the wire,' they said. 'He is our
prisoner and a target for our justice.'

Against the timeless silence of the valley, underlined by the
inconspicuous loquacity of a thousand tributary waterfalls,
we heard the rifle-shots of momentary anger. We knew that
somehow a life had been cast out, by the mechanics of a
tube of steel. The Drava clutched the body in its strong
peasant fingers, and thrust it down to the Red Army and the
Danube plain. And we who had come from Durham and
Mile End saw only the pity of it and our own mortality.
For we had not yet learnt the imperative of human anger,
extinguishing the indignity of war; nor could we share the
creative hatred of the people of Europe, cultivating the
future like the wheatlands of the Drava, and killing weeds
like men.

MR ATTLEE AND THE GADARENE SWINE*

Dr Kenneth Morgan's book is entitled *Labour in Power, 1945-51* but it could more properly be called the Labour *Government* and, for extensive sections, simply the Labour *Cabinet*. The account which is offered is derived largely from Cabinet, Treasury and other Ministry papers, seasoned with some reference to private accounts (published and unpublished), such as little malicious asides from Hugh Dalton's diaries.

As a result the definition of the historical questions is overwhelmingly 'official': that is, problems are seen from within the perceptions of the small governing group and of the civil servants who served—or in some cases ran—the Ministers. This is a necessary exercise and Kenneth Morgan's book will be useful, for purposes of reference, to all modern historians. Especially in the book's second half Morgan brings to light important new evidence as to the reasons why Attlee's government, in the final two years, entered into doldrums and decline until waterlogged with an impossibly-ambitious rearmament programme imposed upon it by the United States, it sank in full view of the electorate with the loss of all hands. The only survivors were Aneurin Bevan, Harold Wilson and John Freeman who had taken to the lifeboat of resignation a few months before.

One problem of writing history from sources limited to the perceptions of the governors is that it assumes as a given

* *Guardian*, March 3rd, 1984, reviewing Kenneth O. Morgan, *Labour in Power, 1945-51* (Clarendon Press, Oxford, 1984).

239

exactly those historical problems which it should be our business to define and to explore. We are immersed at once in the day-to-day decision-making process—the memoranda arriving on ministerial desks, the emergencies crashing through the Cabinet door—until it appears that events took place, or policies were formed, in simple surrender to the pressure of established facts.

Yet if we were to redefine the theme, not as the Labour Government, but as Labour Britain in these years, then there are certain analytic problems which Morgan's book scarcely addresses. Three questions which I would define—and I am writing this not as a professional historian but simply as a politically-conscious citizen who lived through those years—would be the profound symbolic importance of Labour's victory in 1945 in registering a shift in political and class relations: the tenacious loyalism of Labour's popular support over the next six years, which must be examined in its sociological dimensions: and (in contradiction) the acute spiritual and political malaise which had struck a chill into Labour's heart by 1948, which was already freezing up the currents of voluntary activism and reducing its socialist aspiration and intelligence to ice.

The election of 1945 registered shifts in political con-sciousness which had been going on in the previous five years. I would estimate myself that the highest tide-mark of this swelling radical consciousness was in 1944: it had already peaked before the election took place. There had been startling premonitions in by-elections, where radical candidates who challenged the electoral 'truce' swept back in safe Conservative seats: Common Wealth in Skipton and in Chelmsford, Tom Driberg as an Independent in Maldon.

While Labour was the main beneficiary of this radical shift in the 1945 general election, there were other and perhaps more 'freakish' results which suggested not plain 'Labourism' but a leftish volatility. Tom Wintringham, a former commander of the British battalion of the Inter-national Brigade in Spain, polled over 14,000 votes for Common Wealth in (of all places) Aldershot. (Admittedly, Labour stood down in his favour.) Over 100,000 votes were distributed between 21 Communist candidates, with two MPs returned, and surprising results, such as 10,058 votes for the Communist candidate (as against 12,015 for Labour) in Hornsey. When the other parties, in piety to the wartime Prime Minister, neglected to oppose him in Woodford, an unknown Northants farmer, Mr Hancock, stepped in on the eve of poll and took off over 10,000 votes.

Dr Morgan has no space to discuss such psephological marginalia. Yet they are relevant to the understanding of the background of national political consciousness which also was to fix the limits of the politically possible. From 1945 onwards it simply was not 'on', in political terms, to return in government to the class arrogance of the Tory squire or of the Liberal mill-owner. When Conservatism returned to power, in 1951, it had perforce tamed its arrogance, democratised its style—and also had had to sit on Sir Winston Churchill's head.

A great deal of political life takes place in the theatre of symbolism. That symbolic victory—and one, moreover, underscored by the Service vote—perceptibly altered social relations in the whole country. Bankers and shareholders, property-owners, newspaper magnates, industrial employers— all were on the defensive and were minding their manners in a quite uncustomary way for a long while. Only behind their walls of secrecy were the senior civil servants able to vent their alarm and to plot how to circumvent the electorate. Orme Sargent, shortly to become head of the Foreign Office, saw the election results as presaging 'a Communist avalanche over Europe, a weak foreign policy, a private revolution at home and the reduction of England to a 2nd-class power.'

The support of an alert and expectant political consciousness in the country made it easy for Labour to govern. There were, of course, hair-raising difficulties of material shortages, stricter rationing, indebtedness and sterling outflow—some of them, as Dr Morgan documents, exacerbated by the hostility of American financiers and statesmen towards 'Socialist' Britain. But for year after year Labour's supporters in the country were ready to put up with almost anything—bread queues, labour direction, the use of troops in industrial disputes, top-heavy bureaucratic forms of nationalisation.

Dr Morgan emphasises this Labour loyalism, but he tends to see it in parliamentary terms—the ease with which Attlee's government silenced or headed off back-bench rebellion or expelled any heretics. The dimension which he leaves out of account is the sociological roots of Labourism in the country and especially in local government. For it was in the country —and away from Westminster—that the symbolic shift in the terms of class power had been registered most effectively. Labour, which had advanced its position on a multitude of wartime committees, now emphatically consolidated its local and regional positions: on boards of school governors, hospital management boards, on the magistrate's bench, even on Watch Committees, and in the intricate networking of local authority and on the workshop floor and in industrial committees.

Labour had become a national presence and in many urban authorities and some counties a governing presence: and in Durham, South Wales or West Yorkshire there was visible evidence of this, in schools, hospitals and new housing going up which were no longer tainted by charity or the Poor Law but were fit for self-respecting citizens. It was this self-assertion of the rights and prestige of working people which made the disciplining of parliamentary rebels (especially intellectual rebels with outlandish names like Zilliacus) a simple matter. 'Zilly', expelled from the Labour Party for successive revolts on foreign policy, found it hopeless to try and regain his seat in the 1950 election in the face of the Labour machine. His constituency was Gateshead, and he was defeated by a Labour loyalism which could see the new houses and the schools, and which had gained from their 'own' government not so much an improved standard of living as an unprecedented standard of human respect.

But—my third point—the case of 'Zilly' directs us to the profound spiritual malaise which was striking a chill into the heart of Labour throughout these years. The chill came directly from the onset of the Cold War, and in some of its episodes from events far beyond Labour's control. Yet Labour's leading Ministers were active—and, in the case of

Ernest Bevin, eager—accomplices in these developments. Sir Alexander Cadogan, the head of the Foreign Office, noted in his diary on 10 August 1945 that Bevin had 'sound ideas which we must encourage'. But Bevin did not stand in need of the Foreign Office's patronage. A zealous ideologically-motivated anti-Communist already, this able, forceful, and philistine bully (who for some reason Oxford scholars have decided was a 'genius' or—as Dr Morgan has it—a 'transcendant, creative force') was perhaps the leading actor on the Western side in that foul interactive process which led to the Cold War, at least until the moment early in 1947 when Britain (for financial reasons only) suddenly withdrew her forces from Greece. At that point the torch was handed on to the United States, and was accepted by President Truman in a Declaration which claimed American interest in Greece and Turkey, in the 'enduring struggle' against godless Communism—a claim subsequently extended to the Middle East and (by President Carter) to the Persian Gulf.

Dr Morgan's book provides important evidence as to the early stages of this Gadarene progress, with Ernest Bevin cast as Dr Grunter. Bevin had archaic imperialist impulses which out-Churchilled Churchill. Publicly he dissociated himself from Churchill's Fulton Speech but privately he viewed it with 'grim satisfaction'. As the years go by the chorus of the grunting Gadarene swine becomes more vociferous. Morgan clearly shows the Atlanticist political consequences of the Marshall Plan, consequences foreseen and intended by Ernest Bevin. He confirms the role of Bevin as an architect of NATO, and also as a member of the secret Cabinet committee (GEN 163) which (unknown to the rest of the Cabinet) took the fateful decision to manufacture British nuclear weapons.

But the Gadarene stampede only accelerated after Bevin's death. It was in Attlee's disastrous second government (1950-1) that Britain instantly committed forces in Korea. The famous episode of Attlee's flight to Washington to dissuade Truman not to use the atomic bomb turns out to be a murky episode with poison in its tail. Whatever reassurance Attlee received on the bomb (and Morgan leaves that matter unclear) was bought at the cost of a British pledge to almost double 'defence' expenditure (from £3,600m to £6,000m) and also of British assent to German rearmament. That is why the Labour government, waterlogged to the gunwales and with its crew fighting each other, sank in sight of the electoral coast.

Dr Morgan shows us all this, but his reverence for political 'realism' leads him always to downplay motives of political principle. Everything happened as it did because the British economy was drifting onto the rocks and Attlee had to satisfy his American paymasters. His judgements are made off-stage and arrive in the text without supporting evidence. It is all done by adjectives. Attlee, Bevin and Morrison 'represented a matchless combination of experience'. Oh? What experience did Bevin have in foreign affairs? Morgan Phillips, the manipulative *apparatchik* who ran Transport House, is presented as 'authoritative', 'urbane and resourceful'. By contrast critics on the back-benches are described as 'garrulous and difficult' or (Zilliacus again) 'rebellious and generally tiresome'.

That is too easy a way to write history. Moreover it is to misunderstand the political consciousness of the time. Morgan suggests that international issues played no part in the 1945 election. That may be how it appears in top level sources but it was not how it was felt in the country. As a soldier just returned from overseas service I had a walk-on part at several Labour election meetings in rural Buckinghamshire. Packed meetings of suddenly undeferential villagers applauded every expression of hope for a socialist Europe and every reference to the heroism of the European Resistance movements or the feats of the Red Army (which everyone knew had saved what small ration was left of British bacon). In nearly forty years my only similar experience of such a widely-aroused popular concern with international issues—with similar earnest meetings in small market towns—has been in the peace movement of our own time.

This fervent hope for democratic 'popular front' socialist revolutions in East and West Europe was voiced (and applauded) at the Labour Conference of 1945 by a young delegate, Denis Healey. The blighting of these hopes brought chilling consequences not only to Labour but also to general popular consciousness. The chill extended into the stagnant political thought of the time, and thence into the arts and scholarship. The Cold War led the nation into a waste land of the spirit. It led the Labour movement into a weary epoch of manipulative in-fighting—the suffocation of block-vote rule, the disciplinary expulsions and proscriptions of Transport House, the counter-manipulation of Communists in pockets like the ETU. This destroyed any socialist vision, dragooned people into flocks of Atlanticist sheep or pro-Soviet goats, and blocked off any 'third way'.

I will take, once again, Konni Zilliacus as illustrative of this. Morgan describes Zilly in the sloppy terms of today's media lampoons as 'a fellow-travelling Marxist'. That he never was. Zilly was a former secretary to Arthur Henderson and he had been for 18 years a member of the Secretariat of the League of Nations. Zilly, with his large untidy boots, his podgy hands fluttering with notes, his pockets stuffed with *Hansards* (of his own speeches), was a hopelessly unpractical politician, a caricature of an unworldly intellectual set up to be hammered by the chauvinist Labour machine and to be driven out of Gateshead by those electors who felt he threatened Labour's new presence and 'our own government'.

But what Zilly was was an expert, deeply informed on all European affairs (and hence a threat to Foreign Office mandarins like Cadogan and Sargent) and also a man with an indomitable vision of a possible democratic and socialist 'third way'. (For this sin he was denounced, in one of the Stalinist faked trials in East Europe, as an Anglo-American imperialist intelligence agent.) Kenneth Morgan should learn to restrain his dismissive adjectives. For historians should know that the lost causes of 40 years ago have a way of returning as the necessary causes of today. This is the case with the 'third way'—the way for which the European peace movements are now searching—and Zilly has more to say to our times than has Ernest Bevin.

Attlee's first government had two major achievements. It brought into being the Health Service and an attendant

structure of welfare, allowances and insurance. And it registered the independence of India without an Indo-Chinese or
Algerian bloodbath. Dr Morgan supposes that the second
achievement was entirely the work of Clement Attlee, whom
he calls 'an old India hand' (whatever that means). His misunderstandings about India (and about the character of the
India Lobby in Britain) are so large that I cannot hope to
set him right. Let it suffice to say that, in this case, Attlee
recognised the limits of the possible. These limits were set by
the massive presence of the Indian people, but also (in a less
degree) by the impatience of British servicemen to be de-
mobilised and by the education of the British public by
decades of work by an India Lobby from which most of
Labour's 'matchless' leaders had been absent. By January
1947 General Wavell was urging a 'military evacuation' from
India as 'from hostile territory'. It was not 'on' to try to hold
India, either in military terms or in terms of British public
opinion, although (Great God!) if evacuation had been
delayed two years, until the formation of NATO, no doubt
it would have been attempted.

But Attlee, in his quiet way, perceived the limits of the
possible. His choice of Lord Mountbatten as the last Viceroy
was skilful. He extracted the Raj at the last possible moment
from India with dignity, and initiated (with the help of
Creech Jones) the process of decolonisation in Burma and
Ceylon also. And for this he and his Labour Government
deserve credit.

They deserve credit also for the Health Service. And
Aneurin Bevan deserves it most of all. He emerges well from
Morgan's book—neither a consistent nor a skilful politician,
but a man who stuck tenaciously to his post at Health,
immersed himself in constructive detail, fought every inch of
the way for resources wrested from a weak economy, and
founded the Service upon authentic socialist principles: a
free service and 'to each according to his needs'—the principles
upon which he resigned. And only just in time. For *H.M.S.
Gadarene* was then sinking below the Cold War seas which
now surround us on every side.

THE PLACE CALLED CHOICE

i

Crime and compassion, then, statistics, ecstacy,
Struck like a match from chaos. It's all an accident:
This town beneath me meaning no more than stonecrop,
Lichen of banks and offices: fungus on a stone wall,
Spawning into the night a pretty stitchwork of lights
Like swarming midget spiders, bringing someone money.
Widows and acrobats, clowns, suicides:
It's all in the luck of the draw. Man makes what he can get.
The kids play at bandits. Blood issues on the speedway.
The gunmen point from the hoardings, indicating manhood:
Virility slouching in a soft hat and an oil-stained raincoat,
Getting girls at a bargain, going loaded to the cash-tills,
Educating the young in the ethics of business.
The weak get cracked like grapeseed, chewed into digits.
On the corner by the Palace
Without malice or logic
Death waits in a slumped indifferent posture,
Sticking his knuckles in the eyes of all comers.

The applewood is black, bearing fruit at the back of mills.
At Manchester you can find a forgotten half-acre of grave-
    stones,
The grey light blocked by the utilitarian chapel,
The Mechanics Institute, the condemned back-to-back
    terraces.
Soot settles on the cemetery, assuaging its chemical hunger,

Adjusting the stone accounts, writing off our grandparents'
losses.
A good plot lost to the dairyman, the jerry-builder, now to
all memory
Except of the local antiquarian, muffled in Sunday's habit,
Pacing between tilted crosses, tracing some local worthy:
Or once in a leap-year some American returning
To hunt up his ancestors, hoots into the dark passage-way,
Enters the wrought-iron creaking gates. Rain on the head-
stones
Where Jones the Chartist is buried.

                                          Wind crosses the marshes
Fowey, the Cinque Ports, a sand-bar across an estuary:
Silt, mudflats, wormcasts, black posts, rushes, saltings,
Nets rotting in a brackish inlet, a Viking war-way:
The neglected sea-groyne, cork-floats, tar, corrupting bladder-
wrack.
The scavenging gull and the shag lime the clipper's keel
Where picnic-makers throw refuse, sucked half under in sand.

Or buried in a bookshop in an unfrequented quarter—
Bristol, perhaps, or Nottingham—the stack marked down to
sixpence,
The dust rarely disturbed: Cobbett's paper, yellow at the
edges;
The *New Moral World; the Black Dwarf;* Cooper; Bradlaugh.
A find for some collector, more stuffing for a thesis.
Or in the reference library, entombed in the white card-
index,
Paine's *Rights of Man* which once in some high Pennine
valley
The weaver at his handloom, straining by rushlight, read.

Wind crosses the moors. The valley of the last wolf.
Old iron workings. Micre. Quartz. The monotonous peatbog—
Black roots, ling, harebell, the wet relics of a forest.
The gutted stannary. Scrub oak on the old encampment,
Brambles and st-john's-wort. Among the chalk-bits and

pellets,
The droppings of rabbits, a shred of pottery, a flint, a coin.

Or with more grace at Burford, integral with Cotswold stone,
Entering the ceremony of cottages, sweet william and crown
    imperial,
Buried among neighbours and labourers, the Leveller
    corporals.
Riding by night the Roundheads forded the river—
Fifty miles since dawn, Fairfax and Cromwell—
Rested in water-meadows among frog-cup and loddon lily:
Found them and rode them down, their doublets still un-
    belted,
Drowsy at midnight, damp cramping their hips, fatigue
Of freedom's parturition, of a hidden understanding
Nudging their dreams. Damage of horses
Sundering the darkness—sudden clamour of orders—
Tinder-boxes—odour of burned powder, garlic.
Then on the leads time enough for meditation.
Later, in the churchyard—
The round-dance come to an end, the children hailed in-
    doors—
Hard determination was needed for that death in full day-
    light,
Looking at the muskets marking their target,
The soldiers torn in their duty. . . .

                              Wind crosses the cities,
Driving the rain under doors, sweeping the housing estates,
Kicking with ten-league boots at the evening racing special,
The pools slip, the Woodbine carton, the plain cover for
    contraceptives,
Clapping the corrugated sheets on the roof of the garage,
Sluicing the wrecker's yard, the back-axles, the sodden
    cardboard:
Rusted nails, brake-linings, tyres, half-bricks, oddments.

—And now squats in the knotted core of this town
Among the keening smokestacks, the megalithic condensers,

The engines shunting in the yards, the dark bulk
And lighted swarm of the mills. And the wide-eyed child
Listens to the wail in the guttering, watches the street-lamp
Spill and people the walls with shadows, guardsmen, bandits:
The cocked stance of the gunman, the slouched shape on the
    corner—
Sensing enemies as human—the spy and the hunched-backed
    miser—
Never thinking for a moment of the wind at the door, the
    wolf. . .

Wind that is geological time, eraser of familiar landmarks,
Opposing the gait and strike of strata, scouring the faults:
Incessant commentator, stalking the peaks and hursts,
Scanning the smoke of valleys and the straddled cities. . . .
                               Across the alluvial gravel,
Over the Swanscombe skull, crunched among ammonites and
    shells:
Over the tiny crustacea, the bric-a-brac of chalk—
First cousins to our father
Who lies crouched in the abandoned road of memory
Clutching in his stone fist a charm against the centuries:
Trawling the turfs of Fosberry with a net of shadows,
Vaulting the Countless Stones, the barrows, the temple to
    Mithras,
Bursting the hinges of Stonehenge and entering on Halifax,
Howling in the eyeteeth of a boar, through the saurian's
    crutch:
Harrowing our bones now and whatever bones went before
    us:
Wind, crossing peaty headlands,
Crying in pylons,
Questioning the conscience of this island,
Stuck like a white fishbone in the chops of the Atlantic—

                                 If you had suffered
In your own person the pain of the spine's erection:
The brain stretching within the skull, ache of the widening
    eyes:

Pressed south by that tonnage of ice, had your white hide
Sliced into blood by the sabre of the biting tiger,
And now, stooping to put out the bottles on your doorstep,
Or dropping the sports page for a moment to stir the fire,
Suddenly heard that question in the whorl of your ear—
The wash of the sea in the shell, the wet acres, the wind. . .

Would you recall for a moment your figure on the earthwork,
Sweating in brown firelight, hacking with shaped antlers,
Throwing up a wall against tall oncoming strangers:
And the late watch on the dyke while the infernal nightjar
Kept scarring the silence and startling the sentries:
That night on the Sangro
Waiting with corked face and vine-leaves in your helmet
For the canvas boat to be launched among hanging flares?

                              Would you pause and consider
Whether anything was lacking, whether all was in order,
Or some important engagement might have slipped your
        memory—
Some dues outstanding to a half-remembered union?
Sensing within that interthreading of workshops,
In the intricate by-ways and slips between the Palace,
The speedway, the Lyric, and the accountant's offices
Some human bond more strict than the bonds of money,
Warmer, it may be supposed, but more exacting?

England in the grip of suave, competent killers;
Her will weakened by an ethic of money-spiders
And all the cant and claptrap of a vicious individualism,
Masking the lurking coshboys, the slouching gunmen,
Letting in the agents of the ancient antagonist.
Sand silts the narrow roads,
Making obsolete the heroic charts, the old markers of feeling.
The couch-grass and the plantain obscure the white land-
        marks
Of a culture down on its luck, of a nation of hawkers.
The wind knocks for an entry, the waste encroaches,
And on the Pennine uplands

The Chartists march no more with their pikes and torches.

England, buried somewhere under bricks, oddments, worn
    tyres:
Under the shady transactions clinched in the flashy road-
    house:
Buried with Arnald and Lockyer: with Holberry: with Linell:
With the charred bodies of the pieceners scorched in the
    weaving-shed:
With the victims of anthrax: in the back courtyards of
    Bradford
Where the applewood is black, bearing fruit by the oldest
    mills:
Stupified in the smoke of Sheffield, sullen in Derbyshire,
Raking up old grievances and grousing in East London—
Recall the old challenge
Which each generation has no choice but to master:
Flint, bronze, and iron, and the human union—

Or you, on your doorstep,
Turning back to mumble your private solutions,
You will not avoid the slumped figure on the corner:
On the moors of space from the tree of your skeleton
Noosed in your timid and unrealised existence
You will swing in the winds of your death for ever.

ii

The night was full of heaving, matter in labour,
Sucking the vacuum in, expelling at last
With anxious love the tiny identical spawn:
Then vegetables with feelers, climbing toadstools,
Long-haired arachnids, egg-laying creatures
The size of a bank. Beneath the accountant's office
We found the tusks and gills, the horny clashing scales,
And reconstructed the slope and swarm of its carriage—
The brain in the base of the tail and the skull like a teacup.
This was next morning. But that night
At every window was the breath of clawed beasts.

At dawn the noise diminished. Give thanks for that.
We did give thanks, with thirty children's blood,
And their bright heads when dried might keep the demons
    out.
Two men must carry the carved bug of emerald
Which brought our crops fruition, with due sacrifice.
The first light shamed the creatures to the woods,
But still we could see little through the mist
Except for those stone images with beaks
And the terrible ten-armed and helmeted gods.

At nine the Greeks went out, helmeted and cruel.
They came back cruel and helmeted, but radiant.
The place (they said) was good. More sacrifice.
And so, shortly before ten, the man of business
Issued out from the house to set the place in order.

A lot needed attention. Those heathen idols
Were quite unsuited to a man with his professions.
The carved bug went, the cannon did much more.
He created from his rib a well-organised god
With regular office-hours and remarkable files.
It was quite safe to go out now. At half-past ten
The maid banged the gong and we gathered in the drawing-
    room.
We held a brief service of prayer and thanksgiving.

We had all got around the table for elevenses
When—quite suddenly—matter opened its jaws and retched,
Fetching up a great belch in the shape of a mushroom
With curly rootstrings of fire eye-sockets pus
Ricestraw red with abortions cots full of scabs.

Nothing quite so big as this had happened before.
The doorstep was crowded. The distress was painful.
The headline blew its nose and shuffled uneasily.
The concepts of dignity coughed in their hands discreetly.
The treatise on ethics cried 'ah love oh pity'
And went up to bed. The well-adjusted god

Came down in person, flatulent with forgiveness.
For minutes afterwards the sermons were in mourning.

But no-one had done it. The alibis were perfect.
All were indoors—no-one had left the house.
Some suspicion, it is true, fell upon the scientist
Who was rumoured to keep something secret in his lab,
But those who had seen it said the story was nonsense:
He kept it as a pet. The bug was innocent.

The matter stood there. The issue was undecided.
It was not my line of business. I went back to my room.
But I felt, somehow, uneasy. I kept looking at the clock. . .
At five to twelve there broke in at my door
That sandalled runner wet from Marathon,
Leaping the alluvial gravel, skirting the chalk-pit,
Fording the centuries, fresh-scarred from Stalingrad,
Shaking me by the pulse, crying to wake the house:
'Stand to your life! About you, brother, look!'

I looked and the ethics crawled beneath the skirting:
The concepts fell apart and swarmed with gaols:
The emerald headlines bulged with sacrificial blood.
The statesmen wore bright heads to keep the fiend at bay.
Not once or twice only, but everywhere I looked
The putrescence of ideology suppurating its pious pus.

Defilement of life! From each denial,
From the timid evasions and privacies of the good,
From the saurian's crutch, the successful man of business,
The pointed tool of the gunman,
From the lusting speedway, from each sale to the bank
Of the bonds of human choice, there issues this spawn,
Swarming the yard of the world like midget spiders,
Spawn of that fungus settling on every city,
On the walls, the cathedrals, climbing the keening smoke-
    stacks,
Drifting on every sill, waiting there to germinate:
To fetch our house up in one belch.

Already the windows are shut, the children hailed indoors.
We wait together in the unnatural darkness
While that god forms outside in the shape of a mushroom
With vast blood-wrinkled spoor on the windswept snow.

And now it leans over us, misting the panes with its breath,
Sucking our house back into vacuous matter,
Helmeted and beaked, clashing its great scales,
Claws scratching on the slates, looking in with bleak stone
    eyes.

iii
a
What should a poet say?
Poet, a pretty thing,
Philatelist of words,
Playing with sets of rhyme,
Sticking in kings and birds,

Sensing behind the wall
And the technicolour murals
The silverfishes crawl
Nests of digits mate,
Throughout the state
A stench of blocked morals
And at the top of all
The wittol and the stall?

Say first we stand upon
A tributary star,
Issue of chaos, one
In a swarming universe.
Say next that life began
As accidental spawn
Of some atomic war
Within the changing sun.
And last declare that man
(All changing matter alone)

Grew taller than his nurse—
Air, water, stone—
Arose and challenged change,
Chaining the atoms down

But found within his soul
A civil war begun
And felt within his heart
The seeds of fission spawn
Till matter broke apart
Flaming from pole to pole
The star fell in the sun

And while the poet sat
Turning the album of time
Sticking in this and that
To make a set of rhyme
Swarming chaos took
The poet and his book.

                    b.
We are each way defined—
We stand on the crust of a star
Turning about a coal,
Eternity's wind behind
Infinity's moors before.
Man is what he has made,
Carving himself a soul
With bone and cutting blade.
The flint and teaching spade
Revealing what we are.
From each encounter with matter
Man and his needs have grown:
Air, stone, and water
Thought to limit his needs,
But out of the water came wisdom
And song came out of the stone.
First of all I declare

That man is changed by his deeds,
And all within his kingdom
Is stone, water, air

Transformed into a fire
Lighting the moors and blown
By every tempest higher
Until air, water, and stone
In the furnace of the mind
Are changed into desire
And all things are defined.

c.
I stand upon this hurst
Above the straddled town,
Considering water and air
And fire at the core of stone,
Calling to mind the first
Flint arrowhead, shaped antler—
Clumsily fashioned stuff
To master wolf or bear,
And yet it was matter enough
To make man come aware
Of desire and knowledge, vast
As the megalithic altar
Cast from the stuff of his thought:
I stand amazed at the past—
All flint, bone, have taught:
Considering how the steel,
Oil and teaching steam
Reveal unknown desires,
New ways to act and feel—
The fractured atoms seem
In their creating fires
Already to meet and plan
A megalithic man.

It's time to speak one's mind.
I'm sick of an 'anxious age'.
I am fed to the teeth with the cant
Of 'guilt' and original sin.
From all the fires that raged
In England's youth I find
A grocer's timid candle
Is all that is left behind:
And life being unassuaged
By the fuel of cant and cash
Consumes us in the flames
Of unfulfilled desire
Down to sarcastic ash
And threatens to disown
Fire with terrible fire,
Air, water, and stone
Resume what was their own.

Whatever evil there is
I declare was first let in
By timid men with candles
And abstract talk of sin.
Man is what he has made,
Chipping bone with bone,
Shaping the teaching spade:
Urged by his human needs
Changes the world, and then
Transfigured by his deeds,
Changes necessity,
Becoming whole and free.

I stand upon the earth
And watch the hursts of space,
And at last I raise my voice
In the teeth of the swarming wind:
I declare that man has choice
Discovered in that place
Of human action where
Necessity meets desire,

And moors and questioning wind,
Water, stone, and air,
Transfigured in the soul,
Can be changed to human fire
Which man, becoming whole,
Will order and control.

iv.

Crime and compassion, then, statistics, ecstacy,
But mostly crime. At first the fat Cistercians
Engrossing the farms with love. Rascals like Hawkins,
Their sloops steaming with slaves, trading in bibles—
But valiant men in their way, men to encounter the wind.
Then Cromwell with his chaplain, slaying at Burford
Buff-coated passion, was still a fit antagonist,
Swearing by Property and Christ, an honest hypocrite.

Next came the jolly vicar with his sensitive daughters.
The weavers starved in their looms. Silicosis, anthrax:
The hunch-backed children, the pieceners charred in the
    mills:
Black mud and standing water, the craters of Passchendaele,
Men making good with guns. And all those accidents
Fetched up by benevolent progress. Last, that race
Of well-adjusted masters, victims of every wind,
The bloody spoor in the snow, the monster of stone.

Standing above the lamplit town I watch this crime,
Cruel and beaked, crushing all comprehension,
Killing whole streets of men, sticking his horny knuckles
In the eyes of whoever comes. Man, who is changed by his
    hands,
Evolved the man of business, within whose mind
The clawed beast of possession gnawed all bonds until
Man fell apart, and split from self to self,
The acquisitive brain cutting off the creative hands.

Now crime, compassion, have reached the place called choice.
I hear at last the voice of resolution, loud
From the flagstones and setts, the commons engrossed for
   sheep,
From the mullioned windows, the lighted bulk of the mills,
And the living killed in their streets. In the frost-blue flames
Of the handloom weaver's rushlight the heroic shadows leap:
Mellor at Cartwright's mill: Jones on the hustings: names
That merge with anonymous shadows, shaping that man who
   crowds

Every room of the human house, opens the windows, stands
Warming the winds of space at his compassionate hands.

Halifax, October–December 1950

HOMAGES

REMEMBERING C. WRIGHT MILLS*

Wright Mills had few disciples. He didn't ask for intellectual allegiance, nor did he respect those who offered it too readily. His work provoked a critical admiration. We had come to assume his presence—definitions, provocations, exhortations—as a fixed point in the intellectual night-sky. His star stood above the ideological no-man's land between the orthodox emplacements of West and East, flashing urgent humanist messages. If we couldn't always follow it, we always stopped to take bearings.

Mills would have wished his work to be judged within its proper historical context. He would most readily have assented to Blake's warning: 'The man who never alters his opinion is like standing water, and breeds reptiles of the mind.'

In his last years, the stagnant postures of some of his contemporaries called forth his most caustic polemic—those former liberals (but practising conformists) who celebrated institutional devices which had long been rendered irrelevant by changing realities of power: or the 'futilitarians' of the disenchanted Left, so transfixed by their horror of Communism that they were unable, in 1956, to see new human realities struggling within the old doctrinal and institutional forms.

---

* An early version of this appeared in *Peace News*, 22 and 29 November 1963; reviewing C. Wright Mills, *Power, Politics and People* (essays edited by Irving L. Horowitz). Also *Radical America*, July-August 1979.

As life changed, so his own thought changed. We live (he wrote in 1952) in 'a time of irresponsibility, organized and unorganized; when common sense, anchored in fast-outmoded experience has become myopic and irrelevant. Nobody feels secure in a simple place; nobody feels secure and there is no simple place.' To think was to grasp at a reality which changed even at the moment of apprehension.

There were three phases in Mills' intellectual life: an apprenticeship in sociological method and theory; an intensive period of empirical research; 'and third, an effort at combining these interests into a workable style of sociological reflection' (Irving Horowitz). The first phase coincides with the early years of the war. The second, which took him through his studies of trade unionism and the white collar workers to *The Power Elite*, was completed in 1955. The final phase carries us from 1956 to 1962.

These dates have more than a biographical significance. The second phase is that of deepening Cold War, Stalinism at its zenith, and McCarthyism at home. Mills had, perhaps fortunately, been born too late to sink any of his moral capital in the Thirties. He had no intellectual allegiance to the Communist tradition, nor (despite the attempt to affix to him the label, 'Texan Trotskyist') did he feel happy with the obsessional anti-Communism commonly found in American Trotskyist circles.

The McCarthy assault passed him by. And there were fellow-radicals in the States who felt that Mills had ducked under it. I suspect that there was a sense in which Mills felt that the McCarthy battle was off-centre, a distraction. While the mindless ideologues of the American Right jammed the media with their virulent witch-hunting, the real men of power were consolidating their positions in the background, scarcely noticed or criticised by the American Left, which had been thrown into defensive postures or which (still worse) had disappeared in recriminations and self-exculpations.

Civil liberties were to Mills of prime importance. But their importance was to be found, not in their celebration, but in their use. He was also (I suspect) in this phase more of a Texan, more of a political isolationist, than one might

suppose. He saw no place within the international configuration which afforded room for an affirmative stance.
If he had no illusions about Stalinism, he was greatly dis-
couraged also by the post-war record of West European
social-democracy. Hence the implicit pessimism of his out-
look in the early fifties. But hence also his choice of thematic
material. If there were no easy affirmative banners to pick up,
then the intellectual workman must return to his first obedience—to discover and report the truth within his own field
of vision. Temporary disengagement might prepare the way
for a more well-mounted commitment. *The Power Elite* was
among the most substantial counter-blows which Mc-
Carthyism received.

In 1955 and 1956 biography and history came together.
One might suggest that the logic of Mills' work pointed in a
different direction to the one which he chose to take (or
which, perhaps, the context chose *for* him). His early conceptual studies enriched by the empirical research of the
second phase equipped him to return to the work of conceptual analysis at the fullest stretch. He might have succeeded, where so many abstruse claimants have failed, in uniting
in a common theoretical nexus the psychological and
historical dimensions of social analysis, and in developing
those 'theories of society, history, human nature' in which
(he noted in his 'Letter to the New Left' in 1960) we are
still 'weakest'.

I must say plainly that I don't think he achieved this
synthesis. Nor would he have made any such claim. Nor will
it enhance his reputation if the claim is made on his behalf.

He never returned, in his later essays, to a sufficiently high
level of conceptual abstraction to effect such a synthesis.
There is a tension in his writing between the Marxist concept
of 'class', Weber's terminology of 'status', and his own
preferred language of 'structure' and 'elites', which—while
fruitful in descriptive analysis—is never resolved on a
theoretical plane.

There are other loose ends to his thought. The close-up,
contingent sociology of ideas at which he was so expert—
the placing of intellectual workmen within their proper

social milieu, among the pressures of power, employment, esteem—was never spliced into the larger notion of ideological thresholds and ideological drift. His work contains no exacting analysis of Soviet civilisation; the suggestive parallels which he noted between the bureaucratic and militaristic logic of American and Soviet societies were left. . . as suggestions. The splendidly-provocative *The Sociological Imagination* (1959) is the work of an impatient, hurried man. Its critique of the conformist schools of American sociology would have been more telling if he had paused for passages of rigorous conceptual analysis of the kind for which (see his early essays) he was eminently well-equipped.

This is to say that he died far too soon, and left much of his work for others to complete. Horowitz is right to claim that he attained, in his last years, 'a workable style of sociological reflection'. It is a *style*, rather than a comprehensive theory of social process; and it is the style of a responsible and catholic eclectic, playing 'by ear' because the issues were so momentous, the time so short—drawing now upon one, now upon another, of the concepts available in the work of previous sociologists, testing them in practice by their adequacy for the work in hand.

If the world of ideas were autonomous—if even the most abstruse intellectual exercises were not connected by indissoluble organic ties to the world of action—then Mills might have been content in 1956 to return to his academic last. But history overwhelmed his personal biography. He had always been unusual among fellow sociologists in his refusal to assume the largest questions—those of power and social structure. He did not take these things as 'given', and employ himself upon molecular enquiry into this or that fragment of an ongoing social process. He asked those questions which somehow disappear from academic syllabi—why? where is it going? to what purpose? for whose benefit?

The Power Elite disclosed to him the goal towards which (under the celebration of affluence and Growth) one giant civilisation was proceeding at accelerated pace—the cremation of the world. At the centre of power he found, not so much greed or active evil, but emptiness, an emptiness which he

named 'crackpot realism' or 'organised irresponsibility'—
the rational, technologically expert, bureaucratically-intricate
realism of interest and inertia, without a higher will or
directive reason. The compulsive drift towards war was
sustained and justified by a permanent war economy, a
'military metaphysic', according to which all other human
priorities were subordinated to 'a military definition of
reality' and a permanent defensive ideology.

This ideology (he challenged his fellow intellectuals in
the West) was sustained by their 'default'. Stricken by the
disillusions of the thirties and forties, the older generation
projected their own sense of defeat into the future, where
they could see only images of 'sociological horror'. Anti-
Communism in the West served often as the excuse for the
abnegation of all responsibilities, all except peripheral defensive actions. Step by step they had opted for accommoda-
tions with the status quo, private self-immolations; some,
indeed, had become celebrants of the general drift of negation. Among the younger generation he found too many of
the 'young complacents' —men and women who had
surrendered (and without a struggle) their responsibilities
into the hands of the bureaucracies of Government and
business, serving simply as their 'hired men'.

It was not that Mills became 'anti-American', or that he
'sided' with the Communists against the West. It was exactly
this trivial but compulsive vicious-circle of ideology from
which he sought to break free. He was, in an old sense, a
socialist, and he sometimes referred to himself as a 'Wobbly'.
The Wobblies (whose tendency was syndicalist) never fell
into that most dangerous error which supposes that socialist
endeavour achieves some consummation in State Power,
whether 'Workers' or 'People's Democratic' or Fabian-
constitutionalist or however qualified. And Mills' study of
Weber, Sorel, Simmel, Mosca, and Michels had served to
confirm in his mind the wisdom which had come instinctively
to the transport-workers and lumber-jacks of the old IWW.
His notion of socialism entailed the decomposition of state
power.

Thus he was scarcely material for a Communist fellow-traveller, at whatever remove. (These essays are curiously innocent of any considered statement about Communism before the mid-fifties. Perhaps the subject—being, in one way or another, obsessional to so many of his colleagues— simply made him weary.) What excited Mills, and blasted down the inner walls of pessimism, was 1956. Poland, Russia, Hungary—the revisionist ferment among the Communist Parties—it *was* possible for the thing to be shifted, the Monolith could be moved, established power could de- compose. The 'silent enslaved minds' (not Mills' words but Gomulka's) could defy their own conditioning, there were resistances, in life-experience and in minority traditions, which could reply to the centralised propagandist media.

Hence the upsurge of hope—a hope as valid for the Western as for the Communist world. What moved him most deeply was the evidence of intellectuals resuming once again the role of international carriers of disaffection and dissent. As he wrote, in *The Causes of World War III* (1958):

> Western intellectuals should remember with humility, even with shame, that the first significant crack in the cold-war front was not made by those who enjoy the formal freedom of the Western demo- cracies, but by men who run the risk of being shot, imprisoned, driven to become nervous caricatures of human beings. . . Talking in Warsaw and Zagreb and Vienna with some of those who have made the cultural break, I have seen the fingers of such men for two hours at a time continuously breaking up matchsticks on the table before them as they talk of possible new meanings of Marxism, as they try honestly to define the new beginnings in Eastern Europe after the death of Stalin. I have seen the strain and the courage, and now in the inner forum of myself those Poles and Hungarians and Yugoslavs are included. I can no longer write seriously of social and political reality without writing to them as well as to the comfortable and the safe.

But as hope revived within Wright Mills, so it brought with it an enhanced sense of personal responsibility. Before 1956 the great impersonal drift towards war merely deadened the will. 'Most of us,' he had written in 1952, 'now live as specta- tors in a world without political interlude: fear of total permanent war stops our kind of morally oriented politics.

Our spectatorship means that personal, active experience often seems politically useless and even unreal.' After 1956 he felt the critical human predicament with a new poignancy. The devil's finale could be averted. He was astounded by the complacency of those Western intellectuals who met the Communist ferment with an 'I-told-you-so', or who chalked it up as a gain—not to humanity—but to 'the West'. It was their plain duty to move as decisively outside the military and ideological 'metaphysic' of the West as Nagy and Tibor Dery had moved outside that of the East. They must go out to welcome their Eastern colleagues, meeting not in some quasi-official twilight of ideological compromise, but making with them common cause in sharply confronting the twin ideologies of power and mass-manipulation. Together they must fight 'the indifferent professors and smug editors of the overdeveloped societies in the West' and the 'cultural bureaucrats and hacks, the intellectual thugs of the official line. . . in the Soviet bloc'. 'I have feelings of equal contempt for both leading types of underdeveloped cultural workmen of the overdeveloped countries of the world.'

It was at this point that he encountered the Cuban revolution, and through this the needs and gathering ferment of the hungry third of the world. He held the Cuban revolution to be—his friend Ralph Miliband had written—'the best and most decent thing that had ever happened in and to Latin America'. There was much in the Cuba of 1960 to appeal to the Wobbly in Wright Mills: the improvisation, the egalitarian revolutionary tone, the unmanipulated 'self-activity' of the *campasinos*, above all the ideological openness. He encouraged Western intellectuals, of different persuasions, to take up work in Cuba. He even cooked up with Castro a somewhat-bizarre scheme for a 'Seminar on Varieties of Marxism' to which visiting lecturers of the calibre of Deutscher, Lukács, Kolakowski, might be invited, and at which Titoists and Stalinists, Revisionists and Trotskyists, might have face-to-face intellectual encounters.

It was not, of course, the duplicity of Castro or the deep-laid schemes of Khrushchev which hardened this revolution and walled up much of its openness, but, in the first place, the American economic, ideological, and military offensive. Wright Mills saw the Bay of Pigs disaster coming all the way. Privately, yes, he had 'reservations' as to the Fidelists' relations with the Communists, but these were not of a kind which would bring the least comfort to those guilty, in any degree, of any complicity with the siege of Cuba. These— the fair-minded liberals too pure to associate with a 'Hands Off Cuba' committee for fear that they might sit alongside an under-cover Communist, the dogmatists (whether under Trotskyist, pacifist, or radical labels) who smugly prophesied that Cuba would 'go Stalinist' while doing nothing to prevent the State Department from driving her into exactly that logic—he regarded such people as being equally guilty with the men of the Pentagon. 'I am for the Cuban revolution. I do not worry about it. I worry for it and with it.'

He tried, almost physically, to place his body between Florida and the Cuban coast. His *Listen, Yankee* (1960) verges at times on stridency. Analysis and apologetics become confused. But its tone was enforced by the organised hysteria of the great American media—the chain-press, TV, the State Department itself—against which he wrote. These media at last were able to get him within their conventional sights, to hound and lampoon him as a 'Red'. Against medical advice he worked through night after night, during the late autumn of 1960, mastering the history and problems of Latin America, preparing for a nation-wide TV encounter with the State Department expert, A.A. Berle. 'I am bone tired,' he wrote to me at this time:

> I've been running since last February, when I first went to Mexico, then Russia, then Cuba. Too much fast writing, too many decisions of moral and intellectual type, made too fast, on too little evidence. Anybody who is 'non-communist left' today and goes into the hungry nation bloc, he's got one hell of a set of problems. . . Now it looks like I debate A.A. Berle. . . in early December on NBC national TV hook-up (9.30 Sat. night, est. audience 20 million) on 'U.S. policy towards Latin America'. I have to do it: it's my god damned duty, because nobody else will stand up and say shit outloud, but. . . I know little of Latin America and have no help to get me ready for such a thing. But I have to. Then the pressure on me because of Cuba, official and unofficial, is mounting. It is very subtle and very

fascinating. But also worrisome and harrassing. I want to escape to reality, I want to escape to my study, I want 6 months to think and not to have to talk or write. . .

He drove himself, through late October and November, beyond the limits of his strong physique. A few days before the debate he collapsed with a grave heart-attack. Although he recovered sufficiently in the summer of 1961 to visit Europe, West and East, he knew that he was a man living on borrowed time. He was offered academic posts, in England, Poland and elsewhere, in which he might, perhaps, have found some retirement, might even have borrowed from death an extra year. He preferred to return to America.

This is the man who (Professor Edward Shils has informed readers of the *Spectator*) 'was a Manichean who saw power as darkness', who 'really cared very little for humanity', and whose 'self-portrayal' as a man 'who was attacked on every side by overwhelming odds' was 'completely a self-deception':

> Now he is dead and his rhetoric is a field of broken stones, his analyses empty, his strenuous pathos limp. He was a victim of his own vanity and of a shrivelled Marxism, which will not die and which goes on requiring the sacrifice of the living.
>
> (5 July 1963)

This dancing-on-the-grave hurt some of Mills' friends. I think it did so unnecessarily. He would certainly have preferred it to the grudging proprieties and polite devaluations with which the Establishment generally buries its enemies. It would have reassured him to have known that he had drawn blood. After all, was it not of such men as Shils that he had written:

> Their academic reputations rest, quite largely, upon their academic power: they are the members of the committee; they are on the directing board; they can get you the job, the trip, the research grant. They are a strange new kind of bureaucrat. They are executives of the mind. . . They could set up a research project or even a school, but I would be surprised, if, now after twenty years of

research and teaching and observing and thinking, they could pro-
duce a book which told you what they thought was going on in
the world, what they thought were the major problems for men
of this historical epoch. . .

I suspect that there is as much failure of the imagination as
malice in the Professor's obsequies. He really does not understand what Mills was about. What he (and so many others)
can't apprehend is the fullness of the strain taken by a man
of Mills' stature and with Mills' profound responsibility both
before ideas and before the audience which attends upon his
thought, in the nuclear age.

The globe spins, but as they cross the campus to the next
committee they don't notice any movement. The con-
ventions of their ideologies hem them in but they have lived
inside these so long that they don't know it. The world of
politics chunters on from one unprecedented danger to the
next, but the salary still gets paid in to the bank, and pro-
motion (if one keeps one's nose clean) may be round the
corner.

For those who are more open-eyed it is easy to make a
gesture of renunciation, to call down a plague upon both
ideological houses. Neither house is going to be troubled
by that. What is more difficult than any of us realise is to
build, on secure foundations, the house of the future in the
no-man's land between. The Communist revisionist speaks
his mind—and he is hammered by the State for giving comfort
to the enemy. He conforms or falls back into despair. The
Western liberal speaks his mind—and he is hammered as a
crypto-Communist, or becomes a fellow-traveller, or, as
often, is 'taken up' and given a licensed niche as a quaint
protestor. The Fidelists try to break through in their own
way, and the ring of power closes in. At every side there
are traps for the mind or sensibility—well-worn glissades of
complicity or default down which the intellect must slither.

It is more difficult to *think* about the large questions,
independently and to affirmative purpose, than any of us
know. Never before our time have intellectuals who operate
among higher historical generalisations been asked to contain

within their minds so many complexities and tensions—to comprehend simultaneously the inner dynamic and contra- dictions of two, and perhaps three, conflicting social systems. Nor has the outcome of their work been of such moment to the world.

It was this strain which Wright Mills took in his last years, and under which he died. He entered precipitately into the heart of the conflict, and found a world which was in many ways strange. Where he had been most familiar with academic discourse, he now encountered a Babel of voices. Western radicals told him to 'tell Castro. . .' Men from the hungry nations told him to 'tell the West. . .' Embittered Communist revisionists, their eyes full of remembered suffering, warned him against the smoothies of Communist ideological 'co- existence'. Pragmatic Gomulka-type revisionists warned him against the self-flagellant utopianism of the moralistic revisionists. He was solicited by petty factionalists and scorned by proponents of a deflationary *realpolitik;* he attended as readily to little student journals as to men of established academic repute. He had to find his own way, distinguishing the original from the eccentric, the men of integrity from the opportunists. No doubt he made errors of judgment: he was a hard-pressed and impatient man. The important things is that he got the discourse moving. He served in himself as a hyphen, joining the dissenting intellect- uals of two conformist worlds.

To build that house of theory between the camps requires an independence of intellect, and a willingness to call ridicule upon oneself by exposing one's immature notions in public (which Mills called the 'nerve of failure') which can easily tip over into the aridity of self-opinionated isolationism. It requires an openness before changing experience which can tip over into opportunism. 'When events move very fast and possible worlds swing round them,' Mills wrote in 1942, 'something happens to the quality of thinking. Some men repeat formulae; some men become reporters. To time observation with thought so as to mate a decent level of abstraction with crucial happenings is a difficult problem.'

Twenty years on, and the difficulties are greater. It

becomes more evident that the building of that house must be done by many workmen, from the East as well as the West. Theories of society and human nature must be developed adequate to the analysis of both Communist and late-capitalist societies. An utopian goal of a humane, democratic, communitarian society must be projected, to which the greatly-differing societies of East, West and 'Third World' may be directed—and indeed *must* be directed if we are ever to achieve, not a tetchy truce, but the supersession of the Cold War.

Men must discover, East and West, how to decompose power within complex 'over-developed' industrial societies. Addressing himself to this theme, the rise of the 'cheerful robot, of the technological idiot' within the middle-levels of both American and Soviet power hierarchies, Mills wrote in 1958:

> The fate of these types and this ethos, what is done about them and what they do—that is the real, even the ultimate showdown on 'socialism' in our time. For it is a showdown on what kinds of human beings and what kinds of culture are going to become the models of human aspiration. And it is an epochal showdown, separating the contemporary from the modern age. To make that showdown clear, as it affects every region of the world and every intimate recess of the self, requires a union of political reflection and cultural sensibility of a sort not really known before. It is a union now scarcely available in the western cultural community. Perhaps the attempt to achieve it, and to use it well, is the showdown on human culture itself.

That is one reason why Mills sought so earnestly in his last two or three years to open a discourse with the Marxists, to help in unloosing the reserves of experience and sensibility which were locked up within doctrinal forms. When I had the temerity to criticise him (in 1961) for failing to appreciate the extreme sharpness of the encounter between the humanist revisionists and the opportunists within the Communist camp, he replied:

> You might not quite realize. . . that in many ways, just like you, I too am in all that. . . I come to the anguish of it from another position than you, indeed from another way of life, if I may put it

so, but still we are finding ourselves in the same kind of difficulty, I think. As for me, being there makes me feel better, I mean being so generally close to you. Its like Thoreau said: in a dishonest country the only place for a man is in jail. I suppose one could say that what I am talking about is the 'marxism of the heart'. . .

He felt that the Western intellectual must repudiate the ideology of permanent war (at whatever remove) as decisively and as publicly as the scribes of *Encounter* demand that Communist intellectuals should repudiate their origins. No intellectual worth his salt could serve in the echelons of either 'side'; and he should refuse to serve as a mercenary in their bureaucracies. He should live, act, and above all *work*, as already a citizen of a world in which the Cold War had been superseded. His allegiance should be to the healed human consensus of the future, and to no partial—national or ideological—salient. The only 'security problem' which should properly concern him should be the security of human reason.

It was in this sense that he looked toward the intellectuals as hopeful agents of change. He thought that they must take urgent steps to secure their own cultural apparatus, for international as well as national discourse, independent of the intrusions of power. But he did not regard their role in any elitist sense, as his choice of the term 'cultural workman' was intended to emphasise. An 'International' of political or trade union bodies must be mediated (and thereby obstructed and distorted) by *apparatniks* and bureaucrats. But cultural workmen already *were* a diffuse International. Already West and East, South and North, the books were passing, the scholars, writers, and scientists were meeting, the students travelling, the technicians exchanging data.

The intellectual, in his proper role, he regarded, not as an 'expert' (a piece of mystification which drew his fire), but as a *craftsman*. He had no higher claim upon reward or status than any other craftsman, in industry or on the farm. But in the nuclear age his responsibilities and opportunities, in communicating his findings across all barriers, were greater. In one of his finest essays, addressed to industrial designers

in 1959, he defined a 'properly developing society' as 'one
in which the fact and ethos of craftsmanship would be
pervasive':

> In terms of its norms, men and women ought to be formed and
> selected as ascendant models of character. In terms of its ethos,
> institutions ought to be constructed and judged. Human society, in
> brief, ought to be built around craftsmanship as the central exper-
> ience of the unalienated human being and the very root of free
> human development. The most fruitful way to define the social
> problem is to ask how such a society can be built. For the highest
> human ideal is: to become a good craftsman.

Most of all, in his last years, Wright Mills offered a challenge
to his fellow cultural workmen: to stand on their own feet,
and to tell the public what they knew. 'The view that all is
blind drift,' he wrote, 'is largely a fatalist projection of one's
own feelings of impotence and perhaps a salve of guilt
about it.' Nor was it enough to strike alienated postures and
make faces at the Establishment. 'The young complacents
and the angry young men,' he wrote of Britain, 'are quite
free. Nobody locks them up. Nobody has to. They are lock-
ing themselves up. The angry ones in the totality of their own
parochial anger; the complacent ones in their own un-
imaginative ambitions.' By example he helped to end the long
default, and to give back to hundreds of young intellectuals
a sense of the dignities and moment of their trade.

In most of this I report his ideas. I do not, on all occasions,
agree. But I know that he was a wise man and a courageous
one, and that he had need of both qualities. No-man's-land is
a more friendly and more populated place since he has been
at work there, although the house of theory is not yet ready
to receive the human race.

HOMAGE TO TIBOR DERY

In that unanimous agenda of the good
If he should cough the chair would scowl
If he should smile a point-of-order would
Beat out his poems against the wall.
The seven unctious sins had each confessed
To sinning in the interest of all.
He was too old to be self-critical.
He took his platform down and left the hall.

He could no more abide the orthodox.
The lifelike leaders melted in their wax:
Grief fringed the servile squares like grass:
The statues stood on water. Public clocks
Forged in the small hours twelve important chimes.
He beat upon his art twelve answering times
And held a mirror up, of splintered glass:
He bent his pulse to pick their textual locks,

Easing the tumblers of the people's blood
Till something clicked, the formulations swung
Slowly apart, and a colloquial flood
Of common, fallible words got out.
The sweaty facts fell out of the statistics,
The active verbs ran to the brutal young:
Shame, pity, indignation, doubt
Broke protocol and stormed the city's tongue.

The turret summed up sternly for the good
In syllables so big they shut the old man up.
Confessions, concrete, quotas, stronger locks—
He knows what they can do. But can
They formulate correctly that lewd flood
And stuff the verbs back in the lexicon,
Replace the chimes within the fractured clocks
Or stand those statues on a plinth of blood?

1959

Note: Tibor Dery, the Hungarian novelist and short story writer, was a powerful voice of socialist humanism in 1956. After the repression of the Hungarian insurrection he was silenced and then—in 1959— imprisoned.

HOMAGE TO SALVADOR ALLENDE

> 'Our enemies have beat us to the pit:
> It is more worthy to leap in ourselves,
> Than tarry till they push us. . .'
>
> —Brutus at Philippi

Well, comrade president, what is there left to say?
Predicted all the way: and buried in the end
Without the benefit of media, before the mass
Could say its newses over you, the cameras
Squat in your wounds and blow them up.

Failure makes you like us, our kind of man,
Killed by our kind: petrol-pump patriots;
Loyal executives; most loyal constitutional ladies,
Wed to destroyers, setters-on of jets;
Our kindly patient partner, General Fabius,
Who when he strikes strikes hard, getting us in the guts.
Your face was too much common. Money fled uphill
And cost them in their lives who cost your death.

Your art was always an impossible.
Couldn't you learn, with less than half the votes,
The prose of power, the public man's inflation?
You should have been our age, trading their terms
For something less than half a treachery. . .

277

Defective realist, poor loyal sod,
Old silly doctor in a palace on your own,
Knowing the odds were up—
                    Why do you hurt our hearts?

Poetic, Latin man! You do not fall within
Our frames of reference. Transfixed by promises
Pledged to the poor in the high Andean pastures;
The crowd in Santiago; the clasped hand of the metal-worker;
The earnest village schoolmistress, searching your face:
These brought their treaties. You signed them with your life

Which you trade now into myth's ageless reference:
Bolivar, Guevara, Allende. Generous continent!
Accusing hemisphere! But not our kind of men,
As we, back in our prosing beds, stir in our myths,
Recalling such men once. . . and at Philippi one
Who, having fought and failed, took on a Roman end.

                              September, 1973

HOMAGE TO THOMAS McGRATH

i

It would be untrue to suggest that the poetry of Thomas McGrath is without recognition in the United States. On the contrary he has a large and discriminating readership, and the recognition of some fellow poets—even of the odd critic. But the cultural life of the USA is so various, and made up of so many scattered compost heaps, that it is perfectly possible for significant publics to co-exist which do not even know of the existence of each other.

In recent years I have come upon distinguished professors of American literature who did not know of McGrath's work and—more remarkably—circles of socialist or radical intellectuals. The East Coast literary establishment, and its opportunistic cousin the *New York Review of Books*, does not know (or does not wish to know) that his work exists. Since the British accept these agencies as authoritative interpreters, it follows that in this country his work is scarcely known at all.

Yet McGrath's poetry will be remembered in one hundred years when many more fashionable voices have been forgotten. Here is a poet addressing not poets only but speaking in a public voice to a public which has not yet learned to listen to him. Hence not only the poetry but also the reasons for the failure in public recognition demand attention. And this essay must therefore be drawn into a meditation upon obscure alternative traditions within what was once the American Left—contradictions inside a contradiction—a meditation prompted by McGrath's own trajectory.

Let us start by saying that McGrath is a poet of alienation. This puts him at once into a fashionable set. Who, in these latter days, can afford not to be alienated? But, then, McGrath is not, and never has been, a poet in anyone's fashionable party. His trajectory has been that of wilful defiance of every fashion. At every point when the applause— anyone's applause, even the applause of the alienated— seemed about to salute him, he has taken a jagged fork to a wilderness of his own wilful making.

This is not (as some critics might plead) because he is just not quite good enough as a poet. McGrath is a master-poet to his last fingernail. He is self-conscious (sometimes too self-conscious) in poetic technique, catholic in his reception of influence: a political poet, very certainly, but a poet whose politics happen in terms of poetry, within the poems, and not as gestures to an ideology happening somewhere outside them. 'It is always the texture of a poem' (he wrote to me in 1952) 'not what it is "about" that first catches me. . .'

His vices as well as his virtues are those of a poet. He cannot refuse a pun, least of all a pun which induces a metaphysical vibration, even when the logic of the poem may lead in a different direction. The virtues crowd whole poems, like 'Trinc' or 'Praises', with sheer fertility of poetic play:

> The vegetables please us with their modes and virtues.
>   The demure heart
> Of the lettuce inside its circular court, baroque ear
> Of quiet under its rustling house of lace, pleases
> Us.
>   And the bold strength of the celery, its green Hispanic
> ¡Shout! its exclamatory confetti.
>   And the analogue that is Onion:
> Ptolemaic astronomy and tearful allegory, the Platonic circles
> Of His inexhaustible soul!
>   O and the straightforwardness
> In the labyrinth of Cabbage, the infallible rectitude of
>   Homegrown Mushroom
> Under its cone of silence like a papal hat. . .[1]

At times he fusses and clutters the lines with a surplus of association and imagery. He clowns and asses around with terms and typography (as in some late sections of *Letter to an Imaginary Friend*), arousing and destroying expectations and dancing around the reader in a punning courtship-display.

McGrath's is an implacable alienation from all that has had anything fashionable going for it in the past four decades of American culture—and from a good deal of what has been offered as counter-culture also. There need be no suspicion that this alienation is worn as a pose, as the distinguished sorrow of a lonely soul; it is *suffered* with bitterness and with anger; it is *opposed;* and the official culture is seen as (without any qualification) menacing and life-destroying, not only in the most direct political meanings but also to historical and literary values:

<pre>
                              A nation in chains
         Called freedom.
                   A nation of murderers—O say, can you see
         Yourself among them?
                         You?
                               Hypocrite
                                  lecteur
                                     patriot
                                        (Letter, II, 148)
</pre>

But what is this official culture to be opposed *by?* In some part it is judged against a past. McGrath's is a profoundly historical poetry. The history is both personal and public, and often both are entwined. His major long poem, *Letter to an Imaginary Friend* (which after thirty years is only now nearing completion) has an autobiographical structure. But he describes this as 'pseudo-autobiography':

> It is not *simply* autobiography. I am very far from believing that all parts of my life are meaningful enough to be usable in the poem. But I believe that all of us live twice: once personally and once as a representative man or woman. I am interested in those moments when my life line crosses through the concentration points of the history of my time. *Then* I live both personally and representatively.[2]

In *Letter* (as well as in many shorter poems) the personal meditation returns again and again to moments of his childhood in North Dakota: the public meditation returns again and again to moments in the ascendant labour movement of the late 1930 and early 1940s. Returning (perhaps at the end of the Fifties) to the New York docks—the Chelsea waterfront in Manhattan where he had worked in 1941 (he has called this 'the most interesting time of his life'[3])—

. . . the talking walls had forgotten our names, down at the Front,
Where the seamen fought and the longshoremen struck the great
ships
In the War of the Poor.
And the NMU* has moved to the deep south
(Below Fourteenth) and built them a kind of a Moorish whorehouse
For a union hall. And the lads who built that union are gone.
Dead. Deep sixed. Read out of the books. Expelled. Members
Of the Ninety-Nine year Club. . .
* * *
And many thousands gone
Who were once the conscience and pride of the cold streets of the
workers;
Dissolved in numbers is that second Aleph, the Order of Militants,
And the workers defenseless: corralled in the death camps of money
Stoned in a rented dream frozen into a mask
Of false consciousness. . .
lip-zipped
the eyes padlocked the
ears
Fully transistorized
—living a life not their own.
Lost. . .

Still, in the still streets, sometimes, I see them moving—
Sleepwalkers in nightmare, drifting the battlefields of a war
They don't even know is happening—
O blessed at the end of a nightstick,
Put to bed in the dark in a painting by Jackson Rauschenberg.
Machined to fit the print in a rack 'n' gawk juke box, stomped
By a runaway herd of Genet fagots, shot full of holes
By the bounty hunters of Mad Avenue, brains drawn off
By the oak-borers of Ivy League's schools' mistletoe masters.

* NMU: National Maritime Union.

Everything's been Los Angelized. . .
                              Alone, now, in the street,
What sign, what blazed tree, what burning lightning of the radical
    Word
Shall write their names on the wall break down that mind-framed
    dark?

Northern lights in winter; in summer the eccentric stairs
The firefly climbs. . .
                              But where is the steering star
                                                                                  where is
The Plow? the Wheel?
                              Made this song in a bad time. . .
No revolutionary song now, no revolutionary
Party
          sell out
                    false consciousness
                                        yet I *will*
Sing
          for these poor
                    for the victory still to come
RSVP

The reminiscence intermixes anger and elegy. The anger
falls upon what C. Wright Mills called 'the cultural default':

The Committee comes by with its masked performers
To fire you out of your job, but that's expected.
Money breeds in the dark—expected.
Weeping and loss—expected.
          What was hard to imagine were the do-it-yourself kits
With 4 nails and a hammer and a patented folding cross,
And all the poets, green in the brown hills, running. . .
                                                  (*Letter*, I, 96)

Or again:

Blacklisted by trade unions we once had suffered to build,
Shot down under a bust of Plato by HUAC and AAUP.*
Outlaws
          system beaters

---

* HUAC—House Un-American Activities Committee. AAUP—American
Association of University Professors.

> we held to the hard road
> (While Establishment Poets, like bats, in caves with color T.V.
> Slept upside-down in clusters; a ripe fruited scrambling of ass holes.)
> But it's a hard system to beat: working under the hat
> On the half-pay offered to outlaws by the fellow-travellers of
>   money. . .
>
>   (*Letter*, II, 118)

Yet anger demands an alternative. If the alternative be only the elegaic recollection of the past, then anger's alternative may only be nostalgia. And nostalgia, even about the Wobblies or labour militancy, offers no threat to the powers which move in the daytime present. This, too, may be co-opted, rewarded, assimilated. The characters who recur in the *Letter* as points of reference—his father, farming in North Dakota; his brother Jimmy, killed in the war; Cal, the Wobbly farmhand; Mac, the union organiser on the docks—even these threaten to entrap him in a reputable nostalgia:

>   And always, as I go forward,
> And older I hear behind me, intolerable, the ghostlike footsteps—
> Jimmy perhaps; or Jack; my father; Cal; Mac maybe—
> The dead and the living—and to turn back toward them—that loved
>   past—
> Would be to offer my body to the loud crows and the crass
> Lewd jackals of time and money, the academy of dream-scalpers,
>   the mad
> Congressional Committees on Fame, to be put on a criss-cross for
>   not wearing
> The alien smell of the death they love. . .
>
>   (*Letter*, II, 106)

His poetry refuses to permit time to cancel experience like a used stamp. It refuses the past tense (the same incidents from the past recur in each part of the *Letter*, as they revolve and are themselves changed by the changing experience of the present). It refuses the placing of a closed moment of experience with its attendant longueurs, and seeks to extend the past forward through the present into a round dance of the future. This is why, again and again, themes from his childhood recur: North Dakota farmland, a brief episode in which a local civilisation rooted itself, struggled in wind,

snow and debt, and was evicted or emigrated, all within a
cycle of three generations: his grandfather, his father, himself, and each generation hard, only half-fulfilled. It is not
the finished quality of that experience, but the unfinished
quality, the unfulfilled aspirations, which he carried forward:

It is not *my* past that I mourn—*that* I can never lose. . .

—No, but the past of this place and the place itself and what
Was: the Possible; that is: the future that never arrived. . .

(Letter, II, 206)

But how to carry forward that Possible into the future in
the 'man-chilling' American present? The answer has an
effrontery and a chilling courage of its own, in which this
poet, who sometimes supposes himself to be some kind of
Marxist, puts his boot into the usual Marxist stereotypes:

Well—money talks. It's hard
To say 'love' loud enough in all that mechanical clamor
And perhaps the commune must fail in the filth of the American
    night—
Fail for a time. . .
                    But all time is redeemed by the single man—
Who remembers and resurrects.
                            And I remember.
                                            I keep
The winter count.
                            (Letter, II, 119)

This is not the posture of an egotist. (No man is less of an
egotist of the intellect, less of a poseur—except when he
sometimes poses as Tom Fool—than Thomas McGrath).
The claim is of a different order, and perhaps it is of two
kinds. It is made in the Second Part of the *Letter* (written in
the Sixties) in the aftermath of the defeat and also the
(partly self-inflicted) collapse of that part of the Left culture
into which the poet had been initiated in the late Thirties.
The external forces in this defeat ('McCarthyism') are
well remembered, although few who did not endure these
years understand the ferocity of its ideological terrorism and
the remorseless devices employed to hunt down and harrass

individual 'Communists'. What is less well remembered is the
internal collapse of that culture of the Left as it disappeared
into betrayals, self-accusations and disavowals, 'do-it-your-
self' Judas kits, meretricious self-justifications, with the
alienation of friends and the destruction of associative
networks.[4] It was a moment analagous to that of the late
1790s, when a combination of Anti-Jacobin ideological
terrorism and internal disenchantment with the course of
the French Revolution, drove Blake, Wordsworth and
Coleridge (in different ways) into isolation. And it bears
analogies with the predicament of any 'dissidents' isolated
within a conformist society and unable to communicate with
any public, upon whom falls the duty of the redemptive
memory, the 'winter count'.

The claim is being made for the unbreakable power of the
human mind, which mind, in the end, can never be guaranteed
by historicist theories of collectivities, but is an individual
mind which, in the winter night of a hostile culture, must
stand alone. And, in the second place, the claim is being
made for the *poetic* mind, the uncrackable necessity of a
poet to defend poetry's own truth and function. In an
episode which must have astonished his inquisitors, McGrath,
when summoned before the House Un-American Activities
Committee, threw down this claim before them:

> As a poet I must refuse to cooperate with the committee on what I
> can only call esthetic grounds. The view of life which we receive
> through the great works of art is a privileged one—it is a view of life
> according to probability or necessity, not subject to the chance and
> accident of our real world and therefore in a sense truer than the life
> we see lived all round us.[5]

This unexpectedly-Aristotelian view of the function of art
may have surprised not only the House Committee but also
those of McGrath's own comrades who were dedicated to
brutishly-utilitarian notions of art and of its instrumental
functions in the class struggle. It is in the 'privileged' truth
of poetry (uncorrupted by the impurities of chance and
accident) that its power lies not only to remember but also
to 'resurrect' and to 'redeem'. McGrath is not staking a

personal claim, but a high (and very generally abandoned) claim for poetry itself, among the most exacting and necessary disciplines of culture.[6] To this discipline he has the humility of a servitor.

The Un-American Activities Committee had hauled him before it in April 1953, during an investigation into 'Communist activities in the motion picture and educational field in Los Angeles'. The President of Los Angeles State College had promptly decided that he would not have an uncooperative witness on his staff. 'There were student demonstrations etc. but that was it,' McGrath recollected. Then he was entered on 'the Presidents' List' or blacklist. In a letter late in 1956 he wrote:

> Since the Committee got my teaching job I've been working at several things, mostly very tiring and dull—and also bad paying. A very hard period. I wrote a long poem—about 150 pages—last year...

(This was Part One of the *Letter*.) Then, back in Manhattan in 1961, he wrote:

> It's been a hard year. I've been working a lot in documentary and other kinds of film, trying to make enough to buy myself a little time for my own stuff. And so far I've lost three jobs this year as a result of committees, blacklists etc. The first two were in colleges and either of them would have been permanent. I like teaching and the security would have allowed me to write. The latest one was doing documentary work for NBC.* The pay is very good and I had a dream of doing about three months work a year and having the rest of the time myself. The dream lasted just long enough for them to check their files (I never imagined I'd be there since I've never worked for the likes of NBC) and I suppose its a duplicate of the FBI file since its run by retired FBI types. So the dream ended pretty abruptly.

'Thank you,' his letter adds, 'for the kind words about the value of the poetry, it's hard to believe in it sometimes, the way things are and have been. But of course the Muse doesn't let one quit, the grand old bitch.'

---

* NBC—National Broadcasting Company.

              But all time is redeemed by the single man—
Who remembers and resurrects.
                    And I remember.
                                    I keep
    The winter count. . .

Against the intolerant orthodoxy of his times McGrath
affirmed the 'magical' properties of poetry. In the night of a
decadent civilisation moving towards extermination, the
poem might be a charm against evil powers. We have this
written out in that fine poem, 'Against the False Magicians':

    The poem must not charm us like a film:
    See, in the war-torn city, that reckless, gallant
    Handsome lieutenant turn to the wet-lipped blonde
    (Our childhood fixation) for one sweet desperate kiss
    In the broken room, in blue cinematic moonlight—
    Bombers across that moon, and the bombs falling,
    The last train leaving, the regiment departing—
    And their lips lock, saluting themselves and death:
    And then the screen goes dead and all go home. . .
    Ritual of the false imagination.

    The poem must not charm us like the fact:
    A warship can sink a circus at forty miles,
    And art, love's lonely counterfeit, has small dominion
    Over those nightmares that move in the actual sunlight.
    The blonde will not be faithful, nor her lover ever return
    Nor the note be found in the hollow tree of childhood—
    This dazzle of the facts would have us weeping
    The orphaned fantasies of easier days.

    It is the charm which the potential has
    That is the proper aura for the poem.
    Though ceremony fail, though each of your grey hairs
    Help string a harp in the landlord's heaven,
    And every battle, every augury
    Argue defeat, and if defeat itself
    Bring all the darkness level with our eyes—
    It is the poem provides the proper charm,
    Spelling resistance and the living will,
    To bring to dance a stony field of fact
    And set against terror exile or despair
    The rituals of our humanity.

                                        (*Movie*, 121-2)

This poem is given an uncomplex dialectical structure. The thesis of the first verse (the wish-fulfilment of romanticism) is easy, fluent, uncluttered. The antithesis of the second verse (realism) opens with a memorable image: 'A warship can sink a circus at forty miles.' One remembers Mr Sleary's circus in *Hard Times* (which, however, was not in the end sunk by the batteries of utilitarianism); but today I always think also of the tanks rolling in to extinguish the Prague Spring. If realism surrenders to the contingent ('the chance and accident of our real world') then it betrays the privileged view of life of art and has no terms for 'the potential' ('a view of life according to probability or necessity'), falling back in the end upon the lost fantasies of romance. In the final verse McGrath affirms the true magical properties of poetry ('the charm which the potential has'), moving through a commonplace pathetic image to the sustained and impassioned synthesis in which the reality of human spiritual forces is affirmed ('in a sense truer than the life we see lived all round us').

The poem has an enduring validity. We need not try to fasten it down into a local context. But it can also be seen within the particular context of Communist cultural circles to illuminate an internal hullabaloo in which McGrath was rejecting both of the barren alternatives, 'socialist romanticism' or 'socialist realism', which were being debated. The argument had been rumbling and sputtering on since the late Thirties. If critics and historians will only lay aside their orthodox or post-Trotskyist almanacs for a while and look into the evidence, they will find that the real history is many miles away from the stereotypes. McGrath at this moment was in the belly of a decaying Popular Front whale, but he was kicking violently at the blubber around him. This is the way in which most cultural mutations arise—from the contradiction within the contradiction.

ii

To explain this I must take a detour: first, into a political reflection, and then into biography.

The reflection is this: I find, rather often, a curious amnesia within American radical culture as to certain moments in its own past. There are matters which, if not forgotten, are rarely talked about or are falsified in memory. Not only some part of the 1930s but a large amount in the 1940s has fallen out of polite discourse.

Orthodox academicism and post-Trotskyist criticism and historiography have obliterated this moment under some general theory of the universal contamination of 'Stalinism'. Because the American Communist Party and associated 'front' organisations exerted rather extensive influence in the Left press, in cultural journals, films, some trade unions and civil rights movements, a wholesale bill of contamination is issued on all. The errors and illusions of the time are endlessly rehearsed (although, curiously, some of these have a way of returning in more fashionable garb) and the positives pass unremembered. In consequence of this—and also of commonplace pressures upon individuals in their careers—strategies have merged which avoid confronting the historical experience, and which sometimes also (one has to say) avoid confronting or avowing personal histories.

Similar strategies can be observed in Europe, but we do not have the same sense of caesura in our history. It is impossible—although some writers have attempted it—to pronounce the whole history of the Resistance in Italy or France or Spain or Greece or Yugoslavia as contaminated because Communist Parties played a most active role in it. Nor is it possible to hold the hand over the history of Communist Parties themselves, as a distasteful subject fit only for moralistic exercises, when repeatedly these movements have thrown up heresies and heretics. Yet America in that same moment had a very vigorous and influential Left with an international cultural presence. How come that all this, in retrospect, can be analysed down to an irreducible spoonful of Stalinist tar?

But. . . there is no way that I can get further with this essay except through biography. And a bit of autobiography also. I first met Thomas McGrath when I came across the Atlantic, an aged war veteran of 22, in 1946. McGrath had spent some part of his war in the Aleutians. We were both

Communists which, please remember, was not only an international 'conspiracy', a formal Comintern structure, an auxiliary of Soviet diplomacy, etc. etc., but was also an international fraternity and sorority. Our meetings and occasions and circulations were much like those of other human beings in an affined network. They were not—as a contemporary student might suppose—all structured within 'cells' and disciplined according to rule. We found each other out without the benefit of any Org. Sec. In liberated Italy I would mooch around the town, find the blacksmith's shop—the oxen lifted on a hoist to be shoed—notice the PCI posters, introduce myself as a comrade, and in a trice I would be seated on a bench, incongruous in my British officer's uniform, sampling the blacksmith's wine. It was the same with my comrades in India, Iraq, Egypt. (One good friend of mine, masquerading as a sergeant-major, was able to second himself to work for some weeks with the Communist Party in Calcutta—against British rule!) It was the same also with many of our American comrades, who were moved by the same internationalism and optimism. A million informal transactions and discourses were going on in those years, which historians will never recover and which the hard-nosed Party organisers knew nothing about.

I was passed on to Tom by a mutual friend, an American Communist and poet then soldiering in England. Saul (this friend) had found his way to the offices of *Our Time*, a cultural monthly in London, been introduced to the local beer and company, and thence to myself, and his recommendation took me to the door of Tom and to a week's good lodging in Manhattan. I had just published a short story in *Our Time** and Charles Humboldt, the assistant editor of *New Masses*, liked it well enough to carry it there also. No-one in New York knew that it was my only published story; I had that happy misrecognition reserved for travellers and was taken to be a Writer.

Dizzy with success, Manhattan seemed to me to be electric with life. I caballed with poets and pretended to be one. I

---

* See 'Drava Bridge' in this volume.

attended a great rally in Madison Square Gardens and heard
Robeson, Marcantonio, and Communist councilman Ben
Davis from Harlem. I saw the banners of the Ladies Garment
Workers Union waved in defiance of the new Cold War. (For
the Cold War was happening already, in 1946, at every street-
corner, where the Hearst, McCormack and Scripps-Howard
press were howling for an internal terror against Commies
and for the atom-bombing of Yugoslavia: yes, I still have
my notes). Above all, Manhattan felt to me then as a great
city with an internationalist consciousness; a great anti-
Fascist city, its diversity churning into a common torrent of
solidarities—whereas now, alas, Manhattan sometimes appears
to me as a city of mutually tetchy, self-conscious and self-
regarding and sometimes factitious ethnicities. Yet then I
have to ask myself—was that cultural moment authentically
present, or am I yearning for illusions of my youth?

In 1947–8 Tom and his wife, Marian, came over to
England. He was taking up a Rhodes Scholarship at Oxford,
which he had won before the war. Dorothy and I saw them
often, and they spent Christmas with us in a croft on the
Atlantic coast of the Western Highlands of Scotland. The
dark winter days, the treeless landscape and the wind-swept
sea reminded Tom of the Aleutians. It may be here that he
first formed the idea of 'Remembering that Island', with its
terrible conclusion:

In a dream as real as war

I see the vast stinking Pacific suddenly awash
Once more with bodies, landings on all beaches,
The bodies of dead and living gone back to appointed places,
A ten year old resurrection,
And myself once more in the scourging wind, waiting, waiting,
While the rich oratory and the lying famous corrupt
Senators mine our lives for another war.

(Movie, 100)

The friendship between Tom, Dorothy and myself founded at that time has stuck for more than thirty years. It was a
solidarity fiercer than we understood at the time, a commit-

ment to courses which we could not yet name. The Cold War
was closing off all perspectives like a mist at sea. We forget
how protracted was the rupture in ordinary communications between members of the European and American Left—
for some fifteen years, from 1947 until the early 1960s,
transatlantic travel was severely curtailed. European Communists and ex-Communists insufficiently abject in their
penitence could not get visas to the USA. American Communists (or ex-Communists) suffered travel restrictions
and the withdrawal of passports.

> Defenceless under the night
> Our world in stupor lies;
> Yet, dotted everywhere
> Ironic points of light
> Flash out wherever the Just
> Exchange their messages...

During those years, whether just or unjust, we exchanged
ironic points of light. At some time around 1960 McGrath
at length touched England again, conversed in our New
Left coffee bar and trod the Aldermaston road. Then the
messages came to us not only from North Dakota but from
Greece, Yugoslavia, Mexico. We have been poor correspond-
ents. Yet we have felt—certainly Dorothy and I have felt—
that all this time we have been walking shoulder to shoulder.
And I am proud to find, in a letter from Tom of 1961, 'I
think of you both there as one of the few solid things in the
world.'

I do not mean—and it is important to say this—that we
have adopted identical political or intellectual positions.
But there has been a congruence of ulterior values and
commitments, which arose from within the same double-
contradiction. McGrath has reprinted in his Collected
Poems 'Ars Poetica':

> Oh, it's down with art and down with life and give us
> another reefer—
> They all said—give us a South Sea isle, where light my
> love lies dreaming;

> And who is that poet come in off the streets with a look
> unleal and lour?
> Your feet are muddy, you son-of-a-bitch, get out of our
> ivory tower.
> (*Movie*, 59)

But he has not republished 'Thomas Paradox's Second Epistle to the Philistines' which probably belongs in the same period (between 1948 and 1953?) with its effective verse:

> The poet said to the bureaucrat: man creates
> by the laws of beauty
> The artist creates the heart's face: an image
> of all that's human.
> But he said: I've no time to argue—though it
> sounds like a deviation—
> On a hacienda
> In San Fernando,
> I'm making the Revolution.

That is a version of the poem which appears in a raft of typescripts which McGrath sent us from the West Coast in the early Fifties. My sole contribution to the full annotated text of McGrath's Complete Works in the 22nd Century (which century neither McGrath nor I expect to arrive) will be this. I cannot prove it, for I cannot find the earlier copy, but this is a West Coast, Fifties, variant of a poem which in the late Forties (and Manhattan) had ended the verse in this way:

> Desk-deep in class war
> On the eighteenth floor
> I'm making the Revolution.

The change was made, as the poet has recently acknowledged to me, for political and not for aesthetic reasons: 'by the time the poem got to publication some of the people on the 18th floor were in jail or on their way or gone underground; but there were still a good many *one-time* radicals still alive and making money in the shadow of Hollywood'.[7]

This illustrates the difficulties placed not only before an

editor but also a critic. McGrath's texts often suggest a sub-text which is tactfully diminished or even suppressed because the targets of his intellectual attack—the 'bureaucrat', the instrumental Marxist ideologue—were themselves the objects of persecution by Media and State. Meanwhile McGrath, himself persecuted by the same forces, was involved in sharp disputes within that cultural apparatus which both presented and contained, both expressed and repressed, an influential part of the American Left.

It is a curious situation, at odds with the stereotypes. On one side McGrath was being hounded by HUAC: 'I expect to be fired from my job at the end of this term,' he wrote to us from Los Angeles (1951?):

I'm certain someone will see 'Crooked Mile',* read it and decide I'm n.g. Which could mean (this is not for saying aloud) that I might go to jail. Possible.

But he was writing to us the next year:

All in all I think my career as the best or most promising or what-ever it was left-wing poet in America** is due for some drastic revision. In fact, I feel pretty sure that it is no longer possible for me to publish in the left wing press any more. If that is too pessimis-tic, then I will emend it to say that it is only a matter of time. I suppose I was always suspect for being 'difficult' and for being 'bitter'. . . Unless you versify Daily Worker editorials in degenerate Whitmanesque, you're apt to seem like a formalist, and anything that is not a cliche is examined to see whether it might not be a political heresy. This is not just a lament for my own situation. For Christ sake, if you can get anyone to look into the stinking mess here, do so. All the writers I know regard Sillen and the literary commissars (like Fast) as idiots, but the only reaction to them is cynicism, since no one feels that anything can be done. It's absolute-ly strangling. Unless you are, like Neruda, a senator from Chile in exile, you're in a bad way. If you are Neruda, you get fawned on and editorialized over by bureaucrats who really hate all art but admire anything that succeeds. Help! Help!

---

* *To Walk a Crooked Mile* (New York, 1947).
** A jesting reference to the blurb of *Crooked Mile*.

But if the left-wing press was 'strangling', there was no other:
'My novel I think is done for—the pub. house where it was
just had a red hunt and the editor was fired etc.'[8]

It was at this time that McGrath, Philip Stevenson and a
few friends founded the *California Quarterly*. It got 'a mixed
reception' (he wrote to us in 1953):

> The agit-prop-and-idiot faction write us letters which say that the
> stories are negative and that we have no Negro writers—this group is
> a kind of self-appointed Committee of Public Safety, or better yet
> the Mrs. Grundys of the Revolution and apparently they never read
> poetry. . . Another group gives us hell for being so dedicated to up-
> lift and betterment of the human race that we publish a story for
> its theme. . .
>
> The only salvation of left writing in this country, I think, is to
> try to break the strangle-hold of the blue stockings who run left
> editing and criticism. But other editors are afraid to do anything.
> Unless we hold to orthodox views (views which no left-wing writer
> in the country accepts, but all are afraid to challenge for fear of a
> heresy trial) these editors think that Jerome and Sillen and the high
> panjandrums (Fast et al) will attack and destroy us. . . It's a simply
> sickening situation. Everyone here assumes nothing can be done
> about it, refuse to stand together (that would be factionalism!) and
> adopt an attitude of pure cynicism toward Jerome & Co. regarding
> *Masses & Mainstream* as the idiot child: lame-witted and a little
> shameful to be sure, but nevertheless our own.

I am not competent to unravel the inner history of these
disputes: I must leave this to others. My sympathies are with
McGrath: yet I do not know that he was always 'right',
nor that he would always claim this himself. The protagonists
whom he identified most often, among the party of 'bureaucrats' or 'philistines', were V.J. Jerome, Samuel Sillen and
(on the West Coast) John Howard Lawson; and of his own
party, Milton Blau and the generous-minded (and neglected)
Charles Humboldt:

> Now that Charlie Humboldt and Milt Blau no longer have anything
> to do with *Masses and Mainstream* the present editors choose only
> the most thinned out kind of material. I pray for a new Duclos
> letter on American left criticism, but despair of getting it. When Mao
> wrote it for us (have you seen his pamphlet on Art and Literature?)
> there was what amounted to a suppression of it—no reviews, no

discussion, nothing. Perhaps I am no longer quite sane on the whole subject. The Mao thing especially agitates me, since Mao says the same damn thing about the need for both a tactical and a strategic kind of writing which I have argued is the only solution to the dilemma of left writing under capitalism. . . I say in dead seriousness that we need help in the worst way.

No doubt the control exerted by the American Communist Party over its own cultural apparatus was unusually disciplinary and its instrumental attitudes towards art may have been unusually bleak. And the self-submission of some intellectuals to the mystique of the historical authority of the Party, as the interpreter of revolutionary and class truth, may have been unusually abject. But McGrath was wrong to suppose that he was facing some local American difficulty, and that help might come from the advice of fraternal Parties ('a new Duclos letter'). Duclos was quite as much part of the problem as were Sillen or Jerome. Little help could anyone in Europe bring as Zhdanovism extended its ideological and disciplinary reign throughout the international Communist apparatus. McGrath was contesting with symptoms which he had not yet diagnosed as those of Communism's mortal crisis; like his own workers he and his fellow protagonists were 'drifting the battlefields of a war / They don't even know is happening.' And one must add that not only Party discipline (the 'fear of a heresy trial') but also a stubborn loyalty to a Party—and to comrades—who were the object of incessant public attack inhibited open intellectual confrontations.

Thomas McGrath had rendered his voluntary dues to the Party's Caesar. He had offered to compromise with Caesar's demands, by developing a theory of 'tactical' and 'strategic' poetry. 'Tactical' poetry might be about immediate political events: 'the poet should give it as much clarity and strength as he can give it without falling into political slogans'. 'Strategic' poetry ('a poetry in which the writer trusts himself enough to write about whatever comes along') should be open and exploratory, 'consciousness raising or enriching'.[9] In 1949 he had unleashed a splendid charge of his own tactical cavalry in *Longshot O'Leary's Garland of Practical*

Poesie. The title of this book has probably lost meaning to today's readers, although the fiercely-political surrealism of the poems has enduring vitality. What has been forgotten is the precedent charge of the heavy brigade of T.S. Eliot, stationing their chargers on every campus and in every literary review. After the *Family Reunion* (1947) and the *Notes Towards a Definition of Culture* (1948) had come the reissue of *Old Possum's Book of Practical Cats.* McGrath's contestation with Eliot can be detected throughout his poetry of this decade, as allusion, irony, echo. And against Old Possum he sent out Longshot O'Leary onto the field.

These 'tactical' poems McGrath wrote as immediate polemic. He did not expect them to last. His savage poem on the Marshall Plan, 'First Book of Genesis According to Marshall', is—he wrote to us in 1948—'going to be completely useless in a few months possibly'. But it has, in fact, long outlasted the Marshall Plan, perhaps because of its hilariously-inventive surrealist polemic; and the poet has acknowledged this by including it in his (highly-selective) 'Collected Poems' (*Movie*, 55-56).

But even poems such as these could not get into *Masses and Mainstream* by 1952-3. They were too 'bitter'. And where else could they find an outlet? I cannot, even today, turn away without a wry smile from the recollection of those know-all High Marxists and political Heavies who suppressed verses because they were *too bitter!* 'Comrades, you must be more positive! You must have confidence in the international working-class movement!' And what if that movement was collapsing in ruins and bad faith all around us, did not poets then have the duty to warn?[10]

McGrath was right. But that did him no kind of good. Come 1956 and all that, and surely McGrath was at last liberated, freed from the Stalinist shackles, in touch once again with the new and ebullient radicalism of the 1960s, in accord with an audience once more? Well, no. That wasn't how it was. How exactly it was I do not exactly know. But a little I remember, something is in his letters, more is in his poems.

McGrath's break with the Communist Party was never as

sharp or as polemical as was ours. This was partly plain pig-Irish stubborness. When some of those very commissars of culture with whom he had been wrestling for years (in private) suddenly flaked out in public confessional mood, accusing 'the Party' of their own sins, he sat in the same place and was privately sick.[11] He had never, unless in one or two poems in *Longshot O'Leary*, romanticised the Soviet world.

His stance, in the matter of the Soviet Union, had, and maybe still has, a source in pure curmudgeonly opposition. If the official culture of the US of A, which he found to be foul and mendacious, wanted to name Communism as its Satanic antagonist, then he was willing to vow himself a Satanist and place himself directly in front of Orthodoxy's polished self-satisfied nose.[12]

There was, in any case, a brief moment of honour in the American Communist Party in 1956, a revolt within the *Daily Worker*, a stirring of authentic self-reflection in the Party. He was, with Charles Humboldt, one of the boarding-party who tried to set *Mainstream* onto a socialist humanist course. When the attempt failed he simply removed himself quietly and without public statement from the snarling comrades. In a letter which I cannot exactly date (probably 1961) gave a run-down on the previous five years:

I'm afraid that long letter will never arrive—somebody not paid by the post office dept here must have found it interesting reading. But anyway you must have gathered the main strands—and it's dreary to go over them (some jobs lost thru automation and some thru the high spirits of various quasi-governmental bodies: schools, films, etc. etc. . .) In the last three years I've moved around a lot—hardly six months in any one place—following jobs like a bindle stiff. . . To bring you up to date. For some years I was looked on by the *Mainstream* people as a very bad cat—largely because I had been fighting with John Howard Lawson, the grand panjandrum on the West Coast, a great culture faker. Then it was officially discovered that a lot of mistakes had been made etc. etc. Humboldt went as editor of *Mainstream* and asked me to join up with him, which I did. Then, over a period of time things went back to what they had been; it became more and more difficult for Humboldt to do anything with the magazine; there was a showdown and he lost. So I dropped off also—I was only a 'contributor' whatever that means. I've had no organizational connection with the party for years, and the last years when I did have such a connection—god knows how long ago now—were ones where I spent most of the time fighting expulsion. Since then I've free-lanced in a few tactical things with other dissidents—there are a lot of us but there seems no way of getting everybody in any kind of concerted motion, although a few of us did dream for a while of organizing the Ramshackle Socialist Victory Party (RSVP). Somehow it seems that this might still be done, but I don't see how.

Still, with all the trouble there was with the organization, the fact that it has had such a terrible fight in the last years and has lost so much in members and power (more from bad politics than terror) has left a terrible terrible emptiness in the whole life of the country, an emptiness which I think everyone feels without knowing why. And an emptiness which has left a lot of writers and intellectuals in a bad way. I don't mean the ones who were in the organization (although they've been hard hit too); what I am thinking of is the kind of intellectual who never was with the organization and was always critical of it and even opposed to it. *But* who felt some kind of sense of comfort that on many of the big issues where he himself might do nothing, there was a group that was fighting for good causes. . .

Northern lights in winter; in summer the eccentric stairs
The firefly climbs. . .
                              But where is the steering star
                                                  where is
The Plow? the Wheel?
                         Made this song in a bad time. . .
No revolutionary song now, no revolutionary
Party
            sell out
                         false consciousness
                                        yet I *will*
Sing
         for these poor
                         for the victory still to come
RSVP

                                        (*Letter*, II, 125)

So McGrath returns in the *Letter* back to Manhattan, the 'stone city'—

                         An age of darkness has entered that stone
In a few years between wars. The past holds

Like a sad dream trapped in granite: what foot can slip free what trail
Blaze in that night-rock where the starry travellers search?

(*Letter*, II, 125)

But before he returned to Manhattan (1960-1) something
had happened in his last years on the West Coast: no less than
a Renaissance! In 1958 he wrote to us about 'a whirl of
work'—a speaking-reading tour up the Coast, poetry with
jazz in a nightclub, a record with Langston Hughes: 'meanwhile I'm broke'. Yet as this 'Renaissance' bloomed, McGrath
once again turned abruptly away on his own jagged fork. If
anything he had found the civilisation of the West Coast
more threatening than the East. Los Angeles gets a singularly
savage handling in the *Letter:*

Windless city built on decaying granite, loose ends
Without end or beginning and nothing to tie to, city down hill
From the high mania of our nineteenth century destiny—what's
    loose
Rolls there, what's square slides, anything not tied down
Flies in. . .
              kind of petrified shitstorm.

(*Letter*, II, 112)

He recalled his time on the West Coast as:

Ten years—doing time in detention camps of the spirit,
Grounded in Twin Plague Harbor with comrades Flotsom & Jetsom:
Wreckage of sunken boats becalmed in the Horse Latitudes
Windless soul's doldrums LosAngeles AsiaMinor of the intellect
Exile.

(*Letter*, II, 111)

The 'exile' was made the more anguished by the loss of his
two most valued and sustaining relationships: with Marian,
and then with his second wife, Alice. It was made endurable
by the small 'commune' of resistance, the 'Marsh Street
Irregulars', the circle of friends, fellow-outlaws and poets,
which he was later to recall in elegiac mood.[13] But the
pervading memory is one of nightmare, the nightmare of
The Gates of Ivory, The Gates of Horn (1957), his only

published fiction. This terrible futuristic extrapolation of a capitalist consumerised subtopia, governed by the invigilations of a surrealist HUAC, ought never to have passed out of print. Very much superior to *Animal Farm* (that exemplary case of ideology masquerading as art), its fertile symbolic code disallows any simplistic ideological printout—when published in Czech it was no doubt read as a savage satire upon Stalinism. It carries no local political 'message' but a warning that human creativity was under threat from external repression and internal self-betrayal, and that civilisation might pass 'into some kind of surrogate existence'.

McGrath's hostility to West Coast civilisation extended not only to its dominant consumer culture but also to a good part of the self-styled oppositional culture also—an 'opposition' which he often gestures at as one of 'culture-fakers', exhibitionists, egotists, and 'the dreamers, crazed, in their thousands, nailed to a tree of wine' (*Letter*, II, 116)—an 'opposition' only too easily to be bought or co-opted by money and power. What happened to destroy McGrath's accord with the West Coast 'Renaissance' I do not know. But he explained some part of it to us after his return to New York in 1960. For a while he had 'had some hope' for 'the Beat mob':

> There was in fact a lot of social critical thinking in the group (never a group, just a bunch of people who were on the scene). Then *Life-Time* discovered the thing and invented their own version of it. The censors helped by making *Howl* and Ginsberg into an icon. Barney Ross of Grove Press and Lawrence Lipton (he wrote a book called *The Holy Barbarians*) cut the balls off the 'movement', substituting 'disaffiliation' and (as if there weren't enough to go around) 'alienation', dada, obscenity etc. etc. The Beat Movement became a little club of crazies, very exclusive; and the younger ones accepted 'disaffiliation' etc. etc. as the official program, grew beards, went back to the big war against their parents and all social content was lost. All positive social content any way. What a son-of-a-bitch Rimbaud was! He gave a program to a century of petit bourgeois psycho-anarchists.

> What! All those years after the Annunciation at Venice
> And no revolution in sight?

                             And how long since the lads
From West Stud Horse Texas and Poontang-on-the-Hudson
Slogged through the city of Lost Angels in the beardless years
Led by a cloud no bigger than an orgone box, whence issued—
Promising, promising, promising (and no revolution and no
Revolution in sight) issued the cash-tongued summons
Toward the guru of Big Sur and San Fran's stammering Apocalypse?

I do not know how long this thing can go on!
—Waiting for Lefty, waiting for Godot, waiting for the heavenly fix.
In my way of counting, time comes in through my skin—
Blind Cosmos Alley, charismatic light
Of electric mustaches in the Deep Night of the Gashouse gunfire
From enormous imaginary loud cap pistols of infinitely small calibre
Anarcholunacy—how long, in that light, to read what signposts?
When all that glows with a gem-like flame is the end of Lipton's
     cigar?[14]

For a year or two (1960-1) he was back in New York
(now with Genya), an unaffiliated and agnostic revolutionary:

I remain unconvinced of everything except that (under what auspices
now I cannot imagine) the revolution has got to come. And it had
better come pretty soon here or we will have passed into some kind
of surrogate existence—unless we have already—in which regenera-
tion is impossible. . . We live in Manhattan—lower East side—lower
than it's ever been, very poor, luminous poverty and a phospho-
rescence of non-literary alienation in the streets. We have a terrible
sort of place. Would be unbearable to think of living here for a long
time—but I feel that way about the whole city.

And, in the same letter:

No movements about. The pacifists keep fairly busy and I've given
them a hand on a few things now and again. The biggest thing I
think that has happened in quite a while is the action which the
women took a couple of weeks ago. Demonstrations took place all
across the country, some of them pretty sizeable (a couple of
thousand Americans involved in a *good* cause is pretty sizeable to
us nowadays).

Several letters exchanged at this time related to his attempt
to visit—perhaps to stay a while and work—in Cuba. We
furnished credentials from *New Left Review* for Tom and

Genya to serve in Cuba as, respectively, journalist and photo-
grapher, but to no avail: the State Department evidently
consulted up-to-date files and permits were refused.

It is at around this time that McGrath's pessimism about
urban American civilisation appears to deepen: 'I don't
belong in this century—who does?'

> Now, down below, in the fire and stench, the city
> Is building its shell: elaborate levels of emptiness
> Like some sea-animal building towards its extinction.
> And the citizens, unserious and full of virtue,
> Are hunting for bread, or money, or a prayer,
> And I behold them, and this season of man, without love.
>
> If it were not a joke, it would be proper to laugh.
> —Curious how that rat's nest holds together—
> Distracting. . .
>   Without it there might be, still,
> The gold wheel and the silver, the sun and the moon,
> The season's ancient assurance under the unstable stars
> Our fiery companions. . .
>   And trees, perhaps, and the sound
> Of the wild and living water hurrying out of the hills.[15]

Later, back in North Dakota, in one of his rare essays on his
poetic intentions, he discussed the matter:

> What is there, out here on the edge, that makes our experience
> different from that of the city poet? First there is the land itself. It
> has been disciplined by machines but it is still not dominated. The
> plow that broke the plains is long gone and the giant tractor and the
> combine are here, but the process of making a living is still a struggle
> and a gamble—it is not a matter of putting raw materials in one end
> of a factory and taking finished products out of the other. Weather,
> which is only a nuisance in the city, takes on the power of the gods
> here, and vast cycles of climate, which will one day make all the area
> a dust bowl again and finally return it to grass, make all man's
> successes momentary and ambiguous. Here man can never think of
> himself, as he can in the city, as the master of nature. Like it or not
> he is subject to the ancient power of seasonal change; he cannot
> avoid being *in* nature; he has an heroic adversary that is no abstract-
> ion. At a level below immediate consciousness we respond to this,
> are less alien to our bodies, to human and natural time.
> The east is much older than these farther states, has more history.

But I believe that that history no longer functions, has been forgotten, has been 'paved over'. In the east man begins every day from
himself. Here, the past is still alive and close at hand—the arrowheads
we turn up may have been shot at our grandfathers. I am not thinking of any romantic frontier. The past out here was bloody, and full
of injustice, though hopeful and heroic. It is very close here—my
father took shelter with his family at Fort Ransom during an Indian
scare when he was a boy. Later he heard of the massacre at Wounded
Knee. Most of us are haunted by the closeness of that past, and by
the fact that we are only a step from the Indian, whose sense of life
so many of the younger people are trying to learn.[16]

> Why my grandmother saw them—
> And saw the last one perhaps: ascending the little river
> On the spring high water in a battered canoe.
> Stole one of her chickens
> (Herself in the ark of the soddy with the rifle cocked but not arguing)
> Took the stolen bird and disappeared into history.
>
> (*Letter*, II, 190)

But it was not only that in the cities the sense of history
was 'paved over'. McGrath also argued—and perhaps still
argues?—that urban civilisation in the USA had entered into a
'surrogate existence':

Supposing he already knows the facts of life and the class struggle,
the poet has nothing to learn from the city. Where once it was a
liberating place it is now a stultifying one. Only in the ghettos is
something 'happening', as the great proliferation of Black, Chicano
and Indian poetry shows. For such poets the ghettos are a source of
strength. But the white poet can enter the ghetto only with great
difficulty and in any case the ghettos are only beginning to work
through to revolutionary politics. At the moment they are still
involved (with important exceptions) in cultural and political
nationalism, dead ends which it seems must be explored before a
serious politics becomes possible. When that time comes the cities
will again be the place of the central experience of the time and
the poets will have to go back. . .
   The point is to find, during these years of 'wandering in the
desert', the link with the revolutionary past in order to create,
invent, rescue, restructure, resurrect the past. This may be our gift
to the city.[17]

Yet McGrath did not retire from New York to North
Dakota gracefully and in elegaic mood. He stormed out with

the first number of an irregular journal, *Crazy Horse*, 'edited
by a dead Sioux chief'—the chief who helped to defeat
Captain Custer. *Crazy Horse* announced that it wasn't
interested 'in either the shrunken trophies of the academic
head-hunters nor in those mammoth cod-pieces stuffed with
falsies, the primitive inventions of the Nouveau Beat. We
believe that poverty is real, that work is real, that joy and
anguish and revolution are real.'

> We, the Irregulars of Crazy Horse, Ghost Dancers of the essential
> existential Solidarity, now summon into being the hosts of the
> new resistance. Give up those bird-cages built for lions! Alienation
> is not enough![18]

McGrath's own poems and those of Alvaro Cardona-Hine
came closest to meeting the extravagant prescriptions of
the manifesto. There is a violence of desperation, a mood of
wilful self-isolation, invective and blasphemy about this
moment: a total rejection.

Crazy Horse was published sporadically over the next years,
from North Dakota, and then passed from Tom and Genya's
editorship into other hands. McGrath half turned back to his
own state and he was half-driven there. First the University
of North Dakota and then Moorhead State University
(Minnesota) to their honour (and their own good fortune)
found places for this most distinguished poet. In the past
twenty-odd years there have been dark patches and patches
of sun, and in all times McGrath has continued to be prolific,
innovative, poetically 'Live-O'. The *Letter* has passed through
Part Two (completed in 1968) to Part Three, only three
sections of which have been published. These years are still
too close to both of us to discuss with objectivity.

iii

As I have followed the tracks of this remarkable poet through
a dozen tiny and short-lived journals on the margins of
official (or 'official' oppositional) culture it has been impossible not to reach for a comparison. The experience of
isolation, of the loss of relations with a public, of black-

listing and of survival through a succession of casual jobs,[19]
is one which calls into mind the experience of many Czech
intellectuals who were evicted from their professions in the
'normalisation' which succeeded upon 1968. McGrath has
been the outlaw of American normalisation.

Of course, the proper and important qualifications must be
made. McGrath was hounded around the place but he was
not imprisoned, his work was not actually suppressed (except
by the self-regulating censorship of editors and publishing-
houses), and if he was hounded at length back into North
Dakota, Dakota—he would be the first to insist—is no
Siberian *gulag*. He has even, of late years, received a little
recognition: an Amy Lowell and a Guggenheim Fellowship
came his way.

Yet, for all that, the trajectory of his life and work offers
the sharpest kind of critique of the dominant culture. His
work has been barely permitted to continue, sometimes
circulating to a readership of a few hundreds, on an outlaw
margin. Students in the next century may savour the 'metaphysical' wit of the poet who, hounded from one job to
another in California in the 1950s, wrote 'Figures in an
Allegorical Landscape' from his temporary refuge as a board
marker on the Stock Exchange:

> Where number farmers plant their hope
> In the dark of the moon of ignorance,
> He guards their fractionated sleep:
> A sad vaquero, riding fence
>
> Like a good shepherd. Sacred cows
> Graze on the ranges of his lack.
> In his high patrol he binds the strays
> From Anaconda to Zellerback,
>
> While all Dow's children clap their hands
> For the Eucharist of their golden feast.
> But he is bound in stocks and bonds,
> Who writes the Number of the Beast.[20]

And I will predict with greater confidence that students will
read with pride McGrath's multi-faceted refusal to cooperate

with the House Un-American Activities Committee in 1953,
as a teacher, poet and citizen; a statement which commences:

> As a teacher, my first responsibility is to my students. To cooperate
> with this committee would be to set for them an example of
> accomodation to forces which can only have, as their end effect, the
> destruction of education itself. . . I am proud to say that a great
> majority of my students. . . do not want me to accomodate myself
> to this committee. In a certain sense, I have no choice in the matter
> —the students would not not want me back in the classroom if I
> were to take any course of action other than the one I am pursuing.[21]

And they will note with pleasure that McGrath's students
fulfilled his confidence in them, publishing a tribute to him
in the form of a collection of his own poems, *Witness to the
Times!* In a 'Comment' prefaced to the collection, McGrath
wrote:

> I hope that the poems will be a witness to a continuing liaison with
> the world, an affair that is not without its up and downs but which
> is as secure as a sacred marriage. I believe that this figure of the
> world's lover is the best image for the poet—that he may succeed
> where the Neutral Man (whom it shall not profit to gain his soul if
> he lose the world) is certain to fail. The poet always has this task,
> it seems to me: to bear witness to the times; but now especially
> when the State is trying by corruption, coercion, and its own paltry
> terror to silence writers, or dope them or convert them into the bird
> sanctuaries of public monuments—now especially the artist should
> be responsible to the world.

McGrath's good friend and mentor, Charles Humboldt,
had a more savage comment on 'the witnesses' who made
their terms with 'the confessors of the sacred state':

> Now they are kind to children and at the least
> Rebuff burst into tears, reproach and follow
> The hunted as though *they* were being holloed
> Through halls and borders like a tired beast.[23]

'Why does the persecution in mass of Communist and progressive intellectuals arouse no protest among the partisans

of "the liberty and integrity of the individual"'?', he asked. And he indicated the 'latent conservatism' of even the 'pseudo-revolutionary' movements of modern art, 'self-absorbed and devoid of all realistic material perspective':

> Their goal was freedom *from* society, not freedom *within* society to be won in alliance with its progressive forces. After all, one could still crawl in the cracks of the police state. So the fire eaters now drink at their masters' tables while the prophets compose cautious prayers for their own salvation.[24]

McGrath perhaps will have said 'amen' to that, yet it will not have satisfied him. He was not euphoric about 'the progressive forces' of society, and his 'realistic material perspectives' lay more in the past than in the present or future:

> I sit at the beach, in the light of a gone day,
> And I wait for the hunters.

'Dark, now, all the States, / And night on the west coast. / Darkness and exile. . .'

> For they will hunt you, O revolutionaries!
> Hunt you in darkness—the slogan chalked on the wall
> Is your magical sign, icon of terrible love,
> The dark of the calendar. They hunt you, listening
> For a sound of gunfire.
>
> But, now, the silence, and the neutral stars on the sea.
> Sirens. Waiting. The waves' long lamentation.
> Endured by millions—this darkness and the hunting:
> Capture   Death   Victory. Like the struggle, the
>   changeless sea,
> Like the constant stars: Endure   Resist   Endure[25]

Here, waiting for the hunters, he turned inward upon himself and commenced the *Letter to an Imaginary Friend*. In such a moment of isolation and defeat, Wordsworth at Goslar in 1799 commenced *The Prelude*, a poem to which *Letter* can be justly compared. There is the same autobio-

graphic structure (and the same indefiniteness as to bio-
graphic detail); the same recovery of childhood experience,
seen both through the child's eye and the adult poet; the
same central concern with political experience, the same
strenuous attempt to settle philosophical accounts with the
poet's own time.

Yet to mention *The Prelude* in the same breath as *Letter*
is not only to provoke academic hilarity. It is also to snag
one's foot on the widespread misunderstanding that *Letter*
(in its 'valid' parts) is some kind of 'pastoral' offering from
'the West'. It is this (I suspect) which has closed the urban
and academic readership against a due recognition of the
poem: it is difficult to perceive that a poem with 'agrarian'
themes, by a poet who has chosen to 'withdraw' to North
Dakota might possibly be addressed to their immediate
history and their own malaise. When McGrath published
The Movie at the End of the World, a selection from a
lifetime's verse, the *New Republic* noted that this revealed
the poet as 'an old-time dustbowl radical out of the Dakotas
of the '30s' who had passed through 'characteristic romantic
progression from illusion to disillusion'. (April 21, 1973).
Seven years later the *New York Times Book Review* got
around to awarding the same book the high fame of a seven-
line notice (April 13, 1980) which said that 'the spirit that
animates [the poems] is of the West, whether it is in the
form of tough modern verse or that of the simple, oldtime
ballad'.

The misrecognition here is spectacular. McGrath's first
published poems belong to the last years of the thirties. His
first volume, *First Manifesto*, was published by Alan Swallow
at Baton Rouge in 1940, and a brief scrutiny will show that
dominant influences upon the poems were those of Hart
Crane and of the English left-wing poets of the thirties:
Auden, Day Lewis, Spender, MacNeice. It is not so much
the 'old time ballad' as Auden's reinvention of it in *Look,
Stranger* and *Another Time* which gave to McGrath an
inspiration for his own reinventions in *Longshot O'Leary*.
In McGrath's subsequent poetry he draws upon Western
agrarian themes and a Wobbly vocabulary, but the poetic

and intellectual influences are in no way 'regional'. A very long way back there may be Whitman, or the voracious appetite and universal self-licence of Whitman, but—

> Whitman, he thinks, deserves to be sung.
> His imitators should all be hung.[26]

Influences which I have myself noted include Lorca, Elouard, Neruda, Brecht, Pasternak. The strongest intellectual influence of 'Marxism' came to him, not through Marx, but through Christopher Caudwell:

Longshot O'Leary Says a Square Is a Person
Who Cannot Read Caudwell[27]

Among his contemporaries he was clearly in touch with the group of British poets of the Left around *Our Time* and *Arena* (some of whom he had met in 1947–8): Edgell Rickword, Randall Swingler, Jack Lindsay, Hamish Henderson, Arnold Rattenbury, Jack Beeching, Roy Fuller. And close poetic colleagues and friends in America are often summoned into the round-dance of his verse: among them Charles Humboldt, Edwin Rolfe, Naomi Replansky, Don Gordon, Alvaro Cardona-Hine, Robert Bly. My imperfect knowledge of North American poetry prevents me from going further.

But I have written myself into a ridiculous corner: in noting influences which might be overlooked, I have suggested far too narrow a grid of reference for this deeply-cultured mind. He has received, no doubt, two hundred influences per week, and some he has received and rejected (as Eliot, Pound and Beckett) while others, like the *haiku*, he has submitted himself to as a discipline.[28] His poetry is enriched by sufficient mythic and literary (as well as political) allusion to keep, alas, whole Eng. Lit. Faculties at work through the 21st century. I wish only to emphasise that Part Two of the *Letter*, which some people suppose to be 'about' North Dakota, is signed off 'North Dakota-Skyros-Ibiza-Agaete-Guadalajara, 1968'. It is true that McGrath's *politics* are given a very distinct American location; they are not the extra-

polation of some theorised cosmopolitan prescription. But
these are interpreted through a poetic grid of reference
which, if not universal, is as universal as his selection of
poetic values allows it to be.

As he insists, 'North Dakota is everywhere'. And what
is 'everywhere' is not that complacent and self-important
entity, 'the human condition', but the condition of men and
women in their labour, in their love and their loss, in their
'somatic' relation to nature, in their exploitation and oppression, in their thwarted aspirations for 'communitas' (their
faculty for dreaming and myth-making), and at times very
specifically in their common imbrication in the capitalist
nexus.[29]

Nevertheless, it is *Dakota* which is 'everywhere', and if we
are to understand the *Letter* that is where we must start.
The history of the Dakotas and the biography of the
McGrath family is an extraordinarily compressed episode,
almost a parable of capitalism. His grandparents on both
sides were Irish and on his mother's side (the Sheas) they
were Gaelic-speaking. His maternal grandfather came, by
way of Ellis Island, up to North Dakota, working on the
railway, carting and freighting. His paternal grandfather
came through Canada, carrying with him savage anti-English
recollections of the Great Famine; he also came following
the railway, doing freighting work with a contractor of
oxen. Both pairs of grandparents became homesteaders,
the Sheas in the neighbourhood of Sheldon where McGrath
grew up. The family passed on to the growing poet a vigorous
inheritance from the Irish oral tradition. His paternal grandfather was a notable 'curser'[30] and his father a great teller of
'tall stories'—such stories as recur in the *Letter*, as when the
winds from the dustbowls of the West darken the Dakota
skies—

And the dust blowing down your throat like a fistful of glass—
And *that* not so bad, but pushing down on your hat
Were the vagrant farms of the north: Montana, Saskatchewan,
With the farmers still on them, merrily plowing away,
Six inches over your head. . .

                                                      (*Letter*, I, 47)

In the evenings at the farm, when the battery-set ran out, his father would entertain the children with songs and stories, some traditional, some (about local personalities and events) of his own making. To this McGrath could add the scanty resource of the local school—Pope's *Iliad*, Halkett and Laing versions of the classics, *The Burnt Njal:* and the ambiguous inheritance of the Catholic church, which is now being resurrected and roasted in Part Three of the *Letter:*

And now comes the Holy Father a-flap in his crowdark drag![31]

The Dakota farms are laid out like geometric patterns on a drawing-board, allocation upon identical allocation. They seem to have been planted on top of the natural environment, not to have grown up in relation with it. Here and there are densely-packed clumps of woodland ('woodlots'), for homesteaders who agreed to raise timber received a small additional grant of land. The trees do not follow the lanes and hedges, they are simply dumped into isolated corrals: utility plants for fuel. Here a civilisation was planted, with immense hardship, in one generation: struggled to maintain itself in the face of dust-bowls and mortgages in the next: and gave way to collapse and emigration in McGrath's own generation. Moreover, the first generation entered into that hard world of labour only after expelling their forerunners:

> It was here the Sioux had a camp on the long trail
> Cutting the loops of the rivers from beyond the Missouri and Mandan
> East: toward Big Stone Lake and beyond to the Pipestone Quarry,
> The place of peace.
> A backwoods road of a trail, no tribal
> Superhighway; for small bands only. Coming and going
> They pitched camp here a blink of an eye ago.
>   *   *   *
> From Indians we learned a toughness and a strength; and we gained
> A freedom: by taking theirs: but a real freedom: born
> From the wild and open land our grandfathers heroically stole.
> But we took a wound at Indian hands: a part of our soul scabbed
>   over:
> We learned the pious and patriotic art of extermination
> And no uneasy conscience where the man's skin was the wrong

Color; or his vowels shaped wrong; or his haircut; or his country
     possessed of
Oil; or holding the wrong place on the map—whatever
The master race wants it will find good reasons for having.
                                        (*Letter*, II, 189-190)

And, even more savagely, in Part Three:

                              . . . the deep, heroic and dishonest past
Of the national myth of the frontier spirit and the free West—
Oh, nightmare, nightmare, dream and despair and dream!

A confusion of waters, surely, and pollution at the head of the river!
Our history begins with the first wound: with Indian blood
Coloring the water of the original springs—earlier, even:
Europe: the indentured. . .[32]

It was in his father's generation that this episode came to
its climax. Yet the climax was not one of promised prosperity
after hardship and toil, not that of prairie middle peasantry
or New England individualists. What took place instead was
a climax of exploitation, by banks, millers, dealers and rail-
ways, leading these Irish, Scandinavians, Germans and
assorted Americans into a huge social movement of wrath
and solidarity. The Dakotas and Minnesota, so easily to be
seen from the East or West coasts as being way out there
beyond the uttermost sticks, were in fact the heartland of a
great and effective popular movement, inadequately described in the misty all-inclusive term as 'populist'. It was an
active and democratic movement; the North Dakota Non-
partisan League was socialist in its origins, and demanded
the state ownership of banks, grain elevators, etc. In 1919
the NPL caucus dominated the state legislature, created a
state bank and grain elevators, imposed income and inheritance taxes, introduced assistance to home buyers, legalised
strikes and brought in mines safety regulations. In the judgment of a contemporary historian 'no more dramatic demonstration of democracy has occurred in American history'.[33]
This movement was one of the few great impulses on the
North American continent in the 20th century which afforded premonitions of an American socialism or 'communitas'.

And it contained within it even sharper forms of political consciousness. McGrath's father read the *Industrial Worker* and the migrant farm-hand, Cal, so important in the structure of the *Letter*, is a Wobbly and McGrath's childhood mentor. It is from Cal also that young Tom first encounters the savage scepticism of the freethinker in the face of the Catholic formation of his boyhood: 'All peace on earth for about five seconds.'[34]

These are some of the materials for the 'pastoral' (or sometimes 'anti-pastoral') themes of McGrath's poetry. And there are in fact many themes, which the urban reader— encountering coulees and horses and Indians and the stars— allows his eye to pass across too inattentively. Not one of them should be treated with that kind of disrespect, and least of all McGrath's horses, which are sometimes horses, sometimes nightmares or outlaws, and very often Pegasus, the Crazy Horse. (In one of his first published poems he noted: 'I have known personally horses / Who were more alive than many college professors.')[35]

Within this 'pastoral' mode we find, certainly, the keenest eye for natural beauty and for the rightness, but also mercilessness, of natural things; a 'somatic' sense of human transience, a cutting-down of humankind to size against the cyclonic weather and the stars; a sense of contest, the small farmsteads pitted against the vast Dakota winters. And we find other things also. We find the central theme of labour, a male world of agrarian labour with its glimpsed solidarities; and the theme of exploitation, for the winds which blow incessantly over Dakota are two, the wind of nature and the wind of *money*, of mortgages and interest-rates and bankruptcies, 'continual wind of money, that blows the birds through the clocks' (*Letter*, I, 92). There are other themes also, among them the glimpsed 'communitas' of the Farmer-Labor alliance and the Wobblies—a communitas which found, in the thirties, a further and sadder extension in the moments of solidarity of the unemployed.

So this is not altogether what one has come to expect from the term 'pastoral'. '*Letter* is not a poem that comes out of the sensibility of the city middle-class intellectual'.[36] Yet this is not pastoral's negation, anti-pastoral or urban face-making either. The moments of agrarian experience—of joy, terror, hardship in labour—are unqualified values. In *Letter* I there is a moment of sudden transition when McGrath moves (1939) from Dakota to his first contact with High Culture in Louisiana:

> And they got hold of Agrarianism—
> Salvation—40 acres and a mule—the Protestant Heaven,
> Free Enterprise! Kind of intellectual ribbon-development. . .
> *   *   *
> And all of them
> On Donne. Etc.
>   And all of them sailing on the Good Ship Tradition. . .
> For the thither ports of the moon.
> High flying days
> I'll tell you right now!
> And me with my three ideas
> With my anarchist, peasant poverty, being told at last how bright
> The bitter land was.
> How the simple poor might lift a laud to the Lord. . .
> *   *   *
> O architectonic colloquy! O gothick Pile
> Of talk! How, out of religion and poetry
> And reverence for the land the good life comes.
> Some with myth, some with Visions out of
> That book by Yeats would dance the seasons round
> In a sweet concord.
> But never the actual seasons—
> Not the threshing floor of Fall nor the tall night of Winter—
> Woodcutting time—nor Spring with the chime and jingle
> Of mended harness on real and farting horses,
> Nor the snort of the tractor in the Summer fallow.
> Not the true run of the seasons.
> (*Letter*, I, 60-62)

Labour, then, the 'real and farting horse' (which might still be Pegasus), exploitation (the 'wind of money'), glimpsed communitas—

> But I was a peasant from Sauvequipeuville—
> I wanted the City of Man
> (*Letter*, I, 60)

all these are at odds with customary urban expectations. For McGrath's pastoral verse lacks one almost-obligatory element, that of ultimate reconciliation (of man with nature, or of men and women in a shared consensus). I can point to this by means of a contrast with Robert Frost's *The Code*, a poem which I highly regard. Frost often acknowledged in his poetry dimensions of labour and of hardship. In this poem we have a moment of sudden conflict between a small working farmer and his hired hand. Storm clouds threaten the taking-in of harvest: the farmer urges on and chides his skilled labourer who, sharing equal commitment to the task and equally aware of the weather's threat, knows better than to change his steady measured pace, since there is no way in which that long-learned pace can be mended. At length the labourer is goaded to throw down the whole load upon the farmer's head. But, then, notice how the poem ends:

'Weren't you relieved to find he wasn't dead?

'No! and yet I don't know—it's hard to say.
I went about to kill him fair enough.'

'You took an awkward way. Did he discharge you?'

'Discharge me? No! He knew I did just right.'[37]

The poem has established conflict to the edge of murder, but has then reconciled that moment within a shared consensus of values, of shared agrarian skills, which are acknowledged by both master and man.

Contrast this with the episode of Cal at the opening of Part One of *Letter:*

                        Then, one day—windy—
We were threshing flax I remember, toward the end of the run—
After quarter-time I think—the slant light falling
Into the blackened stubble that shut like a fan toward the headland—
The strike started then. Why *then* I don't know.
Cal spoke for the men and my uncle cursed him.
I remember that ugly sound, like some animal cry touching me
Deep and cold, and I ran toward them

And the fighting started.
My uncle punched him. I heard the breaking crunch
Of his teeth going and the blood leaped out of his mouth. . .

(Letter, I, 18)

The episode violates any notional consensus of agrarian
values, not only as between employers and hands, but also
carrying the conflict right into the poet's own family, for
McGrath's father quarrels with his brother:

Outside the barn my father knelt in the dust
In the lantern light, fixing a harness. Wanting
Just to be around, I suppose, to try to show to Cal
He couldn't desert him.
                              He held the tubular punch
With its spur-like rowle, punching a worn hame strap
And shook the bright copper rivets out of a box.
'Hard lines, Tom,' he said. 'Hard lines, Old Timer.'
I sat in the lantern's circle, the world of men,
And heard Cal breathe in his stall.
                                          An army of crickets
Rasped in my ear.
                        'Don't hate anybody.'
My father said.
I went toward the house through the dark.

That night the men all left.

There is a reconciliation here between son and father, for
both carry the conflict unresolved inside them. But for that
conflict itself there is no resolution:

There were strikes on other rigs that day, most of them lost,
And, on the second night, a few barns burned.
After that a scattering of flat alky bottles,
Gasoline filled, were found, buried in bundles.

(Letter, I, 18-24)

And never, in any poem, is it resolved. That past is never
'paved over' and finished. It remains, tormented by conflict,
but also pregnant with 'the possible that never was'. It is

this which confronts the expectations of pastoral verse and which prevents McGrath's *Letter* from being nostalgic, a retrospective meditation upon or a celebration of a finished way of life. Both conflict and potential co-exist in the poem's present tense.

The theme of the potential indicates the point at which McGrath departs from prevalent notations—and also anxieties—as to what is called 'populism'. He has always been more watchful, more accusatory of the 'cultural default' of the intellectuals than the default of 'the people'. Where the Western intelligentsia has increasingly found refuge in theories (some of these even in the form of Marxisms) which predicate the inexorable determinist force of structures to expropriate the people of self-activity and to stamp upon them an ideologically-confected false consciousness—hence offering a view in which 'populism' is always threatening and only the islands of intellect, the reviews and academies, are able to liberate themselves from determinist process—McGrath has, in contrast, held this intelligentsia in his eye as themselves co-partners of the expropriators and co-authors of false consciousness. Even the revolt of the *New York Review of Books* intelligentsia during the Vietnam War did not convince him:

> Out of so much of this temporary 'war politics' rises a terrible spiritual smell which signals to the enemy: 'I'm not really like this. Just stop bombing Hanoi and I will go back to my primary interests: flowers, early cockcrow, the Holy Ghost, wheelbarrows, the letter G, inhabitable animals, the sacred mysteries of the typewriter keyboard, and High Thought including the Greater, the Lesser, and High, Low, Jack-in-the-goddam-game mysticism.' Worthy enough subjects in themselves. . .[38]

I am not wholly clear what is being argued here. Perhaps it is that the 'revolt' engaged with certain symptoms— symptoms too embarrassing to ignore—but did not identify nor engage with the cause? Perhaps that the cause, if identified, would have indicted the artificers of false consciousness themselves? Maybe the criticism is even more bluntly political?

> I suppose I ought at once to name the villain who has stolen our past—or tried to steal it: we don't admit anything but temporary defeat—in order as soon as possible to activate the rage of those critics and those readers who feel that politics is vulgar and revolutionary marxism anathema. The villain is capitalism in all its material and magical forms. How sad for me that I cannot name something nicely and safely metaphysical![39]

Yet McGrath's political stance derives less from revolutionary marxist theory than he may himself suppose, simply because it does not ultimately derive from theory at all: 'in the beginning was the *world!*'[40] And the 'world', the experience in which his politics are rooted (and which his poetry strives to recover) is 'a very *American* kind of radicalism':[41] not that of 'populism' but of the most radical—sometimes socialist, sometimes anarcho-syndicalist—and the most militant anti-capitalist affirmations within Labor–Farmer, Wobbly, and early American Communist traditions. In retrospect he has become critical of the Popular Front of the thirties and early forties: 'the more sectarian politics before the Popular Front were more "American" than the politics which followed':

> In the '20s the Left had many of its origins further west than New York, and out there some of us had been living with the dark side of American experience for a long time. In the late '30s and even more the '40s the Left got coralled in the Eastern cities. And I think some of the writers were unprepared for the late '40s and '50s because they had taken in too much of the Popular Front and watered down their radicalism. . . It led people into an optimistic notion of what *was* going to happen, although after 1946, it should have been perfectly plain what was going to happen. Perhaps it was some sense of this that made me, if not prepared for the long night, at least unsurprised.[42]

The radical intelligentsia inhabited an exciting metropolitan culture, taking some of their bearings from a cosmopolitan Communist mythology, and found themselves quite unprepared for the 'man-chilling dark' of subsequent decades. They were unprepared for the mercilessness of American capitalism 'in all its material and magical forms'. Nor were they sustained by the experience of the solidarity of anti-capitalist struggle (although the poet himself had found this in dockside Manhattan in 1940) and its glimpsed 'communitas'. For Radicalism had begun to drift, from the Popular Front onwards, into complicity with the same divisive ego-psychology that is the legitimating operative drive of capitalist ideology itself: the multiple 'I wants' of the claims to equality of ego-fulfilment. And working-class militancy itself was engulfed as the full employment and easy money of the war years dissolved the bonds of solidarity:

> Out of the iron thirties and into the Garden of War profiteers.
> Once it was: *All of us or no one!* Now it's *I'll get mine!*
>
> (*Letter*, II, 146)

'Here's the first / Sellout from which the country is a quarter century sick,' and one made the more possible because Popular Front radicals turned away from the class war to 'that other war / Where fascism seemed deadlier and easier to fight—but wasn't.' (*Letter*, II, 148).

Against this loss of militancy and solidarity, McGrath's poems perform their incantatory charms, searching backwards for the 'we' of shared labour and hardship, the 'we' of active democratic process, the 'we' of historical potential, the 'we' of casual labour sawing wood in the bitter cold of a Dakota winter, when 'the unemployed fished, the fish badly out-numbered'—among the coffee-guzzling Swedes, the moonfaced Irish, the lonesome deadbeats:

> Those were the last years of the Agrarian City
> City of swapped labor
> Communitas
> Circle of warmth and work
> Frontier's end and last wood-chopping bee
> The last collectivity stamping its feet in the cold.
>
> (*Letter*, I, 45)

'The solidarity of forlorn men'—

> The chime of comradeship that comes once maybe
> In the Winter of the Blue Snow.
>
> (*Letter*, I, 46)

This sense of solidarity. . . in the community is one of the richest
experiences that people can have. It's the only true shield against
alienation and deracination and it was much more developed in the
past than it is now.[43]

Communality or solidarity—feelings which perhaps are more important to us than romantic love. . .[44]

So he recalls—writing in Los Angeles in 1955—the rising
mood of militancy, solidarity and hope of the late thirties,
in a poetic mood half-angry, half-elegaic:

Wild talk, and easy enough now to laugh.
That's not the point and never was the point.
What was real was the generosity, expectant hope,
The open and true desire to create the good.

Now, in another autumn, in our new dispensation
Of an ancient, man-chilling dark, the frost drops over
My garden's starry wreckage.
                            Over my hope.
                                         Over
The generous dead of my years.

                                  Now, in the chill streets
I hear the hunting and the long thunder of money. . .
              *   *   *
                                  To talk of the People
Is to be a fool. But they were the *sign* of the People,
Those talkers.
                                  Went underground about 1941
Nor hide nor hair of 'em since. . .
                                  (*Letter*, I, 52-3)

                              iv
As I have gone over this lifetime of work and have touched
upon some moments when the poet's life intersected with
the crises of his own society, I have been more and more
possessed by a sense of the stature of McGrath's achievement.
I will say without qualification that we are dealing, with
McGrath, with a major talent. To sustain over forty years a
principled alienation from the dominant culture; to turn
away from every seduction which could have co-opted him to

the modes of an official opposition, a 'two-party system'[45] of Academy and anti-Academy which the dominant culture could accommodate; to face directly the terror and defeat of those years in which that culture seemed to move inexorably towards an exterminist consummation; to refuse romanticism or easy answers, and yet at the same time to refuse the options of pessimism or empty face-making—all this is an achievement to which I do not know an equal.

A major talent, who has marked his trail through the forest of forty dark years with the blazes of his poems. But can we say that the achievement of his art has matched the achievement of his integrity? It is my own view that we can; that McGrath must be measured as a major poet. But I am perhaps too close both to the poet and to the times to be the necessary 'Good Critic who, even now, may be slouching towards' his poems.[46] His shorter poems employ the whole keyboard of technique and tone: lyrical, polemical, satirical, meditative, elegaic, metaphysical. They convey, cumulatively, a unique and consistent view-of-life, and, with this, an inversion of official descriptions of reality, a demystification of American normalisation:

> The street rolls up till his office reaches him
> And the door puts out its knob and drags him in.
> His desk-trap is baited with the kill of the day.
> He sets it off by touching it and can't get away.[47]

From this 'Poor John Luck' of the forties to his most recent poetry, there is a characteristic McGrathian imagery of determinism, in which persons are acted by impersonal forces—

> The streets bulge with ambition and duty—
> Inhaling the populace out of exhausted houses.
> The drowsy lion of money devours their calendars...[48]

—until the metropolitan civilisation itself carries its inert human freight to disaster:

> Below me the city turns on its left
> Side and the neon blinks in a code I can all too clearly
> Read. It will go down with all hands.[49]

And yet, with swift inversions, these massive determinist structures themselves are seen as resting upon the frail spiritual and emotional powers of those who inhabit them:

> The city lifts toward heaven from the continent of sleep
> This skin of bricks,
>   these wounds,
>   this soul of smoke and anguish,
> These walls held up by hope and want. . .
>   *   *   *
>   insubstantial
> Structures, framework of dream and nightmare, a honeyed static
> Incorporeal which the light condenses.[50]

I do not know any contemporary poet with comparable range of tone and theme, and sureness of touch with all. Nothing is predictable. On one page we have a hilarious celebration of beer ('*Guinness Stout* with its arms of turf and gunfire'),[51] on another a meditation upon the Heisenberg Principle.[52] The characteristic imagery invites by turn the description 'metaphysical' (by bringing into conjunction opposing mythologies or belief-systems) and 'surrealist' (by implanting will and intention in inanimate objects): one is tempted to coin, for McGrath, the term 'metasurrealist'.

From start to finish of his *oeuvre* there is one recurrent theme: war, the losses of war, the threat of nuclear war, the celebration of war and the means of war in the official culture, the 'heavy dancers'. And here also 'Dakota is everywhere', for, if Dakota were to secede from the United States, it would be, with its battery of Minutemen, the third most powerful nuclear state in the world:

> As in the silos waiting near Grand Forks North Dakota—
> O paradise of law and number where all money is armed![53]

But even this terrible theme—and a distinct essay would be

needed to follow its development—is handled with extraordinary versatility, like a crystal tossed into the air so that
the sun glints now from one facet, now from another. He can
move from lament to jest to invective to the quiet and
beautiful 'Ode for the American Dead in Korea' to the low-
keyed meditation of 'The Fence Around the H-Bomb Plant':
'the fence proclaims / A divorce between yourself and a
differing idea of order':

> . . . it creates out of your awareness a tension
> Wire-drawn, arousing a doubt as to whether
> It is the bomb that is fenced in, you free,
> Or whether you mope here in a monster prison
>
> As big as the world may be; or a world, maybe,
> Which has everything but a future. . .[54]

A world 'which has everything but a future'. Is it possible
for a poet who is ever-sensitive to that threat to write great
poetry? It is a question which McGrath has asked himself;
he has spoken with respect of poets (his contemporaries)
who, overcome with the sense of political emergency, set
aside their talents for more direct forms of engagement.[55]
And the cost of living in such times can be sensed within his
own poetry. The times offered to him few affirmative
evidences capable of carrying authentic symbolic power.
There are such evidences to be found, for example moments
in *Letter II* when the movement of the sixties can be felt—

>   I tell you millions
> Are moving.
>   Pentagon marchers!
>   Prague May Day locomotives
> With flowers in their teeth!
>
>   (*Letter*, II, 107)

But the weight of evidence falls always the other way, and he
has been too honest to romanticise the record.

He has turned in his verse to three kinds of affirmatives.
First, to the elementary alphabet of love, of work, of the
rightness of natural things, and, more recently, of his growing

son, Tomasito. This is always effective. Second, to a more
metaphysical assertion of the exploited as the absolute negation of capitalist process: 'Labor His Sublime Negation', 'the
accursed poor who can never be bought',[56] who must
ultimately confront their exploiters. This (it seems to me)
comes through with increasing strain, as a proposition whose
confirmation by history is continually postponed, and hence
can only be affirmed by recourse to the past, and sometimes
to an antique Wobbly vocabulary of 'bindle-stiffs' and
'jungling tramps'. McGrath has perhaps less emotional insight
into newer and more complex forms of social contradiction:
his world of labour and of exploitation is predominantly
male, and (as we have seen) he has considered 'cultural and
political nationalism' to be 'dead ends' which must be
worked through before 'serious politics' is reached:

> At the congress of the color blind
> I put up the communist banner my father signed and sang:
> LABOR IN A BLACK SKIN CAN'T BE FREE WHILE WHITE
> SKIN LABOR IS IN CHAINS!
>
> (*Letter*, II, 130)

The third affirmative is central to the organisation of the
Letter to an Imaginary Friend. It consists in the magical or
'charm' properties of poetry itself:

> It is the charm which the potential has
> Which is the proper aura for the poem. . .

The poet, in revealing the human potential, is the vector of
(we remember) 'a view of life. . . in a sense truer than the life
we see lived all round us'. He prefaced to *Letter II* a passage
from Claude Lévi-Strauss as a figure of the poet:

> The man who wishes to wrest something from Destiny must venture
> into that perilous margin-country where the norms of Society count
> for nothing and the demands and guarantees of the group are no
> longer valid. He must travel to where the police have no sway, to the
> limits of physical resistance and the far point of physical and moral
> suffering. Once in this unpredictable borderland a man may vanish,

never to return; or he may acquire for himself, from among the immense repertory of unexploited forces which surrounds any well-regulated society, some personal provision of power; and when this happens an otherwise inflexible social order may be cancelled in favour of the man who has risked everything.

This rather grand prescription is perhaps cited, not as an exemplar for the poet so much as an indication of poetry's function. But it is important that McGrath sees the 'immense repertory of unexploited forces' as lying in the unrealised *past*. It is the past which is the reservoir for potential for the present and the future.

I am only a device of memory
To call forth into this Present the flowering dead and the living
To enter the labyrinth and blaze the trail for the enduring journey
Toward the rounddance and commune of light. . .
                                        (*Letter*, II, 103)

McGrath has stressed the importance of Hopi myth and the function of the *kachina* ritual in the *Letter*. I do not feel competent to explore this, although, to be honest, I would say that the actual operative effect of myth and the *kachina* in the structure of the poem is less (for the reader) than the poet attributes to it. I would in any case interpret the poet's stance a little differently, and would derive it, in the first place, from the decisive influence upon him of Christopher Caudwell's *Illusion and Reality*, and perhaps the discussions around this in England and in New York in the late forties.

Caudwell's was a heavy book to throw at the heads of the philistines and bureaucrats of the Left, it provided a full charter against utilitarian views of art, and the most complex and dignified claims for the function of the artist then available in the Marxist tradition. (It is of interest that one of the targets of 'Zhdanovism' in the British CP was to be Caudwell.)[57] To simplify, *Illusion and Reality* offered a materialist interpretation of the primacy of spiritual forces in human development. The function of poetry and art was seen as partly 'adaptive', socialising and adapting the

'instincts' to changes in real life; and partly that of summoning up the spiritual energies of the group prior to any social
action. Caudwell's speculations on the earliest origins and
functions of art were enforced further at the end of World
War II by advances in scholarship; by the discovery of the
rich cave-paintings at Lascaux, and by the publication (1948)
of G.R. Levy's *The Gate of Horn*, with its examination of
Totemism and cave art. The Totem is 'a focus of the life-
energy of a group embodied in the immortal ancestor':

> That is why art is necessary to such a religion, and why approach
> to the forms or symbols is so strictly guarded, since they are nearer
> to reality than the separated lives.[58]

I suggest that it was in the post-war excitement and
debates around Caudwell and Lascaux[59] that McGrath
grounded his materialist vindication of poetry's spiritual
power and function. In his encounters with utilitarian
'politicos' he was able to argue 'that I was the *real* political
type and that they were vulgar marxists'. He refused to
accept the loftier authority of the political Theorist: 'it
would be a good thing if both sides recognised that while
they're both political animals, one is dog and one is cat'.[60]
And this will have predisposed him to borrow from Hopi
myth those symbols of renewal and resurrection which recur
in *Letter* II and III, symbols which are 'concerned with the
offering of evidences for a revolutionary miracle and with
elaborating a ceremony out of these materials to bring such
a miracle to pass'.[61] Yet these 'evidences' consist in resurrect-
ing the spirits of the past, 'that power of the dead out of
which all life proceeds' (*Letter*, II, 104),—a task:

> . . . not so much of rescuing the past (and not just my own) but of
> *creating* it since it was stolen from us, malformed, a changeling
> substituted. I do this, of course, as do all my comrade Kachinas
> and resurrectionists, to rescue the future.[62]

And the 'ghost dances' or *kachinas* of the Hopi provide a
perfect vocabulary of symbolism for this, since '*kachinas*

are properly not deities. . . They are respected spirits: spirits
of the dead. . . spirits of all the invisible forces of life.'[63]
Tom's father and Mac and Cal and all the *dramatis personae*
of *Letter* may therefore be called up into the dance. A blue
star will signify the transition from the Hopi's Fourth World
(McGrath's capitalism) to *Saquasohuh*, the Fifth World:

> The Blue Star Kachina will help these powers to bring in the new
> world. All of us should help to make this Kachina. I think of the
> making of my poem as such an action. In a small way the poem
> *is* the Kachina.[64]

It is a happy conceit to warm the poet at his work, but I
am less certain that so artificial a conceit can operate as
warmly on the feelings of the reader.

Is *Letter*, whether finished or unfinished, a major poem,
a 'great' poem? How can anyone tell yet? Such matters
take time to settle. I have my own difficulties with it. There
are places where the poet himself appears to lose direction
and to struggle to find his way on the paper; some passages
of 'mock-hearty hoorahing' (his own self-criticism).[65] The
tendency to fall back upon incantation of the past ('to
free the Bound Man / Of the Revolution', *Letter*, II, 209) in
place of a more arduous resolution may perhaps indicate an
ulterior philosophical or political irresolution—an inhibition
against working through in public his accounts with the
illusions and selfbetrayals of the Left? (He does not work
through the experience of Stalinism as Wordsworth worked
through that of Godwinism.) The 'Bound Man of the
Revolution' is posed as self-evident proletarian Natural Man
who is everywhere in chains; yet those who, with the poet,
have watched over the history of Socialism in the past
half-century know that there is no such Natural Man. Hence
the *Letter*, while reimagining and recreating the past, loses
the magic power of imagination when it turns towards the
future: we are pointed towards the blue haze of *Saquasohuh*,
the Fifth World.

Nevertheless. Other major poets try our patience sometimes also. Blake's prophetic books disappear into labyrinths

more private and more self-indulgent than anything in
McGrath. Wordsworth is guilty in *The Prelude* of major
evasions and of a few passages of pseudo-philosophical
waffle. But this scarcely diminishes the poems. *Letter to an
Imaginary Friend* is a remarkable achievement. It tears down
all the curtains which lie between 'poetry' and 'life'; it opens
directly upon the pandemonium of reality, the living issues of
history, work, morality, politics. It discovers a long, broken,
accented rhythm of extraordinary versatility, which can pass
into invective or humour or polemic and which can pass
back into lyrical or contemplative mode. It has markers
throughout which will be followed by future historians.
Letter II is superbly constructed and is a definitive statement
of the deathward-tending malaise of a civilisation. And in the
unfolding of *Letter*, the only poem I know of which is built
to the size of our times, the miracle of resurrection of the
past actually begins to take place:

> It is *not* daybreak
> Provokes cockcrow but cockcrow drags forth the reluctant sun   not
> Resurrection that allows us to rise and walk but the rising
> Of the rebel dead founds resurrection and overthrows hell.
>
> (*Letter*, II, 210)

In this resurrection an alternative present begins to appear;
if we cannot see an alternative future through the blue
kachina haze, we can see the elements from which that
alternative might be made. In despite of the 'man-chilling
dark', Thomas McGrath has fashioned an alternative self-
image for America. He has deployed his poem as 'a conscious-
ness-expanding device':

> The most terrible thing is the degree to which we carry around a
> false consciousness, and I think of poetry as being primarily an
> apparatus, a machine, a plant, a flower, for the creation of real
> consciousness. . .[66]

In a letter to us of 1949, when he first reached the West
Coast, McGrath describes sharing a house and garden in Los

Angeles with friends; since they had no access to an auto-
mobile 'we are pretty well cut off from everyone, and it is a
little bit like being all alone on an island, although we are
only about five miles from Hollywood'. And I have thought
of the extraordinary juxtaposition at that time, and through
the ensuing 'Great Fear' in Hollywood, with Ronald Reagan
and Thomas McGrath almost as neighbours and as visitants
within the same hysteric culture; and of the genesis of
opposed self-images of America.[67]
The future President was at that time steadily working his
way up the 'levels' of Los Angeles:

<blockquote>

                          . . . at the ten
Thousand a year line (though still in the smog's sweet stench)
The Johnny Come Earlies of the middling class:
                                    morality
                                      fink-size
Automatic rosaries with live Christs on them and cross-shaped
    purloined
Two-car swimming pools full of holy water. . .
                              From here God goes
Uphill.
        Level to level.
                    Instant escalation of money—up!
To Cadillac country.

        Here, in the hush of the long green,
The leather priests of the hieratic dollar enclave to bless
The lush-working washing machines of the Protestant Ethic
    ecumenical
Laundries: to steam the blood from the bills—O see O see how
Labor His Sublime Negation streams in the firmament!
                                        (*Letter*, II, 113)

</blockquote>

Here was manufactured the approved self-image of America,
as television opened its 'poisoned eye' within the heads of
millions, carrying that poison image from Hollywood to far
Dakota:

<blockquote>

        The houses blacked out as if for war, lit only
With random magnesium flashes like exploding bombs (TV
Courtesy REA)
            Cold hellfire
                screams

</blockquote>

> Tormented, demented, load the air with anguish
> invisible
> Over the sealed houses, dark, a troop of phantoms,
> Demonic, rides: the great Indians come in the night like
> Santa Claus
> down the electronic chimneys whooping and dead...
> *(Letter*, II, 192)

And so those lush-working washing machines laundered the 'American dream' and washed the blood out of the American past. It was McGrath's neighbour who won, and who, in his triumph, threatens the whole world. At the lowest level, the poet sat by the beach and waited for the hunters. But, with the help of the 'Marsh Street Irregulars' and the network of little resistance magazines, McGrath commenced his long labours of fashioning an alternative self-image. And America is moving today, surely, towards a moment of contradiction, of confronting images? 'Everyone everywhere in the States' (McGrath wrote in 1972) 'senses that the whole system is finished, though it may endure for a time. Meanwhile there is this great emptiness that can never be paved...'[68]

If this moment should come, then it will be in such material as *Letter* that an alternative America will discover her features. It is still possible that a miracle will take place, and that the hunted poet will triumph over the powerful impostor—as Blake wrote, when discussing miracles, did not Paine 'overthrow all the armies of Europe with a small pamphlet?'

The world may now be too old and lost for such miracles. But, confronted with McGrath's lifetime of loyalty to his Muse, 'the grand old bitch', I can only celebrate his stamina. His loyalty has been not only to his own talent, at a time when in the scanty *samizdat* of hunted outlaws, poetry itself seemed to be an obsolescent trade. It has been also a loyalty to a notion of poetry as still, despite every evidence of defeat, a major art, a major vector of consciousness, and a major guarantor of an unextinguished human potential:

                            All time is redeemed by the single man—
Who remembers and resurrects.
                            And I remember.
                                                        I keep
The winter count.

He has kept the count well. Homage to Thomas McGrath.

NOTES

There is a valuable Selected Bibliography by Fred Whitehead in *North Dakota Quarterly*, Fall 1982, a *festschrift* issue for McGrath. This also includes many useful memoirs and essays. *The Movie at the End of the World* (Chicago, 1972) is sub-titled 'Collected Poems', although it is in fact an economical selection from earlier collections. Parts One and Two of *Letter to an Imaginary Friend* (Chicago, 1970) have been followed by sections of Part Three in *Passages Toward the Dark* (Port Townsend, 1982) and *Echoes Inside the Labyrinth* (New York, 1983). These are abbreviated in text or notes to: *NDQ; Movie; Letter; Passages;* and *Echoes.*

It will be unusually difficult to establish any canon of McGrath's work. From typescripts sent to us in the fifties I have found poems which appear in *Movie* as 'new poems'; and one or two of them turn up in *Passages* or *Echoes*. This might sometimes be important to the historian, perhaps also to the critic: Warning, handle each 'new poem' with agnosticism as to its genesis and context. The poet himself appears to have lost some of his own copies which, however, survive in the hands of friends or in the pages of scores of little journals in which he has published.

1. 'Trinc', is in *Echoes*, 13-18. 'Praises' in *Movie*, 157-8.
2. *Passages*, 93.
3. See Joe Doyle's interesting essay on 'Tom McGrath's Years on the New York Waterfront', *NDQ*, 32-40.
4. The evidence is fully presented in Victor S. Navasky, *Naming Names* (New York, 1980).
5. Reprinted in *NDQ*, 8-9.
6. 'Probability or necessity'—McGrath here and elsewhere is grounding his view on Aristotle, *On the Art of Poetry*, Chapter 9, 'Poetic Truth and Historical Truth': 'It is not the poet's function to describe what has actually happened, but the kinds of thing that might happen, that is, that could happen because they are, in the circumstances, either probable or necessary. . . For this reason poetry is something more philosophical and more worthy of serious attention than history; for while poetry is concerned with universal truths, history treats of particular facts': T.S. Dorsch (ed.), *Classical Literary Criticism* (Penguin, 1965), pp. 43-44.
7. McGrath to author, 27 November 1980. Of his cultural 'bureaucrats', V.J. Jerome was imprisoned under the Smith Act and John

Howard Lawson was one of the 'Hollywood Ten'. Navasky (op. cit.) has a valuable discussion in Chapter 9, 'The Reasons Considered', of the internal cultural disputes of the CPUSA, especially the 'heresy trial' and recantation of Albert Maltz (with Maltz's own recollections). When I first met McGrath in the summer of 1946 the Maltz case had already taken place, and I remember his anger about it.

8. A subsequent letter (1952?) notes that 'novel now being considered by Liberty Book Club, but editor there wants Sam Sillen to read it to get his opinion—and I figure Sillen will kill it off.' It remains unpublished.

9. When McGrath first tried out this not-very-threatening revision in *New Masses* he got a terrific shower of shit as a result': see interviews in *Another Chicago Magazine*, 5, 1980, and in *Cultural Correspondence*, 9, Spring 1979, *NDQ*, 28. I have not tracked down the original exchanges in *New Masses*.

10. McGrath recalls the years after 1946: 'There was nothing to do to prepare, except as an isolated individual. All one could do was to warn, and those were warnings that no one wanted to hear, often seen as a kind of pessimism or defeatism': *Cultural Correspondence*, 9, p. 43.

11. Tom does not recall exactly when he left the CPUSA. Around 1955-7 he was quarrelling with West Coast organisers about cultural matters and trying to transfer from an 'intellectual' to an industrial branch. When this failed, his membership lapsed but he continued to write for *Masses and Mainstream* and *People's World*. He became a sort of 'charmed quark' on the unaffiliated far Left, and was interested for a while in the Progressive Labor Party until it turned out that his main contact was an FBI spy: conversation with author, 1980.

12. See *Letter*, II, 150:

      . . . having come by blacklist degrees
    To the bottom: dropped out of the labor market as unsafe
    To a government at wars ie the cold, the Korean, the Pretend
    (Against Russia) the Holy (against Satanic citizens the likes of Myself).

This suggests that the Pretend war against Russia was only a cover for the Holy war of internal social and intellectual control. Cf *The Gates of Ivory, The Gates of Horn* (New York, 1957), p. 100, where the generals come and ask the Sybil 'How long will the Pretend War last?' and the Sybil replies: 'How long do you want it to last?

13. See 'Return to Marsh Street', *Movie*, 142-4; *Letter*, II, 120-122; Gene Frumkin, 'A Note on Tom McGrath—The Early 50s', *NDQ*, 46-55.

14. 'After the Beat Generation', in *Crazy Horse*, 1, no date (but published from Tom and Genya's address at 220 East 14th Street, New York, which they left in 1961 or early 1962; also *Movie*, 162.

15. Poem', *Movie*, 130-1. But I think this poem also dates back to the fifties.

16. 'McGrath on McGrath', *Epoch*, 22 (1973), p. 217; also in *NDQ*, 11-28.
17. *Epoch*, op. cit., pp. 218-219. see also 'Poetry and Place', interview McGrath and Mark Vinz, in *Voyages to the Inland Sea*, 3, ed. John Judson (La Crosse, 1973), pp. 33-48.
18. Most of the *Crazy Horse* manifesto is in *NDQ*, 10. I am indebted to the archivists at the poetry collection in Brown University Library, where I consulted some numbers of *Crazy Horse*, the *California Quarterly* and *Witness to the Times!*
19. McGrath's work ranged from some pulp-writing and movie moonlighting (see Mike Hazard, *NDQ*, 101-6) to casual labour and semi-skilled work in furniture and ceramics workshops. He found the physical work ('if it is not too bloody physical') pleasant and compatible with writing poetry. He commenced *Letter*, Part One, while working 'in a little factory for making decorative sculpture'— 'the things we were working on were beautiful things. . . it was a very good situation'—and completed it in a few weeks: interview in *Dacotah Territory*, cited in *NDQ*, 122 and McGrath to author, 1980.
20. 'Figures in an Allegorical Landscape: Stock Brokerage Board Marker', typescript in my own collection. Ironically his job as board marker was one of the only ones he was not blacklisted out of: he was simply 'automated out'.
21. *NDQ*, 8-9. McGrath refused to cooperate with HUAC as a teacher and as a poet. 'When I was notified to appear here, my first instinct was simply to refuse to answer committee questions out of personal principle and on the grounds of the rights of man and let it go at that.' However, on 'further consideration', and to support the stance of other witnesses, he also cited the first, fourth and fifth amendments.
22. *Witness to the Times!*, a typescript mimeographed publication 'conceived and edited by students of Thomas McGrath' Los Angeles, 1953. Or 1954.
23. *California Quarterly*, Vol. II, no. 1, Autumn 1952, p. 50.
24. Ibid., II, 2, Winter 1953, pp. 8-9.
25. From sections 1 and 4 of 'The Hunted Revolutionaries', first published in *California Quarterly*, IV, 1, 1955. Sections 2 and 3 are republished in *Movie*, 172-3, dedicated to Henry Winston, the black national chairman of the CPUSA who lost his eyesight while in prison under the Smith Act: see Frederick C. Stern in *NDQ*, 108. I do not think that sections 1 and 4 have been republished.
26. Alice McGrath, 'Longshot O'Leary Says It's Your Duty to Be Full of Fury' (November 1952) in *NDQ*, 45.
27. Ibid., 44.
28. See *A Sound of One Hand* (St. Peter, Minnesota, 1975) and *Open Songs* (Mount Carroll, Illinois, 1977).
29. See interview in *Voyages*, note 17 above.
30. Extravagant play upon his grandfather's alliterative cursing is in *Echoes*, 101-3.
31. *Echoes*, 114.
32. *Passages*, 127.
33. David Montgomery, in *In These Times*, October 8-14, 1980.

34. *Echoes*, 110.
35. 'Letter to Wendell' in *First Manifesto* (Swallow Pamphlets No. 1, Baton Rouge, 1940).
36. Note in *Passages*, 93.
37. Robert Frost, *Selected Poems* (1936), p. 190.
38. *Epoch* (see note 16 above), 214.
39. *Measure* 2 (Bowling Green State University, 1972), unpaginated.
40. *Epoch*, op. cit., p. 213.
41. *Voyages*, op. cit., p. 38.
42. *Cultural Correspondence* (see note 8 above), p. 43.
43. *Voyages*, op. cit., p. 41.
44. *Passages*, 93.
45. McGrath, 'Some Notes on Walter Lowenfels', *Praxis* 4 (1978), p. 90.
46. *Epoch*, 208.
47. 'Poor John Luck and the Middle Class Struggle', *Movie*, 89.
48. *Echoes*, 45.
49. *Movie*, 138.
50. *Passages*, 9.
51. *Echoes*, 17.
52. *Passages*, 148.
53. Ibid., 99.
54. For lament see among other examples his poems for his brother Jimmy, 'Blues for Jimmy', *Movie*, 73-78, and 'The Last War Poem of the War', ibid., 180; for jest, see 'Mottoes for a Sampler', ibid., 159; for invective, see 'Song for an Armistice Day', ibid., 161 and *Letter*, II, 147-8. 'Ode for the American Dead in Korea' (subsequently changed to 'Asia') is in *Movie*, 102-3, and also (180-1) 'Reading the Names of the Vietnam War Dead' ('thousands of dense black stones fall forever through the darkness under the earth'). 'The Fence Around the H-Bomb Plant' is in *Passages*, 56.
55. *Cultural Correspondence*, op. cit., p. 42, and *Praxis*, 4, 1978, where he writes 'there are some particularly interesting examples in England', perhaps thinking (among others) of Edgell Rickword's long poetic silence?
56. *Movie*, 57.
57. I have discussed this moment in 'Caudwell', *Socialist Register*, 1977. McGrath has not revised his high opinion of Caudwell.
58. G.R. Levy, *The Gate of Horn* (1948), p. 39.
59. Randall Swingler, an editor of *Our Time*, whom Tom met while at Oxford, published in 1950 'Reflections on the Walls of a Palaeolithic Cave' in *The God in the Cave* (1950).
60. *Another Chicago Magazine*, 5, 1980, p. 73.
61. Note preceding *Letter* I.
62. *Measure* 2 (see note 39).
63. Frank Waters, *Book of the Hopi* (New York, 1963), p. 167.
64. *Passages*, 95.
65. *Echoes*, 113.
66. *Voyages*, op. cit., p. 48.
67. This should have been clearly expressed in the title of his remarkable collection, *Figures From a Double World* (Denver, 1955) which, as he explains in a Note prefaced to *Movie*, was a publish-

er's error for *Figures of the Double World*, 'the emphasis on the dialectic, on process, on states of the world rather than states of mind'.
68. *Measure* 2.

MY STUDY

King of my freedom here, with every prop
A poet needs—the small hours of the night,
A harvest moon above an English copse...

Backward unrationalised trade, its furthest yet
Technology this typewriter which goes
With flailing arms through the ripe alphabet.

Not even bread the pen is mightier than.
Each in its statutory place the giants yawn:
I blow my mind against their sails and fan

The mills that grind my own necessity.
Oh, royal me! Unpoliced imperial man
And monarch of my incapacity

To aid my helpless comrades as they fall—
Lumumba, Nagy, Allende: alphabet
Apt to our age! In answer to your call

I rush out in this rattling harvester
And thrash you into type. But what I write
Brings down no armoured bans, no Ministers

Of the Interior interrogate.
No-one bothers to break in and seize
My verses for subversion of the state:

Even the little dogmas do not bark.
I leave my desk and peer into the world.
Outside the owls are hunting.   Dark

Has harvested the moon. Imperial eyes
Quarter the ground for fellow creaturehood:
Small as the hour some hunted terror cries.

I go back to my desk. If it could fight
Or dream or mate, what other creature would
Sit making marks on paper through the night?

September, 1973

ACKNOWLEDGEMENTS

My thanks and acknowledgements are due to the journals and publishing-houses where some of these materials appeared before (sometimes in different forms): *California Quarterly*, City Light Books, Griffin Productions, the *Guardian*, *Il Manifesto*, the *Nation*, *New Society*, *New Statesman*, *Our Time*, *Peace News*, *Radical America*, the *Spectator*, Spokesman Books, Verso/NLB; also to Thomas McGrath and his several publishers for permission to quote from his poems. I cannot begin to list all those who have helped me in this work, including colleagues in END and CND and in the European and American peace movements. But I must thank in particular two helpful and long-suffering publishers, Martin Eve and André Schiffrin; two helpful editors, Paul Barker and Viktor Navasky; Dorothy Thompson; Evy King; Cathy Fitzpatrick; W.H. Ferry; Jan Kavan (and the Palach Press); and Gay Clifford, Jesse Lemisch, Peter Linebaugh and Warren Susman who offered helpful comments on 'Homage to Thomas MacGrath', although they are not responsible for my conclusions.

E.P.T.